GENESIS

Text copyright © Gerald West 2006

The author asserts the moral right to be
identified as the author of this work

Published by
The Bible Reading Fellowship
First Floor, Elsfield Hall
15–17 Elsfield Way, Oxford OX2 8FG
Website: www.brf.org.uk

ISBN-10: 1 84101 314 5
ISBN-13: 978 1 84101 314 5

First published 2006
10 9 8 7 6 5 4 3 2 1 0

Acknowledgments
Unless otherwise stated, scripture quotations are taken from The New Revised
Standard Version of the Bible, Anglicized Edition, copyright © 1989, 1995 by the
Division of Christian Education of the National Council of the Churches of Christ
in the United States of America, and are used by permission. All rights reserved.

Scripture quotations taken from The Revised Standard Version of the Bible,
copyright © 1946, 1952, 1971 by the Division of Christian Education of the
National Council of the Churches of Christ in the United States of America, are
used by permission. All rights reserved.

A catalogue record for this book is available from the British Library

Printed in Singapore by Craft Print International Ltd

GENESIS

THE PEOPLE'S
BIBLE COMMENTARY

GERALD
WEST

A BIBLE COMMENTARY FOR EVERY DAY

INTRODUCING THE
PEOPLE'S BIBLE COMMENTARY
SERIES

Congratulations! You are embarking on a voyage of discovery—or rediscovery. You may feel you know the Bible very well; you may never have turned its pages before. You may be looking for a fresh way of approaching daily Bible study; you may be searching for useful insights to share in a study group or from a pulpit.

The People's Bible Commentary (PBC) series is designed for all those who want to study the scriptures in a way that will warm the heart as well as instructing the mind. To help you, the series distils the best of scholarly insights into the straightforward language and devotional emphasis of Bible reading notes. Explanation of background material, and discussion of the original Greek and Hebrew, will always aim to be brief.

• If you have never really studied the Bible before, the series offers a serious yet accessible way in.

• If you help to lead a church study group, or are otherwise involved in regular preaching and teaching, you can find invaluable 'snapshots' of a Bible passage through the PBC approach.

• If you are a church worker or minister, burned out on the Bible, this series could help you recover the wonder of scripture.

Using a People's Bible Commentary

The series is designed for use alongside any version of the Bible. You may have your own favourite translation, but you might like to consider trying a different one in order to gain fresh perspectives on familiar passages.

Many Bible translations come in a range of editions, including study and reference editions that have concordances, various kinds of special index, maps and marginal notes. These can all prove helpful in studying the relevant passage. The Notes section at the back of each PBC volume provides space for you to write personal reflections, points to follow up, questions and comments.

Each People's Bible Commentary can be used on a daily basis, instead of Bible reading notes. Alternatively, it can be read straight through, or used as a resource book for insight into particular verses of the biblical book.

If you have enjoyed using this commentary and would like to progress further in Bible study, you will find details of other volumes in the series listed at the back, together with information about a special offer from BRF.

While it is important to deepen understanding of a given passage, this series always aims to engage both heart and mind in the study of the Bible. The scriptures point to our Lord himself and our task is to use them to build our relationship with him. When we read, let us do so prayerfully, slowly, reverently, expecting him to speak to our hearts.

CONTENTS

PBC GENESIS: INTRODUCTION

It is a scary thing to write a commentary on any book of the Bible, knowing that others will use it as a guide to their understanding. The responsibility is overwhelming. This is especially the case with the book of Genesis. This book of beginnings shapes so much of our theological thinking; indeed, even if we would not consider our-selves particularly theological people, the book of Genesis has left its mark on us. From Sunday school to modern cinema, from popular culture to classic literature, from art to activism, Genesis permeates our conception of the world. When we touch Genesis, we touch something close to us, whether we can explain the closeness or not. So commentary writers, beware!

Those of us who are Christian or Jewish or Muslim bring a great deal of theological heritage (and so 'baggage') to our reading of most biblical texts, but particularly to the book of Genesis. This is not wrong or inappropriate, but it does often get in the way of a close and careful reading of the text. This commentary is designed to facilitate an engagement with the text. Once we have really 'heard' the text, we can then decide what to do with it theologically. But let us not pre-determine what the text says.

So this commentary is no substitute for the text. It is assumed that readers of this commentary will have read the portion of text being commented on and will have the Bible open at this passage as they read the commentary. Indeed, this commentary is a companion to your own reading of the book of Genesis.

A literary product

The commentary begins with the presupposition that the book of Genesis is a literary product. As we will see, it is a complex literary product. But it is a literary product. We must therefore pay careful and close attention to the text. The translation that we will follow in order to do this is the NRSV. Where necessary (and this will happen fairly regularly), we will depart from the NRSV to try to get a feel for the Hebrew text itself. In many of the stories of Genesis there is a play on words, which is often missed in translation. Generally speaking, however, the NRSV does a pretty good job and will prove a worthy basis for our reading. Having said that, although the NRSV is the English text usually referred to, any translation can be used together with this commentary. Indeed, more than one translation will be most helpful.

Biblical scholarship on the book of Genesis has been dominated by historical and, more recently, sociological concerns. This has tended to fragment the text, dividing it up into different 'sources'. However, the process that led to these concerns came from a close and careful reading of the text. It was as scholars attempted to make sense of the text that they noticed tensions and discrepancies in the text itself. This, together with the emergence of modern science and various historical discoveries in the 19th century, generated an interest in the socio-historical dimensions of the text.

Given that biblical scholarship continues to be dominated by these socio-historical interests, commentaries tend to begin with this perspective, depriving the reader of the chance to follow the path that the commentators themselves have trod. This commentary attempts to follow that path by beginning with the text itself. We will read the text and try to make sense of it as it is. We will therefore allow the reading process to generate its own questions. When we encounter something that we cannot make sense of from our own reading of the text, we will then begin to delve into the socio-historical dimensions behind the text, to see if they can explain our reading experience.

The stories of the book of Genesis individually and the book as a whole demonstrate a quite remarkable literary quality. This is what has made them so memorable. The language and images are rich and complex and worthy of our careful attention.

A composite book

Having said this, even a cursory reading of Genesis makes it clear that we are dealing with a composite text. Genesis is composite in a number of ways. First, the book of Genesis consists of different kinds of literature. There are many different genres, including narratives, poetry and genealogies. Among the narratives there are also a number of sub-genres, including long novellas, like the Joseph story (chs. 37—50) and short sagas, like the series of connected stories about Abraham (chs. 12—25).

Second, Genesis is composite in that its literature comes from different socio-historical contexts. The earliest stories would have started their life as oral accounts, and probably go back to the very earliest periods of the ancestors of Israel. There are also stories that come from considerably later periods and quite different sociological contexts, such as the exilic and post-exilic times. Different parts of the book of Genesis come from periods reaching back as far as 1300BC, and up to about 200BC. The socio-historical locations during this timespan are also considerable, ranging from the context of rural nomadic herders to the context of the courts of the kings of Israel and Judah, to the context of the exile in Babylon, to the contexts of the Persian and perhaps even Hellenistic occupations in Palestine.

Briefly, the history of Israel includes the following formative periods.

- An ancestral but historically difficult to determine period.
- A tribal/clan period from about 1300 to 1200BC.
- A period of political consolidation against the city-states of Egypt and Canaan from about 1000BC.
- The united monarchy under Saul, David and Solomon, from about 1000 to 930BC.
- The division of the monarchy after Solomon, with Israel in the north and Judah in the south, from about 930BC.
- The conquest and exile of the northern kingdom, Israel, by the Assyrian empire in 722BC.
- The conquest and exile of the southern kingdom, Judah, by the Babylonian empire in 586BC.
- Exile in Babylon from 586 to about 538BC.
- The return of some exiles to Judah under Persian colonial control from 538 to 332BC.
- A shift from Persian colonial control to Hellenistic colonial control of Judah from 332 to 140BC.

During each of these very different periods, texts that make up the book of Genesis were produced.

The third way in which Genesis is a composite text is closely related to the second. Not only does the literature come from different socio-historical times and locations, but the literature was also constantly revised and reworked during these periods and in these places. Texts from earlier periods and places were collected, included into larger narratives, and these larger narratives were then themselves revised and reworked by others in still later times and locations. Two primary concerns can be discerned in this process of constant revision and reworking. They are collection and composition.

Ancient communities were great collectors of stories, poetry, genealogies, legal and other texts, whether written or oral. Such literature was remembered and passed down from one generation to another. Very little was abandoned, although its shape may have changed with the constant retelling. At certain moments in the history of a community, however, there was a need to combine these collected resources into a more coherent account, in order to tell 'the story' of the community. In the emergence of 'Israel'—and the inverted commas are deliberate, for the book of Genesis does not overtly deal with 'Israel' in any clearly defined or demarcated sense—there were a number of defining moments when it was necessary to reflect on its identity. The most important of these moments were probably the period of the united monarchy, when 'Israel' was for a brief moment a regional power, and the period of the exile, when the leaders of 'Israel'—really Judah—found themselves exiled from the land that God had promised them. Such moments would have led to serious theological reflection and would have generated the need for some kind of coherent account. But none of these accounts were static; they were always dynamic, constantly being revised and reworked by various composers (or, to use the scholars' term, editors or redactors).

Among the more famous of the compilers or redactors of the book of Genesis are those known as the Yahwist or 'J' (because of the preference for the name 'Yahweh' for God), the Elohist or 'E' (because of the preference for the name 'Elohim' for God), and the Priestly writer or 'P'. Pick up almost any commentary or scholarly work on Genesis and you will come across them. They are, of course, the constructs of scholars. Scholars have postulated them to account for the different 'sources' that make up the book of Genesis. What complicates the matter somewhat is that each of these composers, J, E and P, themselves used various 'sources' in their compositions. In scholarly terms, however, the major 'sources' underlying the book of Genesis have traditionally been J, E and P. They can be detected, scholars have argued, by the names they use for God, their vocabulary, and their theological orientations. So, for example, J prefers the name 'Yahweh' for God, tends to use the name 'Israel' for the patriarch Jacob, and often portrays God anthropomorphically. Much of this argumentation is circular, however, for we only know what J's characteristics are when we can identify J. And how do we identify J? Well, we look for the characteristics of J! This does not mean that compilers like these did not exist, for there is clear evidence of multiple composition by different hands. We do well, though, to be circumspect about dogmatic conjectures about these hypothetical constructs.

This kind of recognition—namely, that the book of Genesis is a composite text put together by generations of collecting and composing—has produced copious amounts of scholarly work, as biblical scholars have endeavoured to understand a complex process. What seemed fairly certain 50 years ago is less certain now, however. The more we learn, the less certain we have become. Part of the problem is the difficulty of exact socio-historical reconstruction. We simply do not have enough external evidence to be sure about dates and places.

What is clear is that the book of Genesis draws on a range of resources from each of the various periods and locations of its formation. Genesis belongs to its socio-historical context, difficult as it is to determine these contexts accurately. There is no doubt that the various texts making up the book engage with the world that produced them. What is also clear, however, is that successive generations brought their own, new questions and concerns to the texts they inherited. These people were not as constrained as we are with texts, so constantly revised and reworked them in order to express their own understandings.

The book of Genesis is like a beloved patchwork quilt that has been handed down from generation to generation for more than a thousand years. Some of the original patches can still be seen, although they too have probably been retouched. Panels of patches have been sewn together in an attempt to convey a message, and have then been unpicked and resewn in a different order or with new patches included. From time to time, borders have been added, to try to show the design of the whole, but these borders have also themselves been unpicked, reworked and then resewn, providing fresh perspectives and understandings of God's purposes.

Theological contestation

The various 'hands' and 'voices' that we encounter in this complex text are not innocent. They each have something to say. As we know, history tends to be written by the winners, so it is not surprising that the priestly community that came to dominate and control 'Israel' after the exile had the final word. In terms of our metaphor, they did the final work on the quilt, providing it with its final shape. After them, the book achieved its present canonical form and was no longer allowed to be altered.

Recent biblical scholarship has attempted to interpret the book of Genesis as the product of this priest-controlled community, with fascinating results. Perhaps the best example is Mark Brett's book, *Genesis: Procreation and the Politics of Identity*, in which he argues that Genesis in its final form is a direct response to the ethnocentrism of the Persian period. After the exile in Babylon, those who returned to Judea became excessively focused on their ethnic identity, and began to exclude those who were not considered 'pure' Judeans. But the book of Genesis, which came to its present form during this same period, rejects this narrow understanding of what it means to be a Judean/Jew. The way Genesis does this, Brett suggests, is by embodying theological contestation. So while the final form does represent the voice and hand of the priestly community who were in control, it also preserves what they inherited, giving different voices a presence. By paying close and careful attention to the text, therefore, we can hear multiple voices and see different ideologies. The book of Genesis, in other words, resists restriction to a single message.

This is important, because Genesis is a dangerous book. As Clare Amos says in her own commentary on the book of Genesis, in the so-called Middle East today, 'real people really get killed in part because of beliefs some human beings may hold about the book of Genesis'. 'I will never forget,' she says, 'my incredulity at being told by a Palestinian friend of mine, an educated Christian woman from Ramallah, a town on the West Bank, how on a visit to Jerusalem she had had a conversation with a Western tourist. On discovering that she was a Christian living on the West Bank, this person had informed her, quite categorically, that "she couldn't be a real Christian, because if she were a real Christian she would of course have been willing to leave her home town, since she would know that God had given the land to the descendants of Abraham, Isaac and Jacob".' A close reading of Genesis shows that Ishmael, the ancestor of Muslims, is included in God's promise. Although the favoured line seems to be Isaac's, there are many indications in the text that God does not abandon Ishmael.

Genesis has also done extensive damage in South Africa and in the world more generally by providing support for racial discrimination. The curse on Ham/Canaan in Genesis 9 and the story of the tower of Babel in Genesis 11 have been used to provide theological under-pinning for the evil political system of apartheid in South Africa. Furthermore, the creation story in Genesis 1, the story of the garden of Eden in Genesis 2—3 and the story of Noah in Genesis 9 have all been used to justify human exploitation of the environment. Genesis 2—3 has also been used to justify the inferiority of women, not least by the writer of 1 Timothy, who has been followed by generations of male commentators. Finally, the story of the destruction of Sodom and Gomorrah in Genesis 18—19 has been read as a text condemn-ing homosexuality. Indeed, Genesis is a dangerous book.

But a close and careful reading of the text suggests a host of other more redemptive interpretations. Genesis does deal with cosmic matters, but on the whole it is about family matters. Most of the stories are about a family, although this family has had to bear the heavy weight of our theological and ideological baggage. They can and do, therefore, speak to each one of us about ordinary but import-ant matters, such as the fear of being unable to have children, the responsibilities of having children, the tensions within a family; they speak about jealousy, envy, lust, love, forgiveness and trust; they speak about leadership; and they speak about God's presence and absence in human life.

Genesis frames our reading of the whole Bible and is therefore a very important book in our theological understanding. It begins with God and ends with the chosen family waiting for God to call them from Egypt. It is intensely theological. The challenge that awaits us as we re-read Genesis with this commentary is to try to hear it afresh, trusting that, as we do so, we will hear the voice of God.

A commentary among commentaries

Of commentaries and books about Genesis, there are many. For those with a historical interest, these are worth considering:

John Skinner, *Genesis* (T&T Clark, 1930). An old commentary, but a fount of information and detail for the serious reader.

Gerhard von Rad, *Genesis* (SCM, 1972). A readable commentary, though aimed at the scholar, with plenty of historical and theological comment.

Walter Brueggemann, *Genesis* (Westminster John Knox Press, 1982). A profoundly theological commentary, suitable to a wide range of readers.

Claus Westermann, *Genesis* (T&T Clark, 1988). A historical commentary aimed at a scholarly audience.

John Rogerson, *Genesis 1—11* (Sheffield Academic Press, 1991). A general overview of how this important section of Genesis has been read through the ages. Accessible by a range of readers.

Clare Amos, *Genesis* (Epworth Press, 2004). A new and engaging commentary accessible by a wide range of readers.

For those with a literary interest, these are worth considering:

Robert Alter, *Genesis: Translation and Commentary* (Norton, 1996). An accessible commentary, but aimed at the scholar.

David W. Cotter, *Berit Olam Studies in Hebrew Narrative and Poetry: Genesis* (Liturgical Press, 2003). A beautifully written commentary, full of literary and theological insight, and suitable for a wide range of readers.

For those with an interest in the final form of Genesis, the following is worth considering:

Mark Brett, *Genesis: Procreation and the Politics of Identity* (Routledge, 2000). A scholarly analysis, but worth the effort.

And for those interested in Genesis and ecology, the following is worth considering:

Norman C. Habel and Shirley Wurst (eds.), *The Earth Story in Genesis* (Sheffield Academic Press, 2000). A range of essays, most of which are very interesting, though aimed primarily at a scholarly readership.

Back to the book of Genesis

Just like our theological baggage, commentaries too can determine how we read a particular text. So while it is possible to say much more by way of introduction to the book of Genesis, sufficient has been said for us to begin reading the text itself. 'In the beginning...'

1 GENESIS 1—11

ADAM *to* SHEM: *an* OVERVIEW

A hundred years ago, the main concern of biblical scholarship was to reconcile Genesis 1—11 with the scientific discoveries of the 19th century. In the 1970s and 1980s its main concern has been to interpret Genesis 1—11 in the light of liberation theology, feminist theology and the ecological crisis.

So writes John Rogerson as he reflects on the changing fashions of biblical interpretation with respect to Genesis 1—11.

Geography and biology

Voyages of trade and exploration in the 15th to 18th centuries raised questions about the world envisaged by Genesis. The world being discovered was much bigger and more diversely populated than Genesis 10 implied, suggesting that this text was not an authoritative account geographically. While doubts were raised about Genesis 10, however, at the beginning of the 19th century it was still generally believed that Genesis 1 was in harmony with scientific discoveries and that Genesis 2—3 was a historically true story about the earliest ancestors of the human race. Geological discoveries and Charles Darwin's theory of natural selection in the mid-19th century generated further questions. Geological study showed that the world was much older than the age suggested by biblical chronology. Evolutionary theory offered an alternative account of how humankind had come into being. So, during the late 19th century, dialogue between the discourses of science and biblical scholarship provided the framework for the interpretation of Genesis 1—11.

Sources and history

Another voice joined the discussion during the same period. In the late 1800s, the discovery of ancient Babylonian texts demonstrated that the creation story in Genesis 1 almost certainly draws upon a Babylonian creation story. At the same time, another Babylonian text was found which showed many similarities with the flood story in Genesis 6—8. The task of biblical scholarship became one of examining the similarities and differences between the texts of this region, and in so doing to attempt to identify what was unique about the beliefs of ancient Israel.

This socio-historical concern continues into the present, with much of biblical scholarship continuing to focus on the relationships between Genesis 1—11 and the socio-historical world that produced it. Interest remains not only in the sources that were used to construct the accounts in Genesis 1—11, but also in how those sources were used and then combined. The 'how' question, it is argued, gives us a glimpse of the theological orientation of those who used the available resources and reworked them for their own purposes.

By locating these texts historically, even if the dates are tentative, scholars provided a base from which to do sociological reconstructions of the world at that time, providing invaluable information on the world that produced the text. So, for example, by dating the creation story in Genesis 1 to the exilic or post-exilic period, scholars were able to examine how the so-called Priestly writer/s used and reworked Babylonian stories to convey their own message.

Literature

Alongside this interest in the socio-historical dimensions of Genesis 1—11, another strand of interest arose in the 1970s. Instead of trying to get behind the text to the socio-historical world that produced it, some scholars began to focus on the text itself. Genesis 1—11, they argued, was not primarily history but literature. As literature, it deserved to be read closely and carefully. Furthermore, while reconstructing the history behind the text is a task fraught with problems, we actually have the text itself! By paying attention to the literary dimensions of the text, we could discern things that socio-historical work had missed. So, for example, a careful and close reading of Genesis 2—3, feminist biblical scholars showed, did not advocate an inferior position for women. Similarly, a literary approach to the flood story placed a different emphasis on it, demonstrating that although the story might have originated from two different sources, what we have is a careful literary composition.

These different methods have brought a great deal of vitality to the study of Genesis 1—11, as have the many and various 'life interests' that different readers bring to the text. One of the most creative has been the relatively recent interest in ecological issues.

PRAYER

We give thanks, our God, that we can bring the questions and concerns that fill our lives to our reading of the Bible.

2 GENESIS 1:1

The FIRST SIGN *of* LIFE: GOD (I)

In the beginning, God was already there. Before the heavens and the earth, God was there. The reader is confronted with a God who has always been there. Genesis 1:1—2:3, the story of the creation of all that is, begins with a God who is not created. God is the creator, and the opening story of Genesis is about this God.

The first sentence

As a comparison of a number of translations of verses 1–2 will show, the first sentence of Genesis is not straightforward. It can be translated either as two sentences or as one sentence with a relative clause which leads into verse 3. An example of the former would be:

(1) In the beginning God created the heavens and the earth.
(2) The earth was still a desert waste, and darkness lay upon the primeval deep and God's wind was moving to and fro over the surface of the waters.

An example of the latter would be:

(1) When God set about to create the heavens and earth——(2) the world being then a formless waste, with darkness over the seas and only an awesome wind sweeping over the water——

The reason for this variety is the first two words in Hebrew, 'In the beginning' and 'he created'. (It is important to note that the use of the masculine pronoun 'he' here reflects the grammatical gender of the verb and the noun 'Elohim', and not the actual gender of God.) The first of these words usually indicates the beginning of something, such as the beginning of the harvest. It is never used to indicate an absolute beginning. The implication of the use of this word here is that what is being described is the first of a series of creative acts rather than an absolute beginning from nothing. Some commentators have suggested that the word implies that God has already created other things, and have speculated that the other things may be the Law or the angels. What seems more likely is that the word indicates that God created the heavens and the earth out of pre-existing chaotic matter, and not out of nothing.

The second word, 'he created', cannot be defined with precision, but includes the following senses. First, it is an act of making/creating that is exclusively divine. Only God is the subject of this verb. Second, the word contains a sense of the extraordinary. Third, its meaning includes a sense of effortless production. And finally, the term is focused on the product and not on the process. The object that follows this verb is always a product of God's creative activity.

God

This brings us to the third word in the opening sentence of Genesis, 'God'. The author does not use the personal name of Israel's God, Yahweh. The generic term for God, 'Elohim', is used instead. This must be a deliberate attempt to avoid any narrow identification of the God who created the heavens and the earth with Israel alone. The second thing to notice about this term for God is that it is plural in form. Because the Hebrew verb used with it is singular, the word Elohim is usually translated as singular. The grammatical ambiguity remains, though, and poses the question of whether the divine is singular or plural. In these verses, and most of the verses that follow, the consistent use of singular verbs suggests that we give Elohim a singular sense. The grammatical uncertainty returns later in 1:26 where Elohim speaks in the plural form, suggesting perhaps some kind of divine council: 'Let us make humankind in our image, according to our likeness.'

The book of Genesis resists a simple, unidimensional sense of who God is. This is evident in the shifting names used for God. The 'Elohim' of 1:1—2:3 becomes 'Yahweh Elohim' in Genesis 2:4 to 3:24, and then 'Yahweh' in Genesis 4. Later in Genesis, there are a variety of other names for the divinity, including El Elyon, El Roi, El Shaddai and others, some of which seem to identify the god of a particular family—'the god of Abraham', 'the god of Jacob', and so on. Genesis 1:1 unsettles settled notions of God, and this is perhaps its initial point. But is this all that it does? Of course not, for in the next sentence the focus shifts to the product of God's creative act.

PRAYER

God of life, God of creation, hallowed be your name,
however we name you.

The FIRST SIGN *of* LIFE: GOD (II)

Within the first sentence, the object of God's creation is 'the heavens and the earth' (1:1). We are also given a glimpse, or a feel, for what was there before.

The product

God creates 'the heavens and the earth'. The use of these two terms designates the totality of all creation. In verse 2, however, our attention focuses on 'the earth', for this is the focus of God's attention. 'The earth', as God contemplates it, is formless and empty: it has no structure and it has no content. God will provide both. The Hebrew words used here rhyme, an indication perhaps of the limits of prose to report God's divine action. Prose cannot capture what God sees and does, so poetry is used. The reader is invited to feel the desolation before God. Next, the reader is asked to see—or, more accurately, not to see, for 'darkness was over the face of the chaotic sea'. There is nothing to see; we can only imagine the chaos. And yet, finally, there is a spark of hope, for 'the spirit/wind/storm of God vibrated/trembled/moved/stirred over the face of the waters'. Implicit in the formless and empty chaos evoked for us is the presence of God. God is present in some way, these verses affirm, even before the heavens and earth are given shape and content.

The *Enuma Elish*

That God is there in the beginning, uncreated, is itself a profound theological statement, contrasting as it does with the conceptions of God or the gods prevalent in the ancient Near East when Genesis 1:1—2:3 is believed to have been written. Careful scholarly research seems to indicate that this first story in the book of Genesis is a relatively recent one, composed by members of a priestly community in exile in Babylon or on their return to Israel after the exile. Part of its purpose, it is suggested, is to provide the existing narratives of the Israelite nation with a creation story that incorporates their own theological perspective over against the dominant creation story of the day—the Babylonian creation story found in the *Enuma Elish*.

The time of the Babylonian exile (587–539BC) was an immensely creative period, both theologically and from a literary perspective. The crisis of being taken by force from their land generated an enormous amount of theological reflection and literature. Much of the existing literature, whether oral or written, was gathered together and edited. In addition, new texts were written, including Genesis 1:1—2:3. Given the similarities between the *Enuma Elish* and the Genesis story, scholars have postulated that the Genesis account was constructed as a polemic against the religion of Babylon.

The *Enuma Elish* is an ancient Babylonian text, dating to about 2000BC. The Genesis account of creation dialogues point by point with the *Enuma Elish*, sharing with it similar images and concerns, but providing a different perspective on each of its assertions about the nature of divinity and the universe. The Genesis account thereby asserts a different theological identity for God and God's people. This is how David Cotter summarizes the relationship between the creation accounts in the *Enuma Elish* and Genesis:

> *Using the template of a story that was both widely known and believed, the author of Genesis 1 describes the same known universe but endows it with a very different theology and anthropology. One eternally existing and uncreated God creates everything without any expenditure of effort. Into a universe that is not founded on the remains of dead and defeated gods and goddesses but is simply an inanimate platform, God places a likeness of the divine person to rule the universe in God's stead. There is one God, not many warring gods. Humanity is good, free, and godlike, not mere slave creatures. Time is holy, not to be feared.*

Doing theology

Israel was not alone in the ancient Near East, so not only are its texts shaped by the context that it shared with other peoples; they are also shaped by the texts of these peoples, whether oral or written. But Genesis 1 is not only a response to the *Enuma Elish*; it is also an articulation of theological views that have a long history within Israel itself. As we consider Genesis 1 in more detail, these theological perspectives will become more apparent.

PRAYER

Speak to us, God of creation, as we read and reflect on your word.

The FIRST & SECOND DAYS

The introduction in verses 1–2 prepares the way for the details of God's creation. God provides form and content. The first four days focus on the form, the infrastructure on which the content depends. The task of the first and second days is to order and limit the primeval chaos.

The first day

The work of God is done through the divine word. God's command creates. The command of God in each case is instantly obeyed (v. 3). God is engaged in, but separate from, the created order. From the primeval chaos, structure is created. The first of the structural elements necessary for life is created: light. With the creation of light, God also creates time (v. 5). With no other observer present to comment on God's work, God is the sole judge of what has been created. Given that the light would illuminate the formlessness and emptiness of the primeval chaos, God's declaration that the light is good (v. 4) is also a sign that more creation will follow. Although there may be an aesthetic element in God's declaration that the light is good, it is more probably a designation of the correspondence between what God intended and what God sees (see also Psalm 104:31). What God had wanted to create has been created.

But the work of God is not yet done, for God now orders the light and the darkness. According to this creation account, darkness is an element of the primeval chaos. With the creation of something new, light, God constrains and limits but does not eradicate the darkness. Darkness and light are 'separated'. The Hebrew word used conveys a sense that each has its own domain or abode (see also Job 38:19–21).

One final aspect of the first day's work remains. God names, signifying God's ownership of what God has created. By naming the light 'Day' and the darkness 'Night', the text returns to the world of the reader. We have read or listened in awe as we are granted a glimpse of God at work. Now we are returned to the present and to the familiar, to the world we know. But we wait eagerly for what is to come.

It is perhaps worth noting that the translation of the Hebrew word for 'day' as 'eon' or 'period' by some authors, so as to harmonize scientific accounts of creation with this account, is most unlikely. There is no warrant for it at all in the Hebrew usage in this account.

The second day

The rhythm of creation continues. Again God speaks (v. 6). However, this command of God is not immediately followed by the product, as was the case with the creation of light. Instead God 'made' (v. 7) what God wanted. God not only speaks; God also 'gets God's hands dirty'! Theologically, God is now more immanent in creation. Whether these two modes of God's activity indicate two different traditions that have been combined here, as some scholars have suggested, is difficult to determine. What is more likely is that the account wants to show that God is both separate from the created order and active in it. When we read that God speaks, we imagine the mouth; when we read that God made, we imagine the hands. These two different ways of portraying God's creative work emphasize different theological understandings of God's work and presence.

What God makes is the firmament or the 'dome' (NRSV). Just as God separated the light and the darkness, so now God creates a structure to separate the primeval chaotic waters. Again, chaos is not destroyed; it is ordered and controlled. Theologically, chaos is part of the created order, although its origins are not explicitly discussed in this account. The grammatical ambiguity of verses 1 and 2 both reveals and conceals. The origins of chaos and darkness and all that they signify are not dealt with here. What is dealt with is their delimitation. They are constrained within God's order.

The firmament or dome is envisaged as an actual structure (see Psalm 104:13; Amos 9:6; Job 37:18), above which are the heavenly waters, and from which the rain descends through windows or doors (see Genesis 7:11; 8:2; 2 Kings 7:2, 19), according to God's pleasure (Psalm 78:23). The dome separates heaven and earth, and fulfils the same function as the light: it orders and draws boundaries for the primeval chaos. The naming of the dome as 'Sky' (v. 8) once again returns the reader to the world we know.

PRAYER

Creator of the universe, we wonder in awe at the work of your words and your hands.

5

The THIRD & FOURTH DAYS

There are a number of ways in which we can analyse the acts and days of creation. One is to follow each act, day by day, as we are doing here. Even as we do so, however, we must try to discern other orderings, for this text is rich in detail. For example, on the first day and the second day, the phrase 'God said' is used only once on each 'day'. Yet on the third day, 'God said' twice, whereas on the fourth day it is again only once. Does this mark the third day as especially significant?

The third day

The work of the third day completes what was begun on the second day. The chaotic waters below the dome are now ordered and consigned to set boundaries (see Psalm 104:7–9; Jeremiah 5:22). The expression 'gathered together' (v. 9) seems to imply that the earth already existed as a solid mass, but that it was covered with water (see Psalm 104:5–6). Alternatively, the language may suggest, supported by 1:2, that God is separating the muddy primeval waters into their two elements, water and dry land.

God's command is obeyed, and the chaotic waters are controlled and bounded. The naming of these two elements, 'Earth' and 'Seas' (v. 10), is a further sign of God's ordering and constraining work. Time and space have now been created. What God sees is how it should be, and so God declares it to be good. There is a contemplative aspect to God's consideration of what has been created: God considers, and acknowledges it to be good.

The work of the third day is not complete, however. The newly revealed earth is now summoned to participate in creation. The feminine grammatical gender of the word 'earth' is suggestive of the earth as mother. God creates a connection between the earth and the plant life that the earth is called upon to 'sprout forth' (v. 11). God mediates; God is the midwife of the plants. The vegetation or 'the greenness' (v. 12) is divided into two primary kinds: plants that yield seed directly and plants that produce seed indirectly through their fruit. Common to both is the ability to be self-sustaining. God mediates, but the earth and its vegetation are designed to be regenerating. Once again, God reflects and considers that what has been done is good.

The fourth day

The fourth day is of special importance, for it brings to completion the basic structure of God's creative work. In a sense, the creation of 'lights in the dome of the sky' (v. 14) continues the work of the first and second days. The light that was created on the first day is now given form, as a greater light, a lesser light, and stars (v. 16). These lights are given functions, namely to designate seasons, days and years, and to give light on the earth. Finally, these lights are allocated a place in God's created order, in the dome of the sky.

Quite deliberately, the lights are not given names—and some scholars even suggest that the phrase 'and the stars' is a later addition. In the ancient Near East, particularly among the Babylonians, the heavenly bodies were animated beings, often associated with the gods. In Hebrew poetry the idea remains (see Judges 5:20; Isaiah 40:26; Job 38:7), but it is not present in this account. The lights here could simply be translated as 'lamps'. They are not the creators of light, but only the mediating bearers of light that was there without them and before them. They become the vehicles for separating the day and the night.

In a way, these lights, like the vegetation, are also a sign of a self-sustaining universe. These bodies of light mediate God's light, day after day, night after night, and season after season. Significantly, the darkness, called 'Night' (1:5), is now given light 'to rule over it'. The boundaries between light and darkness had been set on the first day; now on the fourth day, the state of darkness is permanently altered to include some light, though a lesser light than that of the day. Chaos is being incrementally controlled.

In the first four days, God has established the basic infrastructure for animate life. Time, space and food are now in place. God has 'separated' and distinguished and located the elements of structure necessary for the next step, the creation of life.

PRAYER

Thank you, God our father and mother, for the earth,
the mother of all green things.

6   GENESIS 1:20–25

The FIFTH & SIXTH DAYS

As we have seen, there are a number of ways in which we can analyse
the structure of the eight-act, six-day creation. One way is to recognize a series of parallels between spaces and their inhabitants. Days
1 and 4 are linked, with the space (light) being inhabited by the
lights; similarly, days 2 and 5 are linked, with the waters and firmament being inhabited by the fish and birds respectively. And finally,
days 3 and 6 are linked, with the dry land and the vegetation being
inhabited by land animals, people and food. We consider now the
details of the fifth and the sixth days.

The fifth day

According to this cosmology (and its focus is theological, not scientific), the world is now ready for other forms of life. The earth has
brought forth vegetation with seed, but this is not yet 'life'. God must
'create'—the same verb as was used in 1:1—'life' (v. 21). The waters
and the dome of the sky are called upon by God to play a role in this
(v. 20), but it is not the same role that the earth was summoned to
play. The NRSV translation here is misleading, implying that the same
verb is being used as was used in 1:11. In both cases, the NRSV uses
a similar phrase: 'put forth' (1:11) and 'bring forth' (v. 20). However,
a more accurate translation of the Hebrew would be, 'Let the waters
teem with life'. The Septuagint, which the NRSV may be following
here, does suggest a more procreative role for the waters, but given
the ambiguity with which 'the waters' are viewed in this account, it
is unlikely that they are endowed with a procreative capacity. Furthermore, verse 21 makes it quite clear that God is directly and singularly
the creator of 'life'. According to the Hebrew text, the role of the sea
and the sky is to be receptive to the life that God creates and to
accommodate it. They are the places allocated to the two forms of life
that God creates, respectively marine creatures of every kind and
birds of every kind. In this very act of placing life within the waters,
God is bringing order to chaos. God is bending chaos to the purposes
of God.

    The specific mention of 'the great sea monsters' (v. 21) is a further
indication of this account's dialogue with its world. Even the unruly

embodiments of chaos, the great sea monsters, are merely a part of God's creation. They are mere creatures, not contestants with God (as in the Babylonian *Enuma Elish*). Nothing is outside of God's created order.

What is unique to the fifth day is that God blesses these creatures and gives them the capacity to procreate (v. 22). Having created life, God enables it to be life-sustaining.

The sixth day

The earth is again commanded to 'bring forth' (v. 24, although again the verb used is different from that in 1:11) and so to participate in God's creation. Like the plants, the land animals are conceived of as products of the earth, their bodies being part of the earth's substance. There appear to be three classifications of animal envisaged in this account: wild animals, domesticated animals and reptiles (possibly including insects). A similar classification system has been found on a Babylonian tablet, indicating how the peoples of the ancient Near East may have classified their world.

Everything that has been brought about by God's word on days 5 and 6 is declared to be good (v. 25). The phrase 'And God saw that it was good' is not used at the end of each day, indicating that the division into days is not the only way of understanding God's work. The locations of these phrases of affirmation cut across days, considering not only the work done on a particular day, but the work done up to that point (see 1:12b, 18b, 25b). Perhaps their position indicates the key moments in the creative order: light, vegetation, fish and fowl life, and animal life. The final time the phrase is used will be after the creation of human life.

PRAYER

We marvel, God of all creation, at the works of your words and hands. We are blessed to be a part of what you have blessed.

The SIXTH DAY (CONTINUED)

The last of God's creative acts is the creation of humankind (*adam* in the Hebrew). Before the actual moment of creation (v. 27), we are allowed to overhear God conceiving of the product (v. 26). The plural form that is used here alerts us to something special. For the first time, the plural noun 'Elohim' (God) receives a plural verb ('let *us* make'). The same verb that was used in 1:7 is used here, the difference being that in 1:7 the verb was in the singular, whereas in verse 26 it is in the plural. Another difference is that in 1:7 it was the action of God that was being reported, whereas in verse 26 we overhear God contemplating the project of the sixth day. These are signals to the reader to pay attention.

Is this a recognition of God as plural, which in this instance takes the noun 'Elohim' at face value, as a plural form? This seems unlikely in an account that takes pains to avoid any sense of plural gods. Is it an indication of God's consultation with some kind of heavenly council (see Genesis 3:22; 11:7; Isaiah 6:8; 1 Kings 22:19–22; Job 1:6)? Again, there is no other hint of this in the creation account, so it seems unlikely. Is it some kind of royal 'we'? This is, after all, the first time in the account that we hear God speaking in the first person. Although not an impossible interpretation, it too seems unlikely, for this is not a feature of Hebrew idiom. Is it simply a form of deliberative language, such as the English 'Let's make...', where we use the plural form but clearly intend a singular subject? This is certainly a possible interpretation. Is the plural subject used because a plural object is intended, even though the object (*adam*/'humankind') is a generic, grammatically singular noun? In other words, is the account attempting to convey that there is nothing in the unity and diversity of humankind that does not derive from God? This interpretation is wonderfully suggestive, and links rather well with the rest of the verse.

In our likeness

As indicated, the object or product of the sixth day is 'humankind' (*adam*), a collective noun. But the sentence does not end here. Humankind is to be made 'in our image, according to our likeness'.

There is a vast literature on how to understand the ways in which humanity is like God. Given the other acts of creation, one important respect in which humanity is like God is that humankind is of only one kind! The term for 'kind' used in the creation of vegetation, fish and fowl, and of the land animals, is not used here. This is a remarkable theological position, rejecting as it does the denigration of any part of humankind, whether in terms of race, gender, culture, religion, sexual orientation or affliction (such as HIV/AIDS). Humankind is sacred, like God.

The likeness of humankind to God gives humankind a special position and special responsibilities with respect to the rest of creation. Humankind is to 'have dominion/rule over' the rest of creation. The plural form of the verb is used, making it clear that the singular *adam* is a collective noun. Given human history and the rather precarious state of our planet, how are we to understand this 'dominion'? We need to read on to obtain further information.

Verse 27 is the implementation of God's contemplation. God now 'creates' humankind. The verb used is the same as in 1:1 and 21, signifying God's unique creative contribution (and now that we move into a report of God's work, we shift from the plural to the singular verb). Humanity is like the rest of animate life. The repetition in verse 27 of humankind being created in the image of God makes the point, however, that humankind is also unlike animate life. The use of rhythmic poetic language here is a further indication of something special being done. Having said this, the blessing of humankind by God (v. 28), just as God blessed the first forms of animate life (1:22), is a sign of similarity, as is the command to regenerate. Finally—and this is another way in which humanity is different—God commands that humankind 'fill the earth and subdue it'. Those with ecological concerns might shudder at this combination of verbs! However, when we remember that chaos and darkness are a constituent part of 'the earth', God may here be calling humankind to stand alongside God in the ongoing task of ordering and controlling chaos.

PRAYER

God of humankind, thank you for reminding us that we are all of one kind. Forgive us whenever we consider others less than human.

8

The SIXTH & SEVENTH DAYS

Fill and subdue

That the verbs 'fill the earth and subdue it' (v. 28) do not command exploitation of the earth is apparent in what follows (as well as what has gone before). The marine creatures were commanded to 'fill' the waters (1:22), whereas the birds were not so commanded: they were merely told to multiply. The land animals are given no command to multiply at all, perhaps because they are the procreative product of the earth itself. In 'filling' the earth, humankind obviously has to share it with others (the birds and the land creatures) who have explicitly been given a place in it (1:22, 24–25). Furthermore, human beings are not commanded to 'subdue' other creatures, only 'the earth'. Humankind is to 'have dominion' (1:26, 28) over other animate life. Although the verb is not the same, the sense is perhaps similar to that of 'the two great lights' which were set in the dome of the sky 'to rule over' (1:18) the day and night. Human beings, like God's great lights, regulate life; they do not harm life. This regulating role is further supported by the limitation placed on humankind's food. Like all animate life, humankind is restricted to vegetation as its form of food (vv. 29–30). In this account, animate life, including humankind, is substantially similar in this respect. Implied in this restriction is that blood will not be shed.

Differentiation

We must now return to one other feature of God's creation of humankind: the differentiation of humankind into male and female (v. 27). This follows the repetition of humankind being made in God's image, implying that God embodies both male and female. The grammar of the word 'God'—'Elohim' being a masculine noun and the verbs associated with it taking the masculine form—means that masculine pronouns are used in translation into English. God becomes 'he'. Although this reflects accurately the grammar of the word 'God', however, it does not reflect the gender of God the person. Any gendered reference to God in the Bible is metaphoric. Furthermore, while procreation is clearly implicit in this demarcation of humankind into male and female (see v. 28), it is not their sole or primary responsibility (see 1:26, 28). They are also required, together, to maintain God's order ('to rule') and to constrain chaos ('to subdue').

At the end of the sixth day, when all has been accomplished, God reflects on the product. Looking over all of creation, including the constrained chaos and darkness, God sees that 'everything' is 'very good' (v. 31). The totality, and not just each part, is good. Creation conforms to what God intended in the beginning.

The seventh day

The first verse of chapter 2 summarizes what has taken place. 'The heavens and the earth' as a unity, and in 'all their multitude/diversity', is now complete. But there remains one more thing to do. God rests. For the first time in this account, we read of God's 'work', and it is repeated three times in verses 2–3. Although the creative acts were undertaken with what appeared to be an effortless ease, God has worked. Work is integral to creation—and so is rest.

Work is not conceived in this account as something negative, but it does require rest afterwards. Just as God blessed work, so now God blesses rest (v. 3). God goes even further, doing something entirely new. God 'sanctified/hallowed' the seventh day. The verbs 'to create' (1:1, 21, 27; 2:3), 'to make' (1:7, 16, 25, 26, 31; 2:2–3) and 'to bless' (1:22, 28; 2:3) are found throughout the account, tying it together. What is unique to the seventh day is the verb 'to hallow'. This is where the account ends, with God resting.

It is a day on which work and rest coexist. It is important to note that 'on the seventh day God finished the work', so while this text has been used to support the notion of the sabbath, it is not a day for humankind, in this account, but for God.

In addition, for those familiar with the *Enuma Elish*, that account also ends with a concluding act following the work of creation. In that account, it is the public glorification of the god Marduk in the assembly of the gods, as the chief gods name his 50 names and extol him. How different is the concluding act in the Genesis account! Here there is no fanfare, no public acclamation of God. God simply finishes work and rests, present in creation.

PRAYER

Bless our work and our rest, Creator God of both.

9

From CREATION *to* HUMANKIND

There is a 'pause' in the text after the completion of God's creation. Just as God rests, so the text seems to pause. Verse 4 creates that pause. The first part (usually designated as 4a) could be read as the conclusion of the creation story in Genesis 1, or it could be read as the beginning of the next literary unit. Whether we read it as an end or a beginning does not really matter, however, for as we read on, it becomes clear that we have moved into another literary unit. By the time we get to the second part of the verse (4b), it is apparent that we are reading a different story.

Lord God

Perhaps the clearest signal of a new literary unit here is the change in the name of God. The NRSV faithfully represents this shift (both here and throughout the book of Genesis). Whenever the Hebrew text uses 'Elohim' (as is the case in Genesis 1:1—2:3), the NRSV translates it as 'God'. Whenever the Hebrew text uses 'Yahweh Elohim' (as is the case in Genesis 2:4—3:24), the NRSV translates it as 'LORD God'.

Elsewhere in Genesis these names for God are used separately, either 'Yahweh' or 'Elohim' (translated respectively by the NRSV as 'LORD' and 'God'). In Genesis 2:4—3:24, however, they are used in combination. Apart from its regular use in this literary unit, this combination is only used one other time (Exodus 9:30) in the Pentateuch (Genesis—Deuteronomy). Quite why this syntactically strange combination is used here is not clear, although it does serve to show that there is a clear link between the 'Elohim' of Genesis 1, the 'Yahweh Elohim' of Genesis 2—3, and the 'Yahweh' of Genesis 4. It is the same God, the phrase testifies, although that God is differently named.

The generations

Another signal that we are now encountering a different story is more apparent in the Hebrew than in English translations. In verse 4a we read, 'These are the generations of the heavens and the earth...'. The word translated as 'the generations' is the Hebrew word *toledot*, which comes from a root meaning 'to give birth to'. It is difficult to translate, so even the same English translation does not always render it in the same way on each occasion that it is used in the Hebrew. The NRSV is no exception; it too translates this word in different ways. What readers of the English text may miss as a consequence is the role that it plays in the book of Genesis, for some scholars have argued that this word signals the linking of the various family stories found in Genesis. The word occurs in 2:4; 5:1; 6:9; 11:10, 27; 25:12, 19; 36:1, 9; 37:2. So it is probable that the use of *toledot* in verse 4 signals a transition from one story to another.

Shifts in focus, style and sources

It is clear that we encounter another, although related, story as we read on. Not only does the name of God shift; so too does the focus. We move from creation story in Genesis 1 to a story about the origin of human life and culture. The details of the rest of creation are incidental in this story. The focus is firmly on humankind. God is the grammatical subject, but humankind is the narrative subject. More specifically, the focus of Genesis 2—3 seems to be on what scholars refer to as 'etiologies'. These are stories that explore possible explanations for the origins of particular cultural practices, the most obvious being the existence of two genders, the relationship between the genders, the reason for wearing clothes, the antagonism between humans and snakes, the struggle to bear children and to produce food, and the apparent distance between God and humanity.

There is also a marked difference in style between Genesis 1 and Genesis 2—3. As one commentary has put it, Genesis 1 tells and Genesis 2—3 shows. Furthermore, while in Genesis 1 God is the only speaker, in Genesis 2—3 others speak as well. Indeed, Genesis 3 is characterized by dialogue.

Such clear differences between Genesis 1:1—2:3 and Genesis 2:4—3:24 have led earlier generations of readers to speculate about, and then to postulate, the relationship between these different 'sources'. While Genesis 1 has traditionally (in biblical scholarship) been allocated to the work of P (specifying the Priestly writer/s who, it is suggested, composed this story), Genesis 2—3 has been allocated to the work of J (the Yahwist, a writer who traditionally has been located in the time of Solomon).

PRAYER

Open our ears, Lord God, to hear you speak a new word to us.

ADAM, *the* GROUND-CREATURE

The NRSV captures rather well both the awkwardness and the focus of verses 4b–7. The main clause is verse 7, the forming of humankind, which is preceded by a number of subordinate clauses. These subordinate clauses give the time and setting of God's (Yahweh Elohim's) formation of humankind. Both the time and the setting, however, are presented in the most general terms (vv. 4–6). Interestingly, the general setting, namely 'the earth and the heavens', appears in this unusual order only here and in one other text (Psalm 148:13). The normal order is 'the heavens and the earth'. Here the order is significant, signalling as it does the primary focus: the earth.

The way the earth is characterized has some resonances with the description in Genesis 1, although there are more differences than similarities. The earth is barren (v. 5a). The reasons for this are twofold. First, there is not yet rain, and second, there are no human beings to work the ground. These two components are necessary, the text teaches, to the fertility of the earth. There is a God-given component (the rain) and a human component (tilling). Water is present, but plays no generative role yet. The Hebrew word translated 'a stream' by the NRSV (v. 6) is an obscure word that may mean 'mist', 'vapour', 'stream' or even 'surging of waves'. Again, there is no real detail here, merely a general outline.

Forming the ground-creature

Once we reach verse 7, the focus of the opening sentence, and the story, is clear. Whereas Genesis 1 moved from chaos to the cosmos, Genesis 2 has a much narrower focus on the earth alone—an earth that requires collaboration between God and humankind. In chapter 1, humankind is the climax of God's creation; in Genesis 2, humankind is the centre around which creation is constructed.

After the conditional clauses in verses 4–6, we finally arrive at the first action, the creation of humanity. God is the potter forming humankind from the fundamental element of life, the ground. God forms humankind from the clay or ground. This idea was common in the ancient Near East: there is an Egyptian picture that shows the god Chnum forming human beings on the potter's wheel. God moulded 'man'.

The translation 'man' in verse 7 is extremely unfortunate, for it completely misses the relationship between the ingredient and the product. Literally, God 'formed the ground-creature from dust of the ground'. The dry ingredient—the dust of the ground—is moulded by God into a form, and this form resembles the ingredient and so is named after this ingredient. The ground-creature (ha-adam) is formed from the ground (ha-adamah). In both cases the noun is preceded by the definite article (ha, 'the'). The grammatical gender is masculine, hence the translation 'man' and the use of 'Adam' as a name. But is this product of God's formation a biological male? Or is the 'ground-creature' actually the basis for the later creation of 'man' and 'woman'? We will need to wait until 2:23 to find out.

The focus of verse 7 is not the gender or sex of the creature but the earthly/'groundly' and godly combination. The ground collaborates with God to form the ground-creature. But we are not only intimately related to the ground; we are also intimately related to God. God forms the ground-creature from dry dust and then brings it to life by God's very breath. What an intimate image! God surpasses the potter who can only make a lifeless form. Without God's breath, we are barren ground (like the earth in verse 5). No wonder a more intimate and worshipful name for God is needed: 'Lord God' (Yahweh Elohim).

Locating the ground-creature

In Genesis 2, humankind is the first act of God's creation. Having 'formed' humanity, God's second act is to create a place and a purpose for it. The place is a garden (v. 8) and the purpose is 'to till it and keep it' (v. 15). In the midst of the barren earth, God creates abundant and beautiful plant life (v. 9). Intriguingly, among this plant life are two specifically named trees: 'the tree of life' and 'the tree of the knowledge of good and evil'. Their purpose is not immediately apparent, but becomes clearer later.

The name 'Eden' appears to be the proper name of a place in a designated region ('the east'). The point here is not to designate a particular historical period or place, however. Like the other details in this chapter, the garden's location is vague.

PRAYER

Lord God, we celebrate our connectedness with the ground and with you, our moulder and maker.

HUMANKIND *in the* GARDEN

From the same ground that God used to form the ground-creature, God 'grows' a garden of trees (2:9). No other plants are mentioned; other plants, it seems from 2:5, require human work. God provides the trees and their fruit (and their beauty). God provides all this, but humankind also has a task.

The task of humankind

The primary task of humankind appears to be particularly focused and clear in verse 15: 'to till and keep' the garden. The ambiguity of Genesis 1 in terms of humankind's relationship to the environment is not entirely absent from Genesis 2, however. The references in 2:10–14 to gold, an aromatic resin and gemstones hints at human exploitation of the earth for its natural resources. Verse 15 is clear, though, that humankind's primary purpose is 'to till and keep' the garden in which God has placed it.

The NRSV's use of the word 'till' is perhaps misleading, for this word is associated with cultivation and agriculture. Clearly the 'garden' is not the average vegetable or flower garden, for it is a garden entirely of trees. According to the story, so far, there is no need to 'till' the garden in order to produce food. The trees already provide food (2:9). The 'garden' is a forest of beautiful and food-bearing trees, and human-kind's task is to 'work/serve and care for it'. This translation captures more closely the picture before us. Humankind's task is a modest one, not an invasive one. Made from the same ground as the garden, humankind is to serve and care for the ecosystem in which God has placed it.

The limits of humankind

No sooner is humanity given its task than God sets a limit on human-ity (v. 16). Humankind is substantially but not totally free. All the trees are available for food, including, we must presume, the tree of life. Only one tree is off-limits, the tree of the knowledge of good and evil (v. 17). The fruit of that tree brings death, not life. Why humankind should not eat of this tree is not told, except that it brings death. But this is not a *reason* for why humankind must not eat of the knowledge of good and evil. We are told the consequences but not the reason, although this has not stopped generations of readers from speculating. Some have suggested that the fruit of the tree produces moral choice, but later in the story, the woman, before she eats of the tree, shows that she already has moral choice (3:6). Some have suggested that eating from the fruit of this tree results in the knowledge of sexuality, but the man and the woman obviously already experience this knowledge (2:23–25). Perhaps the limit is an arbitrary one, a sign of humankind's finitude. Humankind is like God, but humankind is also unlike God. Humankind is limited. Indeed, perhaps verse 16 points to the crucial difference between God and humankind: God knows all things, whereas humankind knows only partially. To desire to know all is to lose our humanity, and so to die.

Humankind's companions

The story does not linger on these matters, moving quickly to another important aspect of humankind's identity. Plentiful food and beauty are not enough. The human being needs companions, other creatures like itself. So from the same ground that God used to form the ground-creature and grow the trees, God 'forms' the full diversity of animal life (v. 19). By bringing the animals to the ground-creature, God is not so much giving humankind power over them as asking humankind to recognize them as being from the same source: God and the ground. There is a distinction, here as in Genesis 1, for God does not intimately breathe into the animals, but it is the similarity, not the difference, that is emphasized here. The human being names the animals from the recognition that they share common ground (v. 20).

Behind God's gesture of bringing the animals to humankind is another concern, namely, to see if any of them has the capacity to be an appropriate or fit companion or helper for the ground-creature. But, the narrator tells us, 'for *ha-adam* there was not found an appropriate companion' (v. 20). The animal world is related to humanity and does offer support and companionship but not the kind of intimate partnership that God intends. So God reaches into the ground-creature instead of outside it, to find the fitting companion.

PRAYER

Thank you, Lord God, for reminding us of your intentions for us and of our connections to the world in which we live.

MAN, WOMAN & POETRY

The ground-creature does recognize the vast variety of animal life that God brings before it, and so the ground-creature is able to give each of them a name, identifying them. But this recognition also results in an awareness, according to the narrator, that none of these animals is that appropriate and intimate partner envisaged by God. So God adopts a different creative strategy. Instead of reaching again for the ground, God reaches into the ground-creature.

God puts the ground-creature, the Human, to 'sleep'. The word used here is used elsewhere to refer to a kind of deep sleep that is receptive to an encounter with the divine. God prepares to engage with the Human, *ha-adam*, in a unique manner. When the Human is asleep, God draws out a rib, and from this material makes Woman (*ishah*, v. 22). God then brings this creature, just as God brought all the animals, to the Human. The Human, on seeing this creature, undergoes a further transformation, breaking into poetry and becoming Man (*ish*). English does not cope too well with the wonderful poetry of the Hebrew, so a more literal translation is necessary:

> *The Human (*ha-adam*) said:*
> *This time, she is it!*
> *Bone from my bones,*
> *flesh from my flesh.*
> *This one shall be called Woman/Female (ishah)*
> *for from Man/Male (ish) this one was taken.* (v. 23)

God creates two differently sexed creatures from the one unsexed ground-creature. Now at last there is fit! What was undifferentiated becomes differentiated: male/man and female/woman. The poetry plays with the similarity between the Hebrew words for man (*ish*) and woman (*ishah*), just as the earlier parts of the story played with the similarity between the ground (*ha-adamah*) and the ground-creature (*ha-adam*).

Gender and sex

A distinction is usually made between biological sex and culture-based gender. This story, it seems, deals with both. The fundamental distinction within humanity is male and female, a sex-based distinction. But immediately this distinction is made, the narrator makes a culture-based gender comment: 'For this the man/husband will leave his father and his mother and will unite/join with his woman/wife, and they will be one flesh' (v. 24). What was once one flesh—the undifferentiated ground-creature (ha-adam)—is once again united, but this time the unity is as sexually differentiated beings (male and female) and as culturally differentiated genders (man/husband and woman/wife).

The intimacy and appropriateness of their partnership is made apparent in verse 25: nothing hides them from each other. There is total vulnerability and mutuality. In the Old Testament, 'shame' is usually associated with a defeated enemy. Here there is no shame because there is no enmity or inequality. There is difference, but it is a difference that complements rather than a difference that separates.

Although there are hints of the patriarchal world that produced this text, the Hebrew text emphasizes equality and partnership.

Marriage and sexual desire

While verse 24 can be and has been read as words about marriage, its emphasis is on human sexual desire. If this verse is primarily about marriage, it is very strange that it does not correspond to the patriarchal family custom of ancient Israel. The cultural tradition was for the woman to leave her family and to join her husband's family. This discrepancy has led some to argue that what we have here is the remnant of a matriarchal culture, and this may be the case. It is more likely, however, that the verse is primarily about human sexual desire. 'For this', the Hebrew says, the man will leave his family in order to unite with the woman. What is 'this'? In the context of our story, it is human sexual desire. Ish/male and ishah/female come from and therefore desire to be one flesh. The poetry of verse 23 and the simple statement in verse 25 affirm this.

PRAYER

Thank you, Lord God, the giver of good things, for our sexual desire. May we find the partner who makes us whole.

DIALOGUE *among* GOD'S CREATURES

There is a link between Genesis 2 and 3, established by similarity in sound between the word for 'naked' (2:25) and the word for 'snake' (3:1). For the attentive reader of the Hebrew text, this is a signal of a connection, but quite what the connection is has yet to be established. Although chapter 3 appears, initially, to be unconnected to the story of Man and Woman, they are related.

Chapter 3 begins like many a fable, so we may suspect that we are beginning a new story. We are introduced to an animal character, Snake. However, Snake, we are assured, is one of the creatures that God has made (v. 1). Indeed, Snake is one of the creatures that Human has named. But there is a new dimension to this section of the story. So far in the story, it is only God and Human who have spoken. There has been no dialogue, no conversation. Now the idyll of Genesis 2 is about to be ruptured, and the vehicle is conversation.

The snake said

The snake, or Snake (if we are to sustain the sense of a fable), is characterized by the narrator as 'crafty' or 'clever' or 'wily', more so than any of the other animals. Why this characteristic is foregrounded is not clear, but it is obviously important, for little else is said about the snake. The snake is not presented as evil, simply as clever. Snake, in many a fable or folk tale, is a trickster, a creature with wisdom that lives by its wits. When the snake speaks, it is to try to trick the woman by offering its own wisdom.

Most translations are misleading in implying that the snake asked the woman questions. In fact, we could translate this part of the sentence as follows: 'Ah, and so God has said…'. The snake makes incomplete and incorrect statements, drawing the woman into dialogue as she attempts to correct the snake. She does correct the snake, but in doing so she seems to add a prohibition that was not included in 2:17: she claims that God has forbidden her to 'touch [the tree]' (v. 3). This detail, like that of her describing the position of the tree instead of its designation, may not be significant. What is important is that during the conversation—the first conversation in the book of Genesis—there is miscommunication. This seems to be the main point. The snake adds to the miscommunication by offering its own wisdom, not only about the results of eating the fruit of the forbidden tree but also about God's motives for forbidding it (vv. 4–5). At this, the woman stops talking and starts looking.

Why the woman?

We bear the baggage of centuries of distorted images of women, so it is difficult to 'hear' this text on its own terms. Absolutely nothing is said about why the woman is singled out for the first conversation. Traditional androcentric interpretations point to the woman's inherent moral weakness. More recent feminist interpretations point to her uniqueness. She is the apex of God's creative work and therefore the fullest embodiment of human wisdom. Significantly, the snake always speaks to the woman using plural forms (you plural), indicating that it is clearly targeting both woman and man. So too the woman responds on behalf of both her partner and herself, in the plural.

Another way of approaching the issue is suggested by paying attention to the role of dialogue in this story. When God made the original prohibition, it was made to the ground-creature, *ha-adam* (2:16–17). Taken from *ha-adam*, the woman (*ishah*) embodies humanity in all its fullness, but does she retain what God said to *ha-adam* in 2:17? Or was it the responsibility of the man (for whom the term *ha-adam* is used in this chapter) to tell her of God's prohibition? The centrality of dialogue and conversation in chapter 3 perhaps points to the failure of communication or the incompleteness of communication between this first human couple. The woman's responses to the snake perhaps indicate only a partial communication of the prohibition. By not communicating fully, the man and woman have created an opportunity for the snake to insert its own wisdom—the wisdom of a creature, not of the Creator.

God, not Lord God

Significantly, when the snake and woman speak of God, they do not use the now familiar 'Lord God' (Yahweh Elohim). A subtle distancing occurs, precipitated by the snake (v. 1b) but taken up by the woman (v. 2). God has become less intimate and more remote, and they speak of 'God' (Elohim). Conversation again leads to distortion.

REFLECTION

Read James 3:1–12. What does this tell us about communication?

The COLLAPSE of COMMUNICATION

Perhaps the prohibition in Genesis 2:17, namely, not to eat of the tree of the knowledge of good and evil, is meant less to test humankind than to expose its inherent limits. The prohibition itself limits humankind to partial knowledge. Only God knows fully. Fully knowing good and evil is beyond human capacity. Even contemplating this knowledge, as the woman now does, exposes our limitations.

Another limit of humankind lies in its capacity to communicate, and the snake exposes this limit. *Ha-adam* (the man) has either not listened carefully to God's command, or has not communicated it clearly to 'his' partner, the woman. Communication is constitutive of what it means to be human and at the same time exposes the limits of what it means to be human.

When she saw...

Having offered its wisdom, the snake withdraws, leaving the woman alone to contemplate what the snake has said, what she remembers of God's prohibition, and the tree itself. We already know that solitariness is not a good thing (2:18), so this would be a good time for in-depth discussion with her partner. But communication is over between these first humans, and will not reappear until God reinstates it in verse 9.

The woman *sees* the fruit in its three dimensions (v. 6); she then *takes* the fruit; she *eats* the fruit; she *gives* the fruit to her man. Without any persuasion, he participates. Indeed, he may have been there all along, throughout the conversation with the snake, for the narrator tells us that he 'was with her' (v. 6). He eats. Speech is conspicuously absent. There is communication, but of a non-verbal form.

The effect

The effect of their disobedience is immediate. The snake's wisdom has proved to be both true and worthless. The snake said that their eyes would be opened (3:5), and their eyes are opened (v. 7). But what do they see? Again there is the pun on the words for 'snake' and 'naked'. Their previous and precious vulnerability towards each other—their nakedness—now becomes unbearable. Perhaps they do know more about good and evil, but at what cost!

The snake's knowledge proves to be limited, although later on God will agree with the snake that humankind has become like God, 'knowing good and evil' (3:22). But what is this eye-opening knowledge that God did not intend humankind to have and which belongs (after the humans have eaten of the tree) only to God and humankind? Some commentators on this topic have suggested that it is self-awareness. Self-awareness is what enables humans to experience shame. The man and the woman become self-aware, and so self-conscious of their nakedness. But this is only the outward dimension of human self-awareness. The peril of human self-awareness is that it places humankind at its centre. Self-consciousness leads to self-centredness and self-interestedness. Humankind, not God and God's creation, becomes the dominant and dominating reference point.

Not only do the man and woman hide their bodies from each other; they also hide from God. The way verse 8 is introduced suggests that God routinely joined them in the garden for conversation. Ironically, they try to hide themselves among the trees that God has caused to grow in the garden: their eyes may be open, but they see less than they saw before. God calls to them, asking the first real question in Genesis: 'Where are you?' (v. 9). This is at the same time a routine question and a fundamental question. Where indeed is humankind at this moment?

The man responds, confessing that he was afraid (v. 10). The intimacy between God and humankind is fractured. God immediately discerns that the man has eaten from the forbidden tree (v. 11). The man refuses to answer directly; instead, he blames the woman (and God for giving the woman to him) before acknowledging that he did indeed eat of the forbidden tree (v. 12). The relationship between the man and God is disrupted further, and so too is the relationship between the man and the woman. God turns to the woman, who blames the snake for tricking her before she too confesses to eating the fruit from the forbidden tree (v. 13). Relationships are in tatters, including the relationship between humankind and God's other creatures. Communication is restored, but blaming others, even God, has become its dominant function.

PRAYER

Forgive us, Lord God, for our human self-centredness. Walk again, we pray, with us in the cool of the evening breeze.

47

CONSEQUENCES *of* DISOBEDIENCE

We have already seen the initial consequences of human disobedience; these are now articulated by God. All of the relationships that constitute humankind are disrupted. While the text here appears to be trying to make sense of life as we find it, the text is also deeply theological, articulating the alienation that comes from disobedience to God.

The woman has laid the blame for her disobedience on the snake, and God seems satisfied to start there. The snake becomes the animal that is cursed, and is assigned the body and the habitat that we know today (v. 14). The snake is also made particularly detestable to the woman, with a relationship of mutual hostility (v. 15). Working backwards, God then addresses the woman, once again articulating the disruption that comes of disobedience. She is not cursed, but is trapped between three related realities: painful childbirth, sexual desire and the rule of man (v. 16). Next it is the man to whom God turns, not cursing him but condemning him to be the one who is responsible for the ground's being cursed. Hard work will now be needed to make the ground yield food, and even then thorns and thistles will usually be the result. The play on words remains, but gone is the goodness of the relationship. *Ha-adam* is responsible for the cursing of *ha-adamah*, and *ha-adamah* will now produce only pain and futility for *ha-adam*. Gone is the abundant fruit of the garden; gone is the gentle and harmonious working and caring for the garden; gone is the leisure to enjoy the cool breeze of the evening. From now on, man's destiny is hard labour during his life, and then death (vv. 17–19).

Whoever the authors of this text are, this is the world that they know. It is the hard and unrelenting world of a peasant community struggling to survive in harsh conditions. The land is dangerous, with snakes everywhere, both in the field and in the home. The primary role of the woman is to ensure the survival of the clan by continuing to bear children, notwithstanding the realities of difficult and dangerous childbirth and the demands of the patriarchal household. The man must work in the blazing sun day after day, trying to make the reluctant land yield enough to live on. The only certainty is death.

The story both attempts to explain how this reality came about and to proclaim that this reality is not what God intended. In a way, the story is a lament: it laments a world that might have been. What is truly amazing is that this story does not blame God for the world as we now know it. It teaches that God intended a different world and that it is human disobedience that brought about our world. Humankind's relationships with the earth, with each other and with God have each been disrupted, though not entirely destroyed. Abundant life is gone, but life itself remains.

Naming and making

The man now acts out the dominance that the distortion of disobedience has brought about, for he names the woman (v. 20). This hierarchical act is softened, however, by the name that he gives her. 'Eve' is similar to the word for 'life'. The woman's name embodies their mutual determination to live. Paradise may have been lost, but they refuse to let go of life. Although the relationship with God has been disrupted and has changed, God does not abandon them. God makes them more durable and appropriate garments than they themselves had made (3:7). The world they have begun to inhabit demands more durable clothing. Furthermore, the kind of garment given to them is special (v. 21): elsewhere in the Old Testament, this kind of garment is always worn by one who is in authority, indicating that this man and woman still have a divine task.

Sending out

At this point in the story, we are allowed to eavesdrop on God's thoughts (v. 22). God is perturbed that the knowledge that human beings now possess—their new self-awareness and self-centredness—will do untold damage if they are allowed to eat freely of the tree of life. By placing itself rather than God at the centre, humankind has developed the capacity to cause damage, as we have seen. All of humankind's relationships have become damaged. So God imposes a new limit on humankind, this time giving us no choice. We no longer have access to the tree of life (v. 24). We will struggle to live and we will die.

PRAYER

We lament with you, our God, the loss of intimacy and wholeness, and long for its restitution.

CAIN & ABEL

The poetry of Genesis 2:23 is far behind us. Sexual intercourse is now about bearing children, bringing forth the next generation. The man does his part and the woman does hers. The first child, Cain, is named after the Hebrew verb 'produced' (v. 1). God is acknowledged as part of the process, but the intimacy of the name 'Lord God' is gone: God is now 'Yahweh'. Eve bears a second son, Abel (v. 2), and although we are not told what his name means, anyone familiar with Hebrew would associate it with the word for 'breath' or 'futility'. The abundant and beautiful garden is gone; life is now characterized by struggle.

Modes of production

We are introduced to the two brothers in verse 2 by the different ways in which they wrest life from the earth. Abel is a shepherd and Cain is an agriculturalist. These two vocations coexisted in the ancient world as they do today, but there were constant tensions between them, given their different priorities for how land was to be used.

Understandably, each brother brings an offering to God of what they produce through their labour. Inexplicably, God 'regards' one and not the other. Perhaps there is a difference, not in the substance of what is offered but in the care and quality of the offering. Abel's offering, we are told, is carefully selected and he brings the best he has to give (v. 4), whereas Cain simply brings what is at hand (v. 3). Other explanations have been put forward to try to account for God's preference, but the text is strangely silent on the reason for God's regard of the one and not the other. What this story does focus on—and this is new to the stories we have read so far—is the psychological dimension of humankind's new state. We have seen the disruption that disobedience has brought to our relationship with others, creation and God, but what of our relationship with ourselves?

Psychological analysis

Cain's reaction to God's disregard for his offering (v. 5) is a mixture of anger ('it became very hot to him') and dejection ('his face fell'). God's response is interesting, for it delves into Cain's subconsciousness. Seeing Cain's outward demeanour, God probes what lies inside Cain

(v. 6), analysing and advising him (v. 7). First, God identifies the key problem, the desire to do what is right/good. Cain must desire to do what is good/right. Second, God's diagnosis is that 'sin is crouching' within the very being of Cain, but that it can and must be controlled. Sin resides at our very core, with real power, but it can and must be ruled. As soon as we do not desire to do what is good/right (in God's sight), we give opportunity to sin to wreak its destructive power. Cain may be uncertain about why his offering has been disregarded, but he must desire to keep on striving to do what is good and right. To give up is to give in to sin.

Murder

Cain fails to heed God's guidance. He premeditates the murder of his brother. Again there is no conversation, only an ambiguous 'and he said' (v. 8). In the Hebrew text, there is no indication of what he said. The NRSV follows most other translations by amending the Hebrew text from other available manuscripts which include the phrase, 'Let us go out to the field'. What, according to the Hebrew text, did Cain say to his brother? We are not told. Perhaps Cain was incapable of clear speech, having given in to the beast crouching within him. But we bear witness to what his anger and dejection have become: 'And it/Cain rose up at Abel, his brother, and killed him.' The Hebrew captures both the beast within Cain and Cain himself as together they strike at Abel. This is the first of many fratricides that will follow (see Judges 9; 2 Samuel 2:26–27; 13—14; 1 Kings 2:25). The beast within us must be subdued.

Again God intervenes, not to prevent the murder but to delve more deeply into Cain's psyche (v. 9). God's question is similar to the question asked of ha-adam (3:9). Cain, unlike ha-adam, lies, refusing to face up to who he has become. He refuses to face up to his responsibility for his brother, saying sarcastically, 'Does a shepherd need a keeper?' The answer is not what Cain's rhetorical question implies, for the good or right answer is 'Yes'. But Cain has given in to sin and no longer desires what is right or good. God is appalled (v. 10), for even the ground (ha-adamah) cries out to God! This is the first but not the last time that God will hear the cry of injustice.

PRAYER

Help us, God of Cain, to control the destructive desires that war within us.

The CONSEQUENCES *for* CAIN

We have interrupted God's words to Cain by breaking the narrative at verse 10, for God continues, articulating the consequences of Cain's inability to control the sin lurking within him. Just as God articulated the consequences of the disobedience of the first man and the first woman (3:16–19), so too God now articulates what Cain has brought into being.

Cain is now banished from the very ground (*ha-adamah*) that was used to form humankind. The irony is that it was Cain who tilled the soil in order to bring forth 'the fruit of the ground' (4:3). Now that same ground, having drunk of his brother's blood, denies him its fruits. Cain, as the firstborn son, took up his father's profession, becoming a tiller or server of the soil. But he has failed to serve it, polluting it instead with his brother's blood. The blood has a voice and the ground has a mouth (vv. 10–11), as they join together to cry out against Cain.

Cain's anguish

The fourth and final disruption in what it means to be human is given voice in verse 13. God has spoken and so have the blood of Abel and the ground. Now Cain articulates the final damaged relationship: his relationship with himself. Cain's deep sense of alienation is expressed in his lamentation (vv. 13–14). It begins with a cry of internal torment: 'My punishment is greater than I can bear.' Cain is damaged psychologically. Having learnt something from what has happened, Cain cries out to God. He realizes that he cannot survive separated from the ground, from God and from other people.

Just as God intervened on behalf of the murdered Abel, now God intervenes on behalf of the distraught Cain, marking him so that he will not be murdered (v. 15). The irony is palpable! But God's grace does not take away the consequences of Cain's having allowed sin to rear its head in his heart. Cain must go away, leaving the presence of God. How is he to survive his alienation? The next section provides some answers.

Cain as a city builder

At first sight it seems odd that Cain, 'a tiller of the ground' (4:2), becomes a builder of a city (v. 17). A further oddity is that the building of a city seems to contradict God's judgment that Cain would be a fugitive and a wanderer. However, careful attention to the narrative progression guides our interpretation. Being cut off from himself, the ground, God and others, Cain chooses to abandon life on the land, choosing another kind of life altogether: urban life. Cain surrounds himself with others like himself, exiles from the land, and surrounds himself with city walls for protection. The full consequences of eating of the tree of the knowledge of good and evil now become apparent. Cain becomes autonomous. He chooses to embrace rather than repair his disrupted relationships. The city, both here and elsewhere in the Bible, is an ambiguous place, a metaphor for human autonomy and self-centredness.

In the genealogy that follows (vv. 18–22), Cain is depicted as the founder not only of the city but also of city industry and culture. Cain and his descendants are no longer directly dependent on the ground. Even people such as Jabal (v. 20), the literary context implies, serve the city rather than the land. Cain brings to birth a new and ambiguous form of life, separate from the ground. Fundamental to the life of the city is violence, which is why Lamech is able to boast about his capacity to kill, mocking God's mark of protection on Cain and God's limitation of violence (vv. 15, 23–24).

Not the final word

Fractured though human relationships are, they must be maintained and celebrated. Eve does just this, celebrating the birth of Seth, whose name resembles the word for the sense she has that God (Elohim) has 'appointed' another child in the place of Abel (v. 25). God remains involved with humankind. Indeed, the birth of Seth signals another genealogical line, markedly different from Cain's. Seth's line, we are told as the final word in this story, began 'to call on the name Yahweh' (v. 26). Here we find the promise of a progressive restoration of broken relationships, which comes to its culmination under Noah.

REFLECTION

Do you think that Jesus framed his statement in Matthew 18:22 about forgiving seventy times seven with conscious reference to this passage? If so, how are we to understand what Jesus is saying?

SETH *to* NOAH

Genealogies, like the various characters we encounter in these narratives, are not primarily presented for their historical specificity.
Genealogies and ancestor stories remember well-loved ancestors, but
whatever historical detail may once have attached to them has been
shed with their constant retelling, generation after generation. What has
been retained is what remains important to successive generations. So,
for example, the age-old question 'Where did Cain get his wife?' is not
the concern of the narrative. The narrative and its linked genealogies tell
us what is important about Cain and his line, just as the genealogy in
chapter 5 tells us what is important about Seth and his line.

Contrasting lines

Cain's line was characterized by the kind of work they did, showing the
emergence of urban culture and industry. This way of life was to
become fundamentally exploitative of the 'tillers of the ground' who
lived on the land surrounding the cities. In time, powerful city-states
emerged, which came to control the land around them, exerting more
and more pressure on the peasant farmers to supply the labour, livestock and revenue required by the voracious consumption of the city
economy (see 1 Samuel 8).

Seth's line, in contrast, offers a different picture. Appropriately, it is
introduced by a summary statement similar to that found in 2:4, a
statement that occurs at the beginning of eleven sections in Genesis
that contain genealogical lists. It is as if the narrator wants to send a
clear signal of something new. Although Genesis 1 is clearly alluded to
in verses 1–3, there are variations. 'Adam' (Human) is used here as a
proper name, which was not the case in chapters 1, 2 or 3. Secondly,
God's naming the creature 'Adam' (Human) is also new. Thirdly, the
idea that God's image and likeness passes from one generation to the
next, from Adam to Seth (v. 3), is original to this genealogy. Fourthly,
what is also more marked in this account is its patriarchal emphasis,
which is not surprising given that it is a genealogy. Although it is
affirmed that God made humankind (*ha-adam*) as male and female, the
focus soon shifts and follows God's image and likeness being passed
down the male line.

Characteristics of Seth's line

There are a number of recurrent characteristics in Seth's line. First, all the males mentioned live exceptionally long lives. The hyperbole implies God's blessing. Second, although the genealogy follows a particular line, focusing only on one particular son in each generation, we are repeatedly told that they had 'other sons and daughters', making it clear that they were blessed in this respect as well, with children. Third, two sons are singled out for special mention with respect to their relationship with God. Enoch, we are told rather enigmatically, 'walked with God; then he was no more, because God took him' (v. 24). The implication here is that Enoch was 'taken' by God in an unusual way, perhaps circumventing death. Noah too receives special attention, for it is Noah who is designated as the one who will restore what has been disrupted. The consequences of disobedience will be ameliorated by Noah. The ground, once the fundamental element of God's creative work but which has become cursed through human disobedience, is not irredeemably damaged, nor is the relationship between the ground and humanity. Noah, whose name means 'comfort', will 'bring us relief from our work and from the toil of our hands' (v. 29).

Long lives

The long lives ascribed to the patriarchs in this genealogy cause, in the words of Gerhard von Rad, 'remarkable synchronisms and duplications'. For example, Adam lived to see the birth of Lamech, the ninth member of the genealogy, Seth lived to see the 'translation' of Enoch and died shortly before the birth of Noah, Noah outlived Abraham's grandfather, Nahor, and died in Abraham's sixtieth year, and Shem, Noah's son, outlived Abraham. Indeed, he was still alive when Esau and Jacob were born!

This may have been humankind's 'golden age' as some commentators claim, but it is unlikely that these lifespans are meant to be taken historically. Their purpose is different, which is to affirm the presence and promise of God in Seth's line.

PRAYER

Thank you, Yahweh, for the promise of restoration of the relationships that make us human: our relationship with ourselves, with others, with the environment and with you.

19

HUMAN & DIVINE WICKEDNESS

We will have to wait for the redemption promised in Noah, for before Noah is introduced we are told of increasing wickedness, in both divine and human spheres.

Divine desire

The strange fragment in verses 1–4 concerns angelic beings, 'the sons of God', who desire 'the daughters of humans'. It also contains reference to the 'Nephilim', heroes or, as some translations translate the word, 'giants'. Quite what the relationship is between these two groups of beings is not clear.

Not much is said about the first group of beings, 'the sons of God'. However, there are enough biblical references to them to indicate that God's realm was populated with other divine beings beside God (see, for example, Genesis 28:12; 1 Kings 22:19–22; Job 1:6; 38:7; Psalm 29:1; 82:6; 89:7). Here, these heavenly beings are considered to be male and to have a certain amount of autonomy. In this case, the angelic beings are not explicitly condemned for their actions, nor are they stopped from taking human women as their wives, but God is clearly concerned to set a limit on the lifespan of the resulting offspring. This limit to the human lifespan is then applied, it would appear, to all human life.

The mention of the second group, the Nephilim, in verse 4 seems to imply that they are the offspring of the union of angelic men and human women, although this connection is not explicit. Indeed, the 'heroes that were of old' are portrayed in rather a positive manner.

This fragment poses more questions than it answers, although in terms of its placement in the larger narrative of Genesis, it seems to have been inserted here to explain why the long lifespans of Genesis 5 are no longer the norm. God, this fragment says in a rather garbled fashion, has placed a limit on human life expectancy because the divine–human union and/or its offspring should not live for ever. The precise reason, however, is difficult to determine because the crucial sentence, verse 3, is extremely difficult to understand.

What the inclusion of this fragment does demonstrate quite clearly, though, is the tremendous capacity of these ancient texts to be constantly reworked. We baulk at the idea of anyone adding to or in any way tampering with scripture, but we stand at the end of a long process during which there were no such scruples. These were living texts, so many different communities and voices made their contributions to the living tradition that has become 'scripture'.

Human wickedness

The first introduction to the story of Noah is found in verses 5–8, and it tells of an escalation in human wickedness. Again, the inclusion of the story at this point in the larger narrative of Genesis makes sense, for it comes after Lamech's song in praise of violence and prepares the way for God's act of redemption through Noah.

The force of these two texts (vv. 1–4 and 5–8) together is of a world slipping increasingly into evil. The chaos that was controlled in Genesis 1 somehow seems to have broken loose. Cain's act against his brother now seems to have infected all of humanity (and even the heavens). The promise of redemption in Seth's line now seems far off.

In the story of Noah, of which verses 5–8 are one of the introductions, different names for God are used, indicating perhaps the combination of two different versions of the story, one using the name Yahweh and one using the name Elohim.

Yahweh/God's despair is terrible to contemplate. Yahweh/God looks at what was created good and sees now 'only evil continually' (v. 5). Until now, there has been little comment on human (or divine) wickedness. Nothing was said about Lamech's mockery of God's limits on violence; nothing was said about the behaviour of the sons of God. Now Yahweh/God says it all: 'Yahweh was grieved that he had made *ha-adam* on the earth, and it hurt his heart' (v. 6). The divine decision is then given in all its horror: 'And Yahweh said, "I will wipe away *ha-adam* whom I created from the face of the earth..."' (v. 7). Yahweh/God's grief and despair do not stop there, for such is the bond between humankind and the rest of the creation that everything else Yahweh/ God created must go as well. All that will be left, presumably, will be the dry and desolate earth (2:5). Amid Yahweh/God's grief, there is a word of hope, however: Noah 'found favour in the sight of Yahweh' (v. 8).

PRAYER

Thank you, grieving God, for allowing us to see your despair. May we too find a glimmer of hope in the midst of our grief and despair.

INTRODUCING NOAH

The story of Noah and the flood runs from 6:9 (or 6:5) through to
9:19; it begins with a short genealogy of Noah's sons and ends with a
short genealogy of Noah's sons. In between is a remarkable story, both
in terms of content and composition. In terms of content, it is a story
of redemption, the first explicit story of its kind in the Bible and the
forerunner of many more. In terms of composition, it is a story from
two sources which have been combined with some artistry.

Intertwining stories

From what we have read already in the book of Genesis, it is obvious
that Genesis is a composite text, the product of numerous hands and
voices. What the story of Noah allows us to see quite clearly is how collected stories were combined. Briefly, a careful reading of the narrative
indicates the following difficulties, which can best be explained by the
combination of two sources. There are two different reasons for the
flood, the wickedness of the human heart (6:5) and the corruption and
violence of the earth (6:11–12); two different instructions about the
animals to be taken into the ark, one indicating a pair of each type of
animal (6:19–20) and one indicating seven pairs of clean animals and
one pair of unclean animals (7:2); two different durations of the flood,
forty days and forty nights (7:4, 12) and a whole year (7:6, 11; 8:13,
14); two different explanations of the flood, a great rain (7:12; 8:2b) and
a cataclysmic rupture of the waters below and above (7:11; 8:1–2a); two
different accounts of leaving the ark, one after sending out various birds
(8:6–12) and one because of the command of God (8:15–17); and
finally, two different names for God, Yahweh and Elohim.

Various attempts have been made by scholars to reconstruct the two
sources that have been combined in the present narrative. There is no
consensus on exactly what these sources looked like, and the argu-
ments are to some extent circular. However, this appears to be a good
case of the combination of two previously independent stories or
sources, even though their original form is not clear to us. Attempting
to reconstruct such sources, elusive and tentative though it is, is
important in that it gives us glimpses of the communities of faith that
contributed to the process of constructing scripture. For our purposes,

the focus is on the final form of the story that we now have. What we now have shows considerable artistry in the combination. In other words, this story exhibits the dual concerns of collection and creation. Two traditions are collected, and are then combined into one narrative, incorporating elements from each.

Perhaps the easiest clue to the 'originals' behind the text we are reading is the different names used for God. The NRSV faithfully translates these either as 'God' (Elohim) or 'LORD' (Yahweh). Our concern should not only be for the memory of these originals, however, but also for the narrative before us, which demonstrates considerable coherence. Whatever the author of this narrative used as his/her sources, they have been thoroughly reworked, without eradicating traces of the originals.

A righteous man

The promise of redemption associated with Noah's name (5:29; 6:8) is now fulfilled, although the final effect is not as marked as we might have expected. At last we are to be told the story of the longed-for redemption of humanity and the earth. The story begins with a simple but profound statement: 'Noah was a righteous man, blameless in his generation' (v. 9). Like his ancestor, Enoch (5:24), Noah 'walked with Elohim'. It is not clear whether Noah is righteous and blameless in some absolute sense, or whether he is only righteous and blameless relative to the wickedness of the rest of humankind. The former is grammatically more likely, indicating that it was possible for humankind to remain in relationship with God, which is what prevents God from destroying what was created good. Some goodness remains, and God finds it in Noah. The next person that God declares righteous will be Abram (15:6).

The declaration of Noah's righteousness is followed by a brief genealogy. Why the genealogy is placed here, interrupting the narrative, is not clear, but perhaps it is a suggestion that Noah's righteousness is in contrast not only to those who surround him in the present but also to those who will come after him. If so, it is a bleak reminder of the tenuousness of righteousness.

PRAYER

We give thanks, gracious God, for the righteous among us and for the way in which their presence provides grace for us all.

21 GENESIS 6:11–22

INSTRUCTIONS *for* NOAH

After the introduction, the story of Noah gathers pace, with a reitera-
tion of the problem. Cast in more general terms than before (6:5), it is
the very earth that is corrupt 'in the face of Elohim and full of violence'
(v. 11). The actual violence of Cain and the violence forecast by
Lamech has infected the earth. The reader is allowed to see the earth
as God sees it. The Hebrew text expresses this dramatically: 'And
Elohim saw the earth, and behold/see, it was corrupt...' (v. 12). Here
it appears that the corruption and violence that Elohim/God sees has
tainted 'all flesh', human and animal. This becomes clearer when we
hear of Elohim/God's judgment in verse 13. Elohim/God devises a way
of destroying 'all flesh', except for the remnant that is to be saved.

Quite how the animals have become violent is not clear, but the
image of chaos breaking from its bounds (Genesis 1) is the image that
is being conveyed. Disorder abounds, and it is characterized by violence. Indeed, it seems from verse 12 that even the earth is to be
destroyed, although this is metaphoric rather than geologic. The image
is of God undoing what was done in creation.

The point of view of the narrative now moves from God to Noah. All
is not lost, for God has a plan to preserve a part of the created order.
Elohim/God instructs Noah to make an 'ark' (v. 14). The word used
here is not the usual word for a boat and is used again only in Exodus
2:3–5 to describe the 'basket' used to preserve Moses. The careful
instructions are metaphoric, in that they probably represent a micro-
cosm of the world as it was understood in ancient times, with four
sides representing the directions of the compass, and with the three
floors representing the underworld, the world of human and animal
habitation (the earth), and heaven. The occupants represent a sample
of God's creation. All is to be destroyed, but all is preserved in the ark.

It is only in verse 17 that it becomes clear how Elohim/God intends
to destroy the earth. It is also absolutely clear that God intends to
destroy both human and animal life, 'all flesh in which is the breath of
life'. Although this would seem to exclude plant life, the next phrase,
'everything that is on the earth shall die', may include it. This is unlikely,
however, as there is no direct reference to plant life being corrupted. As
far as this narrative is concerned, 'life' refers to animate life. This con-

ception of life is similar to that found in Genesis 1, which is one of the reasons why this portion of the Noah story is attributed to the Priestly writer, who also uses the name Elohim for God.

Just as God instructs Noah about his plans for destruction, so too God instructs Noah about the plans for redemption (v. 18). For the first time in Genesis, we read of God establishing 'a covenant' with a human. This is the first of many covenants that God will establish in an ongoing commitment to humankind. Elohim/God's plan for preservation includes humans and all the creatures mentioned in Genesis 1 (although the aquatic creatures are not specifically mentioned). Elohim/God tells Noah that his task is 'to keep [them] alive with you, male and female' (v. 20b), thus ensuring the future of every kind of creature. Humankind's task, represented in Noah, remains to care for and keep creation, although the images are derived from Genesis 1 rather than Genesis 2. Practically, Noah must provide food for all the occupants. Just as in 1:29–30, plant material is the basic foodstuff of life.

Noah says nothing, but the narrator assures us that Noah obeys God: 'he did all that Elohim commanded him' (v. 22). Noah's righteousness is based on his obedience to God.

Flood stories

Flood stories are fairly common in the ancient Near East, and one in particular shows many parallels with the story of Noah: the *Epic of Gilgamesh*. The general region from which the *Epic of Gilgamesh* comes was prone to floods, situated as Mesopotamia is between the two great rivers of the region, the Tigris and the Euphrates. The annual flood brought both life and death, enabling the irrigation of Mesopotamian cities but also bringing death if the flood was excessive. Floods were thus a way of life, prompting theological reflection, as is the case in the story of Noah.

Here, and whenever biblical texts draw on the religio-cultural resources of the world of their time, there are both similarities and differences, as these resources are reworked in order to express the theological orientation of the communities they represent.

PRAYER

May we discern your plan for life in the midst of destruction,
God of Noah.

ENTERING *the* ARK

When God speaks, it is Yahweh/God who speaks, commanding Noah to take his household into the ark, and reiterating the reason that he and his family are being spared. The command to take seven pairs of clean animals and a single pair of unclean animals indicates either a refinement of the earlier command (6:19) or the use of another source. We are also given new information concerning a distinction between the animals that has not been indicated before. Indeed, this distinction between clean and unclean animals will not make sense until humans are allowed to eat meat and a sacrificial system is in place, neither of which is present so far. Yahweh/God reiterates the reason for the male–female pairs (v. 3) and gives a specific timeframe for the onset and duration of the flood. The flood, in this portion of the narrative, is to be caused by rain (v. 4).

The age of Noah is given in verse 6, thereby associating him with the longevity of his ancestors in Seth's line (ch. 5). He will be the last to live so long. The repetition in verses 7–9 not only serves to confirm Noah's obedience to Elohim/God, but also slows the narrative pace, building tension as we wait to see what will happen. At the designated time (v. 10), the flood begins.

The sense of tension is heightened when we read that it was 'on the very same day' (v. 13) when Noah and his family entered the ark that the waters were let loose. 'Phew, that was close!' is the sense the narrator wants to illicit from us readers. Again, we have a long repetition of the key elements (vv. 14–16a), and then, abruptly, we come to a new development: 'Yahweh shut him in' (v. 16b). God, significantly, remains outside with the ruined creation, watching and wreaking its destruction. God watches his work being destroyed.

With a rhythm that mimics the rise of the water, the story continues, relentlessly and slowly narrating events as they unfold (vv. 17–24). The ark is safe, borne up by the very waters that drown everything else. The catalogue of 'flesh' that is killed by the flood is given in verse 21. In the verses that follow, the repetition confirms the relentless fulfilment of God's plan. In verses 21–23 there are echoes of Genesis 1 as, one by one, each of the sorts of creatures brought into being by God dies. The unrelenting gaze of the narrator (and so the reader) is nowhere more apparent than in verse 22, where we read that 'everything that had the breath of the spirit of life in their nostrils, everything from the dry land, they died'. We can almost feel the water slowly engulfing us and entering our nostrils.

The phrase translated 'the breath of life' by the NRSV in verse 22 is significant, for it is perhaps a reminder of Genesis 1:2, in which 'the spirit/breath of God' existed within the primeval chaos. There, God's presence amid the chaos brought forth creation; here, 'the breath of the spirit/breath of life' is extinguished.

The story makes it quite clear that nothing remained that was not engulfed by the waters, not even the mountains (v. 20)—nothing except Noah and those who were with him in the ark (v. 23b). The waters, we are told, 'flooded over the earth for a hundred and fifty days' (v. 24).

Chronology

Throughout this story, there is an attempt to provide some kind of chronology, although how the various dates and durations are connected is difficult to determine. One of the things that these chronological indications demonstrate, however, is that it is not just recent readers of the Bible who are interested in charting God's timetable. Some ancient authors and redactors (those who revised and edited the work of others) had this interest, and throughout the book of Genesis we find their attempts to connect everything chronologically.

Theology

Like so much of the book of Genesis, and much of the Bible in general, in this story historical and so-called scientific detail is not important. The stories have been remembered and reworked because of their theological importance. This does not mean that we should not seek to recover and reconstruct the historical detail, but it does mean that this should not distract us from paying attention to what has been preserved for us.

PRAYER

We watch with horror, O God, the destruction of all these creatures, and wonder at the despair that drove you to do this.

EXITING *the* ARK

Elohim/God 'remembers' Noah and the ark, all that remains of earth's once-abundant creation. The phrase 'God remembered' (v. 1) is used a number of times in Genesis, and each time it is significant. In Genesis 9:15–16, God pledges to remember the covenant made after the flood; in 19:29, God remembers Abraham and saves Lot for Abraham's sake; and in 30:22, God remembers Rachel and she becomes pregnant after many years of barrenness. In the words of David Cotter, 'To be remembered by God is to be the object of God's saving and life-giving concern.'

God remembers Noah. It is almost as if God is pulled from the depths of despair by the image of the solitary ark upon the waters. The image perhaps picks up on Genesis 2:18, in which God recognizes that *ha-adam* is alone and so sets about creating a companion. God has made a covenant with Noah (6:18) and so they have formed a partnership. It is this commitment that causes God to act. With further echoes from Genesis, this time Genesis 1, the flood slowly recedes. In words reminiscent of Genesis 1:2, 'Elohim sent a wind over the earth', presumably to begin drying up the water (v. 1). With similar images to Genesis 1:6–8, 'the fountains of the deep and the windows of the heavens were closed' (v. 2). And drawing on the ideas of Genesis 1:9–10, dry land appears. The message is clear: God is creating anew. Although the destruction has been unrelenting, the narrative attempts to convey a sense that creation has been saved from itself. From the perspective of the narrative, this renewal of creation is an act of grace.

Gradual redemption

The time indicators convey the lengthy and gradual process of redemption (vv. 3b–5). Destruction too was drawn out, although in that case the sense of time passing slowly was communicated by the constant repetition and rhythmic quality of the language. The narrative pace is slow throughout the flood story, emphasizing its importance theologically as a new beginning. Noah too is made to wait, for in verses 6–12 he sends out first a raven and then a dove on two occasions to measure the extent to which the waters have receded. Finally, 'the face of the ground (*ha-adamah*)' is dry (v. 13). What was accomplished by God's word immediately in Genesis 1 now takes a full year according to the chronology supplied (see 7:11; 8:13). Incidentally, at this point in the story—Noah's sending out of a raven and a dove—there are close similarities with the *Epic of Gilgamesh*: there too, birds are sent out to scout for dry land. The purpose of the raven in the story of Noah is not that clear, for it does not accomplish anything that the doves accomplish. It may be one of the 'loose ends' not integrated by the author who combined the two flood stories.

Perhaps this narrative of redemption, which takes so long to narrate (and which is not yet over), portrays God's growing patience. God has been remarkably quick to destroy, even though the evidence was not that overwhelming (from the perspective of the reader). The covenant that God makes in chapter 9 confirms God's commitment to be more patient, and the rest of Genesis bears out this change.

New life

The olive leaf that the first dove brings back (v. 11) is both a reminder of God's garden with its food-bearing trees (2:9) and of human cultivation (3:23; 4:3). The olive tree is a symbol of both. Here is a clear sign of new life. Plant life has remained. The basic building-block of life is intact (1:29–30). A full year after the flood began, Elohim/God speaks again. There has been a year of divine silence. When Elohim/God does speak, it is to command Noah to leave the ark (vv. 15–16), just as Yahweh/God commanded Noah to enter the ark (7:1). The leaving of the ark is as even-paced as the rest of the narrative; repetition slows the pace of the narrative, demonstrating at the same time that what God has commanded is done by Noah, exactly as God commanded. Echoing 1:22 (and 1:28), Elohim/God commands Noah to bring out the animals 'so that they may abound on the earth, and be fruitful and multiply on the earth' (v. 17). Significantly, humankind and all the other representatives of creation on the ark are grouped together by this summons of God to be fruitful and multiply. Just as their 'kinds' were destroyed together, so together they must replenish the earth. The image in verses 18–19, captured by the NRSV, is that all God's creatures emerge from the ark family by family, beginning with the human family.

PRAYER
Remember us, God of Noah, when we feel abandoned and alone;
draw near to us and renew us.

NOAH RESPONDS & GOD REFLECTS

Noah's first response on leaving the ark is to build an altar to Yahweh/God and to make an extravagant 'burnt offering' to God of 'every clean animal and of every clean bird' (v. 20). In so doing, Noah follows Abel's form of offering (4:4). Although it was a common form of religious practice in the ancient Near East, none of the narratives we have read explains why God requires this form of ritual worship. Given that God has sanctioned only plant material for food (1:29–30), the slaughtering of animals for worship is anomalous. We must remember, however, that the stories we have read so far were not written in chronological order. Genesis 1, for example, is a relatively late text, while Genesis 2 is probably earlier. In other words, although portraying the very earliest period of Israel's story, the texts that tell the story are themselves products of different and often much later times. So it is not surprising that the concerns and practices of later times have found their way into stories that tell of earlier periods.

As God smells 'the pleasing odour' (v. 21), God reflects. The word for 'pleasing/soothing' is a pun on the name of Noah, which means 'rest' or 'comfort'. Noah, we remember, is the one who would bring relief/rest from the harsh grind of survival (5:29). When Yahweh/God smells Noah's offering, the troubled heart of God comes to a recognition and a resolution. Allowed to eavesdrop on God's interior reflections, we see into the heart of God.

Recognition

God recognizes that humankind is inherently flawed. The heart of God looks into the heart of humankind and recognizes a fundamental flaw, woven into its very being. Just as chaos was woven into the very fabric of creation (1:2), so it seems that 'evil' is a constituent element of humankind, 'from childhood' (v. 21). The inclination or tendency of the human heart is evil. The argument within the heart of Yahweh/God goes as follows: 'I will not repeat to curse the ground (ha-adamah) again because of humankind (ha-adam), even though the inclination of the heart of humankind (ha-adam) is evil, from childhood; I will not repeat again to destroy all life, as I just did.' This literal translation, awkward though it is, captures the logic of Yahweh/God.

Resolution

In recognizing the flawed nature of humankind, God also recognizes that the repeated destruction of it (and the rest of creation, which is integrally related to humankind) will not solve the problem. In modern terms, humankind is genetically prone to evil, so dealing with this evil by destroying it would entail constant cycles of regeneration and destruction. Smelling Noah's offering, God draws back from this vicious cycle and formulates another way. God resolves to allow the cycle of life to continue, flawed though it is, season after season, day and night, as long as the earth endures (v. 22). God does not discuss this with Noah, for humankind could probably not endure this knowledge about itself. Instead, God reflects on the dilemma internally. Recognizing that humankind cannot change, God resolves to change.

The agricultural images used in verse 22 are a reminder of humankind's basic task, which remains to live in relationship with the environment. This is also the first of three short poems (see also 9:6, 13–14) which poetically portray God's commitments to this new beginning. They provide the framework of the new order.

The *Epic of Gilgamesh*

Before leaving the story of the flood, it is worth reflecting briefly on the relationship between our story and the flood story in the *Epic of Gilgamesh*. While we cannot be sure what the exact relationship between these particular texts is, they clearly draw on a similar older tradition, probably one originating among the Sumerians. The Babylonian version tells the story of a council of gods who decide to destroy the city of Shurrupak. This decision is revealed to Utnapishtim, the hero of the story, by the god Ea in a dream. Ea orders Utnapishtim to build a ship, which he does, and so survives a flood so terrible that the gods 'cower like watchdogs' and the goddess of heaven, Ishtar, 'screams as one in travail'. After the deluge, Utnapishtim makes a sacrifice, which is received by the gods, who 'gathered like flies over the sacrificer'. Utnapishtim is then enrolled among the gods. Just as it is clear that the stories have similarities, it is also clear that they are quite different.

PRAYER

Thank you, gracious God, for changing your mind
and for giving us life, flawed though we be.

25

INSTRUCTIONS *for* NEW LIFE

Unlike Utnapishtim, Noah is not taken up to be among the gods. God has a purpose for Noah and his family on earth. Although this is God's 'Plan B', Elohim/God gives similar injunctions to Noah as were given in Genesis 1:28. Like their ancestors, Noah and his family are commanded to be fruitful and multiply and to fill the earth (v. 1). However, the relationship between humans and other creatures is now expressed in more domineering terms than before, characterized by fear and dread (v. 2a). They are also 'given/delivered' into humankind's hand (v. 2b). That a change has taken place becomes absolutely clear in verse 3, for now it is not only all plant life that is given for food (see 1:29–30), but 'every moving thing'. It is almost as if God is forcing humankind to face up to the violence intrinsic in humanity and the renewed creation.

Eating meat

Having given prominence to the violence in the human heart in our very relationship with other creatures, however, God sets limits. God will no longer destroy humankind and the world that its violence and evil have contaminated. Instead, God will manage it. So Elohim/God sets a restriction on and demands a reckoning for human life (v. 5), from all creatures. The poem in verse 6 makes the limit clear. 'Whoever/whatever sheds the blood (Hebrew: *dam*) of *ha-adam*, by *ha-adam* his *dam* will be shed'. The reason for the limit and for prioritizing humankind in this manner is because 'in the image of Elohim, Elohim made *ha-adam*'. Though flawed, we remain made in the image of God (see 1:27).

The prohibition in verse 4 on eating meat that retains its blood appears to be a reminder of this limit. All blood serves as a reminder that God will demand a reckoning for the taking of human life. When humans do eat meat (and God now allows this form of food) they must always pause—as they are forced to do by the preparations necessary to cleanse a carcass of its blood—and remember God's limit.

Verse 7 reiterates what was said earlier (v. 1), focusing on the prospect of new life. The use of 'you' for emphasis at the beginning of the sentence draws attention away from the restriction and forces Noah and his family to focus on the command to participate in God's redemption, flawed though it is. This is Elohim/God's blessing (vv. 1, 7), that humankind will abound on the earth and fill it. Just as the first creation was blessed (Genesis 1:22, 28; 2:3), so too this renewed creation is blessed, although the tone is a more sombre one and the blessing seems to be limited to humankind.

Rainbow covenant

The next stage of Elohim/God's management of a corrupted humankind (and creation) is to fulfil the commitment made earlier (6:18) to enter into a covenant with Noah. The covenant is now extended, however, to include not only humankind but also 'every living creature' (v. 10). The covenant that Elohim/God establishes is that 'never again shall all flesh be cut off by the waters of a flood, and never again shall there be a flood to destroy the earth' (v. 11). The rainbow is assigned by Elohim/God as the symbol of the covenant. Because the rainbow is a physical property of the water vapour and rain, whenever clouds gather or rain falls God will be reminded of the covenant. In other words, it is 'scientifically' impossible, God declares, for there ever to be rain without God remembering the promise to preserve the earth and all that is in it. Of course, the rainbow is also a reminder to humans (and perhaps to the other living creatures) that God will never start again. God will live with this world's violence, although it will be limited and monitored.

Noah's successors

Verse 18 is a summary statement, bringing to conclusion the story of Noah. Whatever sources the author has used, the final product ends where it began in 6:9, with a brief genealogy of Noah. The genealogy is brief because humanity must begin again, under God's covenant of redemption. Any illusions about humanity are gone; we are corrupt in our very core. Yet that is not the end of us, but our new beginning and our new self-understanding, provided we adhere to the limits that God has placed upon us. Seven times between verses 8 and 17 the word 'covenant' is used. Having given us substantial freedom before, God will now manage us, and the vehicle for God's management of humankind will be the various covenants that God establishes throughout the ages.

PRAYER

We recognize ourselves, covenant God of Noah, in this story,
and confess that we are prone to evil; forgive us and guide us
through your covenant with us.

26

The FIRST VINEYARD

This story of Noah is quite clearly a separate and distinct narrative. It has been included here because it is a story that 'belongs' to this great ancestor and because it fits rather well. The flood has passed and Noah has begun to till the soil, like his ancestors before him. Life after the flood continues as before. Significantly, Noah is described as 'a man (*ish*) of the ground (*ha-adamah*)' (v. 20). Noah's first act after the flood was to build an altar; his second act is as important, for he plants a vineyard (v. 20). What God did in the garden of Eden (2:9), Noah does after the flood: he plants trees.

The parallels do not stop there. Just as eating of the fruit of the forbidden tree brought consequences, so Noah's eating of the fruit of the vine brings consequences. Nakedness too plays a role in both.

After the epic story of Noah and the flood, this short account feels almost ludicrous and, at first glance, comic. Noah gets drunk! What follows, however, is far from amusing, for Noah's curse on his son assumes cosmic proportions, and the effects of the story on generations of Africans (and others) has been catastrophic. Whether Noah was celebrating or simply consuming too much wine, the produce of his newly planted vineyard, is not told. Why he was naked at the time is also not revealed, although we know from Genesis 3:7 and 2:25 that nakedness has come to be associated with shame. The absence of detail in verses 20–21 makes it clear that these verses are simply setting the scene for what is to come. One of Noah's sons, Ham, comes into Noah's tent (we must assume) and 'sees' (v. 22) the nakedness of his father. The Hebrew offers us nothing more, although the later phrase, 'what his youngest son had done to him' (v. 24), may suggest that Ham 'did' something other than 'seeing'. Speculation has been rife, with some suggesting castration and others rape. But in the narrative as we have it, Ham is guilty only of immodesty, both in entering his father's tent to look and then in telling his brothers of what he has seen. The immediate and carefully modest response of these brothers is set over against his own behaviour (v. 23).

The story could be read as a story about the loss of innocence. Noah, unfamiliar with the produce of the vine, becomes drunk. Ham, unfamiliar with his father's drunken behaviour, looks into his tent to see what is going on. Confused by what he sees, Ham tells his brothers. The brothers, being older, do the culturally acceptable thing. Noah has learned and so has Ham. But that is not how the story goes. After waking, Noah speaks. Having lived with Noah for so long, we may not notice that Noah has not said a single thing since his name was first mentioned in 5:29. Now that he does speak, it is to curse his son and generations to come.

The curse of Noah

On awakening 'from his wine' (v. 24), Noah launches into a poetic curse on Canaan. There is a fair amount of muddle here. The story is clear that it is Ham who transgresses, and yet we know from the genealogies in 6:10, 9:19 and 10:1 that Ham is the middle son, not the youngest. And yet it is 'the youngest son' who is said to have behaved improperly (v. 24). Furthermore, it is not Ham (or Japheth, the youngest son) who is cursed, but Ham's son, Canaan (see vv. 22, 25). The confusion continues when Noah's curse treats Canaan, Shem and Japheth as 'brothers' (vv. 25–27). Something is clearly amiss.

What appears to be happening here is a rather crass attempt at ethnic stereotyping. The text has been manipulated to serve the agenda of those who wanted to denigrate a particular ethnic group, the Canaanites. This text may date to a period when there was animosity between Israel and Canaan. Interestingly, as we will see, in the rest of Genesis there is generally a very good relationship between the ancestors of Israel and the Canaanites (the indigenous peoples in whose lands the ancestors of Israel wander and make their home).

Canaan is cursed to be the slave of his brothers. The other brothers are blessed; part of their blessing is that they will live together and part of their blessing is that Canaan will be their slave. While we may dismiss this contrived stereotyping of the Canaanites, generations of Africans were made to carry the burden of this text. Designated as 'the sons of Ham' in Genesis 10, they were made to carry Canaan's curse. This text (together with Joshua 9:27) was used in South Africa to justify 'apartheid' (racially based 'separate development') on biblical grounds. Africans, we were told, were decreed by God to be the slaves of other races.

PRAYER

Deliver us, God of all, from racism and all forms of ethnic prejudice.

27

The TABLE *of* NATIONS

The story of Noah is not quite complete. Chapter 10 is framed by reference to Noah and his sons. Noah is a new beginning for the world. Like God, he plants trees, and in obedience to God he and his sons are fruitful and they do multiply and fill the earth (9:1). All humankind now stems from them.

Many nations

The 'Table of Nations', as it has been called, in Genesis 10 is an ambitious attempt to link all of humankind. The generator of this genealogy tries to connect all the known world of his/her time with the sons of Noah. At first glance, the genealogy appears to be about nations. Many of the names have a fairly clear connection to a particular nation: Javan (Greece), Tarshish (Spain), Kittim (Cyprus), Rodanim (Rhodes), Cush (Ethiopia), Mizraim (Egypt), Put (Libya), Canaan, Asshur (Assyria), Lud (Lydia), and Aram (Syria). Furthermore, the genealogy presumes, reasonably logically, that nations are formed through the expansion and genealogical division of extended families. While this view fits the framework of the family-centred narrative of Genesis, it does not correspond to the complex political processes that actually 'construct' nations.

There are also anomalies in the genealogy itself, which make it quite clear that they are not intended to be interpreted literally. For example, Nimrod migrates from Africa to Mesopotamia and in so doing overlaps with a region and places associated with the descendants of Shem (compare vv. 11 and 22). Nevertheless, viewing this genealogy as connecting and charting the nations that derive from the sons of Noah is one point of view.

Socio-political tension

Several scholars have suggested another perspective, namely that we see this genealogy as being organized around socio-political rather than ethnic or nationalistic concerns. A socio-political perspective is instructive in that it connects Noah's genealogy with the texts both before and after it. Cain, we were told (4:17), built the first city, and his descendants were the founders of urban industry and culture

(4:22). The people of the land of Shinar in Genesis 11 are also city builders (11:4). Just as there was a tension between Cain's line, with its base in the city, and Seth's line, with its base in the country, so we can discern this tension in the genealogy of Genesis 10.

Indeed, this interpretation provides another angle from which to understand the curse on Ham (9:25–27). In verses 6–20 the genealogies of Ham and Canaan are given, and although there is not much detail to go on, what is evident is that Ham's descendants move from the country to the city. Nimrod is 'a mighty hunter' who moves from the land to found 'his kingdom', which includes a number of 'great' cities, among them Babel and Nineveh (vv. 9–12). Indeed, Nimrod is credited with being 'the first to be mighty on the earth' (v. 8, in Hebrew). The NRSV's translation of this phrase as 'the first on earth to become a mighty warrior', while not being an exact translation, does convey very well the violence implicit in Nimrod's characterization. Here is another link between the genealogy of Cain and that of Noah. Ham's line, like Cain's, is characterized by the violence endemic to the city and the socio-political control that the city came to exert over the countryside. Cain was the first to build a city; his descendant Lamech was the first to boast of violence (4:23–24). Ham's descendant Nimrod is the first to be called 'mighty' and is the founder of many 'great' cities.

Racial discrimination

What any of this has to do with Africans or black people is not at all clear, and yet, in the history of interpretation of this text, the curse on Canaan has been associated with a curse on 'blackness'. 'Black' has been read as a synonym for 'slave' (9:25–27). But, according to the genealogy in Genesis 10, Canaan's line has nothing to do with Africa. Three of Ham's descendants are linked to Africa—Cush, Egypt and Put—but none of these is cursed by Noah. Significantly, there is no reference or allusion anywhere in Genesis to skin colour or to any other form of racial marker or characteristic.

REFLECTION

In a conversation with the Catholic priest Frei Betto, the Cuban leader Fidel Castro says, 'I was taught that one of Noah's sons was punished by having black descendants. Somebody should check to see if this is being taught today and if it's really proper for religion to teach that being black is a punishment of God.'

The GENEALOGY *of* HUMANITY

As we have seen, the confusion surrounding Ham and Canaan in 9:25–27 continued into 10:1–20. In chapter 9, Canaan seems to be a son of Noah, and yet he is explicitly designated as the son of Ham. Similarly, in chapter 10, although not indicated as one of Noah's sons, Canaan is given his own genealogy (10:15–20), like the other sons. Given the prominence of the land of Canaan in the history and imagination of Israel, this is not surprising. Canaan was the land in which the ancestors of Israel sojourned. Throughout Genesis, as we will see, they are guests of the indigenous peoples, who are Canaanites (though other terms are also used to describe them). Canaan was also the land of a number of large city-states, which would have been experienced as oppressive by 'the people of the land'. It was these 'people of the land' who were the founding 'tribes' or clans of the nation of Israel. And then, when Israel itself became an oppressive city-state (with Jerusalem as its capital) under Solomon, Canaan would have been seen as either a potential political ally or a threat. So 'Canaan' would have meant many different things during the different periods of Israel's history.

Socio-cultural concerns

One way of reading this genealogy, as we have already seen, is from a socio-political or socio-cultural perspective. The descendants of Japheth (10:2–5) are largely 'coastland peoples' and seafarers; the descendants of Ham (10:6–14) are primarily city-based; the descendants of Canaan do not have a designated socio-cultural profile, but are presumably subsumed under the characterization of Ham's genealogy; and the descendants of Shem are mainly nomads.

Shem is singled out for particular attention as both the father of 'all the children of Eber' and as 'the elder brother of Japheth' (v. 21). While the mention of his being the eldest son makes immediate sense, the reason for the reference to his being the father of Eber is less obvious. Eber's name, however, is related to the word for 'Hebrew', a term that was used to designate those of low social status with a nomadic lifestyle. As we will see, the term 'Hebrew' is used a number of times in Genesis, and on each occasion it refers to those with an outsider status, both culturally and socially. The name, then, does not apply to an ethnic or national identity, but to a people living under particular socio-political conditions. Significantly, it is from Eber that Abram will descend (11:16–26). The genealogical 'comment' may suggest, therefore, that these socio-political characteristics are key to God's purposes in choosing Abram's line as the vehicle to bless all of humankind (Genesis 12:3).

A socio-political interpretation of Genesis 10 (in association with the texts on either side of it) points to the implicit tensions between different socio-political orientations in the ancient world, and in particular to the tension between land-based rural life and the city-based power of the great urban empires and kingdoms in Egypt, Mesopotamia and Canaan.

Where is Israel?

While the nations of the known world are mentioned in Genesis 10, there is no mention of Israel. There is not even a hint that a specific line of humanity is of particular importance. It is only in chapter 11 that a particular line is assigned special significance, but even then there is constant contestation of the privileging of this line. Genesis 10, and much of Genesis, emphasizes the unity of humanity.

Theology, not geography

The genealogy in Genesis 10 is a construct that attempts to connect all of the known world of its author to Noah's progeny. Impressive though the attempt is, it cannot be taken as genetically accurate, and vast parts of the world are simply ignored. But its purpose is not geographical. A geographical framework or metaphor is being used to make a fundamental theological point: that all humankind is related. This remains a constant theme throughout Genesis. Humankind is represented as a family. God's promise to Abram therefore makes perfect sense: 'In/by you all the families of the earth shall be blessed' (12:3). The book of Genesis never allows us to forget that this is God's primary purpose in establishing a covenant with particular people. They are merely the vehicles of and for God's primary purpose: the blessing of all humankind.

PRAYER

Help us to know in our hearts, and not only in our heads, God of all families, that humankind is indeed one family.

The TOWER of BABEL

The opening verse of the story of the tower of Babel is at odds with the genealogy that precedes it. Three times, corresponding to each of the sons of Noah (with Ham and Canaan being treated together), we are told in chapter 10 that each set of descendants had their own languages (10:5, 20, 31). The emphasis in chapter 10 is that although humankind is diverse, humankind is also a unity. In contrast, chapter 11 begins with the statement that 'all the earth had one language and common words'. In a sense, then, chapter 11 might be considered a 'flashback' to how human language became diversified.

The juxtaposition of chapters 10 and 11 clearly demonstrates how accepting of difference the compilers of the book of Genesis were. Just as the two very different creation stories in Genesis 1 and Genesis 2—3 are allowed to stand next to each other, so the genealogy of chapter 10 and the story of the tower of Babel are allowed to stand next to each other. Each has its own emphasis, and this is why each has been collected and incorporated. What we must not miss, however, is what is accomplished by this kind of juxtaposition for the larger narrative of the book of Genesis as a whole. Difference and even contestation are part of its design.

There is an important connection between Genesis 10 and 11. Nimrod's cities in 10:10 are located in Shinar, and this is exactly where the building project described in 11:2-4 is situated. Indeed, the story could be read as the story of Nimrod's descendants, were it not for verse 1, which gives the story a universal reference. And, on the surface, the story appears to be about how unity is transformed into diversity, with human language being the tool that accomplishes this transformation. The language of the story is itself full of indicators of inclusion and scattering.

Human activity

The story can be divided into two parallel parts. Verses 1–4 describe human activity, and verses 5–9 describe God's response. What is difficult to discern, however, is the motivation that drives the actions of each. We have already seen that the building of a city is associated with violence, for it is Cain who builds the first one (4:17) and it is

Lamech's line that is associated with the rise of urban industry and culture (4:19–24). In addition, humankind now usurps the language of God (1:26) in saying, 'Come, let us make…'. God will respond in similar terms in 11:7, using the divine plural found in 1:26. All these echoes are perhaps an indication that something negative is happening here. Is this, then, merely another indication that the human heart is prone to evil (8:21)? What is the motivation in building this city?

Verse 4 provides the motivation. There are four elements to it. The first element may be a desire to be less dependent on the land. By building a city, humankind severs its direct relationship with the land. The second element is more overt: it is the desire to be like God. Not only is the language of God's creative work appropriated, but there is also the aspiration to have 'a tower with its top in the heavens', so drawing near to God's own dwelling place. The third element is: 'And let us make a name for ourselves'. Previously it was God who named humankind, and the name God has given it is *ha-adam*, signifying the intrinsic connection between humanity and the ground (*ha-adamah*), the land. Now humankind wants the autonomy to 'make' a name for itself. Here, and in so much of this story, there is play on words. The word for 'name' (*shem* in Hebrew) connects this story with the genealogy of Shem in 10:21–31 and 11:10–30. Shem's line will lead to Abram, who will spend his entire life wandering in a land that is never his. The line that God will choose as the vehicle for the blessing of all humankind will be this line of nomadic wanderers, and not the city dwellers. The desire for autonomy and stability is, then, the third element. The fourth element is a refusal 'to fill the earth' (1:28; 9:1). Instead of going forth, humankind fears being 'scattered abroad'. The concentration of human vision and endeavour—for such is what we see here—in the city is to be its source and site of power.

PRAYER

Thank you, our God, for the capacity to be creative and to collaborate with others. May what we do with these gifts be pleasing in your sight when you come to see what we have done with what you have given to us.

DIVINE RESPONSE *to* BABEL

'And Yahweh came down to see the city and the tower that the sons of *ha-adam* had built' (v. 5). This sentence is the turning point of the narrative. What God sees causes God to scatter them abroad (v. 8) by 'confusing' the language that united them. But why does God do this? What does God see that is a source of concern? First, the very fact that humanity is 'one people' with 'one language' (v. 6) seems in itself to be a problem. God intended diversity to be a mark of creation. Throughout Genesis 1, God creates plants and animals of 'every kind'. Diversity is also a feature of Genesis 2—3 and of the story of Noah. God creates and sustains diversity. From this story, it would appear that God also intends a diversity among humankind (as we find in Genesis 10). Second, God is disturbed by the prospect of what other human enterprises may follow the building of this city. Something in the very nature of what the humans have built worries God.

What humankind builds is a city. In the time of the writers and compilers of the book of Genesis, and much of the Old Testament, the world was ruled by empires whose power lay in the city-state. Each of the great empires of the ancient Near East that succeeded each other, whether it was Egyptian, Canaanite, Assyrian, Babylonian, Persian, Macedonian, Ptolemaic, Seleucid or Roman, based its power on cities. Those who lived on the land outside the cities were considered the raw material for the sustenance of the cities. Structures were put in place that controlled 'the people of the land', as they were called, including various forms of tribute. Indeed, the political economies of the region were characterized by what is known as a tributary mode of production. The concentration of military power in the city enabled the city leadership—including the king, his court, the priests and their temple, and the numerous officials and merchants who served them—to demand tribute from the people of the land in return for protection. The clearest summary of this system is given in 1 Samuel 8. From this brief overview it becomes more readily apparent why God is so concerned about this particular project. The city symbolizes human power and the potential for exploitation and oppression.

The third factor that features in the description of God's concern in verse 6 is human hubris. God is anxious that if human beings succeed in this project, they will be unable to see their own limitations. They will begin to believe their own propaganda!

Given these concerns, God intervenes. The strategy God employs is to 'confuse their language' (v. 7). This has the required effect, scattering humankind 'abroad from there over the face of all the earth' and, most importantly—for it is located at the end of the sentence for emphasis—'they left off building the city' (v. 8).

South Africa's 'Babel'

Ironically, this story was used in South Africa to justify 'apartheid' (separate development). Theologians and biblical scholars who supported Afrikaner nationalism and white supremacist racism argued that in this text God had intentionally 'separated' humanity into distinct linguistic and cultural groups, and that it was God's intention that these groups should live and develop separately. This text became the biblical, theological and ideological foundation of a race-based state policy of segregation. In accepting it as such, white Afrikaners built their own empire, failing completely to 'see' the potentially evil empire that God saw in the similar project in the plain of Shinar. Such is human hubris and the damage it can do.

Scattered humanity

This story concludes, almost, what is known as the primeval history, Genesis 1—11. It seems a rather bleak conclusion, reminding us as it does of humankind's ongoing propensity for evil (see 9:21). It also reminds us, however, of God's ongoing management of humankind. In more theological terms, this story reminds us that God is being faithful to the covenant that was established with Noah (9:9–17). God does not destroy humankind for its arrogant ambition; instead, God remains engaged with humankind. The scattering that God accomplishes by confusing the language of power also brings into being a more 'grounded' kind of people—a people who live in relationship with the land, each other, themselves and God. The stories that follow the genealogy in 11:10–30 reveal that none of these relationships is fully realized, but they also reveal that God never gives up engaging with us.

PRAYER

Forgive us, faithful God, for our improper ambition.

From SHEM to ABRAM

The book of Genesis begins with the story of the first family in Genesis 1, and then takes on more cosmic proportions, culminating in the destruction of the whole world in Genesis 6. We then begin again with another family, Noah's, and this culminates in the scattering of humanity across all the earth. The genealogy in 11:10–32 now narrows our focus once again, until it concentrates on only one family.

Ten generations

There were ten generations from Adam to Noah, and Noah produced three sons. There are now ten generations from Shem to Terah, and Terah produces three sons, one of whom is Abram. The symmetry is typical of oral tradition, in which the ancestors are remembered using rhetorical devices such as this. Minor ancestors tend to get forgotten in the process, with only the major ancestors being honoured in the recitation. There are other rhetorical techniques in this genealogy. From the birth of Shem's son to Abram's migration to Canaan is 365 years, a year of years. Furthermore, Abram is born when his father is seventy years of age (threescore and ten)—a significant number (see Genesis 46:27; 50:3; Exodus 15:27; Numbers 33:9; Deuteronomy 10:22; Judges 1:7; 8:30; 9:2, 4, 5; 12:14; 1 Samuel 6:19; 2 Chronicles 36:21; Psalm 90:10; Zechariah 1:12).

Genealogies are not only lists of generations; they are also signs of an order in life. In the case of this genealogy, we are being told that the significance of Noah is matched by the significance of Abram. We are also assured of a divine order in the very fabric of 'history'. Ancient authors were not as fixated as we are with verifiable 'facts' as the basis of history. History, they knew, is a construct and represents a particular perspective on life. There is always selection and combination, and different people select and combine differently. While we try to set identifiable limits on this process, our ancient compatriots were not as constrained.

A potential problem

The sense of purpose and plan in the genealogy is upset in verse 30: 'Now Sarai was barren'. In case we have missed the significance of this short statement, it is repeated in different words: 'she had no child'. The genealogy comes to its climax not in fruitfulness, but in failure. How will this break in the genealogy be repaired? Will the symmetry of God's purpose be disrupted? This complication in the plot of God's plan is what keeps us reading! Sarai and her inability to conceive are central to the action of the story. The gap that her barrenness brings to the genealogy offers both opportunities and problems.

The journey begins

The rest of the book of Genesis will follow the family introduced to us in verse 31. The line will not always be a straight one, for God is as interested in the margins as in the centre. Although the focus appears to be on this one genealogical line of promise, there are plenty of indications that those on the outside of the family are as important. Indeed, the notion of what constitutes this family is constantly problematized and contested.

The journey to Canaan does not begin with Abram, although it is he who will complete it. The journey begins with his father, Terah. What prompts his move from Ur of the Chaldeans to Canaan is not told to us. As will often happen with Abram, Terah is sidetracked. He does not make it to Canaan, his ostensible destination; instead he settles in Haran. There he dies, leaving the stage set for Abram. It is not as simple as this, however, for according to the chronology provided, Terah dies at the age of 205 (v. 32). According to 12:4, Abram left Haran at the age of 75. Given that he was born when his father was 70 (v. 26), this would mean that he left his father's home 60 years before his father's death. This makes his leaving all the more remarkable, which is where the next story begins.

PRAYER

Thank you, God of Adam and God of Abraham, for all the stories which have been preserved for us. Give us ears to hear and eyes to see your word to us.

32 GENESIS 12—36

ONE FAMILY, THREE GENERATIONS

The stories in this section of the book of Genesis are largely about one family, covering three generations. If we were to include Genesis 37—50, then it would be the story of four generations. So treating Genesis 12—36 as a section is somewhat arbitrary, although it does group together stories that share a number of important common features. While Genesis 37—50 is one long extended story, Genesis 12—36 is made up of many short stories, or sagas, as they are sometimes called.

Cycles or chains of sagas

The term 'saga' is a useful one, because for the non-scholarly reader of the Bible it carries no particular baggage. The term has been used by scholars to designate short stories that have one principal character, and which do not show a great deal of character development. In addition, sagas tend not to contain much historical or geographical detail. This is the predominant type of story that we find in chapters 12—36.

The stories in these chapters are stories about the ancestors, those figures whom later generations venerated as the founders of their family and nation. In Genesis, the ancestors are clearly ancestors of the family rather than the nation. Very few of the stories in chapters 12—26 have any national consciousness. Later generations have read them as the foundational stories of the nation of Israel, but the narratives do not portray themselves as such.

What we have in Genesis 12—36 are stories that have arisen around particular ancestors, the most prominent of whom are Abraham, Lot, Sarah, Hagar, Ishmael, Isaac, Rebekah, Jacob, Dinah and Esau. If we include Genesis 37—50, then we can add Joseph, Judah and Tamar.

These ancestor stories clearly have had a long history, being told and retold generation after generation, which is why they have shed many of their historical and geographical details. They have been collected and treasured and told because they say something about a remembered ancestor. Most of them would have had an independent existence—each story a story in its own right, remembered by a particular part of the family. As time went on, however, these stories would have been collected. So, for example, the various independent stories about Abraham would have been gathered together in order to remember this great ancestor. These oral stories would, at some stage in the history of Israel, have been written down and incorporated into a larger narrative about the nation. This process was a complex one and scholars are not certain about the details of the compilation process, but what is clear is that sagas were connected together into saga cycles or chains of sagas. So, for example, the Abraham sagas were gathered and then linked one to another. The act of linking was itself a creative and theological act, just as was the original composition of the individual saga.

What we have, then, is a historical compositional process in which various communities over time in different contexts have tried to construct a coherent account of the early ancestors of Israel. The various individual sagas have been connected by a variety of means, some quite simple and others more complex, to tell a larger story. Each saga still tells its own story, but, together with the other sagas to which it has been linked, it now contributes to the larger narrative.

Reading the ancestor stories

Given this process of collection and composition, the stories in Genesis 12—36 can be read at various levels. We must pay attention to each of the sagas in its own right, and we must also try to discern the concerns of the larger narrative of which the individual sagas are a part. Because many generations of readers have left their imprint on the texts we are reading, we will encounter many voices as we read. Various authors and editors in different contexts have tried to communicate their theological understandings in the fabric of these stories. To honour and hear them, we must read closely and carefully, for in so doing we also hear the voice of God.

PRAYER

Thank you, God of our ancestors, for these sacred stories
that have been passed down to us through many generations.
Give us eyes to see and ears to hear as we read them,
that we might see and hear you.

GOD SAYS, 'YOU MUST GO!'

God has not spoken for quite some time. Now God speaks again, and like the last time God spoke, God commands someone to 'go'. When God told Noah to 'go' (7:1), however, it was clear to the reader and to Noah why he needed to go. When God tells Abram to 'go', it is not at all clear why he must go.

God's command is not only unusual in that reasons are not given about why Abram must go; the verbal form is itself unusual. This form of the verb 'to go' occurs only one more time in the Hebrew Bible (Genesis 22:2), when God speaks to Abraham for the last time. Given its rarity, it is not easy to translate, but scholars have suggested that it means something like 'You must go!' or 'Go for yourself', or 'Go to yourself'.

Go from

Understood in this way, the command of God to Abram is less about what he has to 'go from' (v. 1) and more about what he has to 'go to' or 'go for'. Nevertheless, there are specified aspects of his life that Abraham must 'go from'. This is made clear by God, for God follows the imperative with a preposition: 'Go from…'. Then come three prepositional phrases, each detailing what Abram must go from. He must go from his country, from his people, and from his father's household. Everything that makes Abram who he is is to be left behind. Even those in our world today who have embraced its call to individualism would baulk at a command like this, so imagine the horror of this call on someone who is defined by these three elements.

Go to

God mitigates the almost incomprehensible command by providing a destination and a promise. The destination is 'the land that I will show you'. With land before him, Abram has the promise of belonging again. This promise of land is followed immediately by a number of further elements of God's promise. First is the promise of 'the land I will show you'; second is the promise 'I will make of you a great nation'; third is the promise 'I will bless you'; fourth is the promise

'I will make your name great'; fifth is the promise 'you will be a bless-ing'; sixth is the promise 'I will bless those who bless you'; seventh is the promise 'I will curse the one who curses you'; and eighth is the promise 'in you all the families of the earth shall be blessed' (vv. 2–3).

God's composite promise is not as stark as it has been represented by these eight elements. The elements are connected and form an argument. The argument is that God will make Abram a great nation and bless him and make his name great *so that* he will be a blessing to others. Similarly, God will bless those who bless Abram and curse those who curse Abraham *so that* all the families in the earth will be blessed through Abram. Abram must go *so that* others will be blessed by God. This is the primary purpose of God's calling, and is con-firmed on four further occasions: to Abraham twice (18:17–18; 22:16–18), to Isaac (26:2–4), and to Jacob (28:10–14).

Abram obeys (almost)

The first part of verse 4 indicates that Abram obeys the command of God: 'And Abram went, as God told him'. But in the very next part of the verse, we read that he only partially obeyed God. He does leave his country, he does leave his people, but he does not quite leave his father's household, for he takes his nephew Lot with him (v. 5). Is this a quibble or is it a substantial point? When Abram is commanded to leave his father's household, whom does the command include? The narrative is not clear about this; nor does it comment overtly on Abram's decision to take Lot with him. Neither, for that matter, does the narrative make any comment on God's command to Abram. From the perspective of the narrative it is self-evident that Abram is expected to obey God. No comment is required. But would Lot be considered a part of Abram's household or a part of his father's household? This could be argued both ways, so for now we will have to leave this matter unresolved. As we read on, it may become clearer whether or not Abram was obeying God fully in taking Lot.

PRAYER

Your word to us is not always easy for us to understand; help us to discern what you want to say to us, God of Abram.

From Haran to Canaan

Abram's journey is not described at all. Having left Haran, Abram and his household arrive in Canaan, the land to which his father Terah had been journeying (11:31). Abraham completes the journey his father had begun; more importantly, Abram completes the journey God has commanded him to make. Abram has yet to become a blessing to others, but he has arrived in the land to which God directed him.

Worshipping together

On his arrival in the land, Abram visits a sacred tree in Shechem (v. 6). This shrine, it would appear, is associated with the Canaanites. At the mention of the shrine, God appears to Abram once again, telling Abram that this is the land that God will give to his descendants. In response, Abram builds an altar to his God, Yahweh, in Shechem and another further on, between Bethel and Ai. When Abram builds altars to his God and invokes Yahweh's name in this land, is it over against the existing shrines, such as the tree-shrine at Shechem, or is Abram placing his religion alongside that of the Canaanites? We will need to read on to answer this question more fully, but from this first encounter with the indigenous inhabitants of the land, the Canaanites, Abram shows no signs of wanting to distance himself from their religion. Indeed, quite the opposite happens, with Abram deliberately seeking out Canaanite shrines as sites for his own worship of Yahweh.

Abram not only recognizes that other people are in the land already (see below), but he also recognizes their religion, showing respect to it by associating his own worship with it. Abram's journey to Shechem, to 'the oak of Moreh', seems quite deliberate. He seeks out a religious site as his first stopping place in this new land, not to destroy it or assert his own religion over against it, but to identify and associate himself and his religion with it. Would that we were as gracious!

A peopled land

In verse 6b, the narrator explicitly informs us that the Canaanites 'were in the land', making it clear that the land was not empty.

Remarkably, given the later animosity between Israel and the Canaanites, there is no sign of any animosity in this text (or, indeed, anywhere in the book of Genesis). Later editors have refrained from tampering with the text here, allowing us to grasp the legacy that Abram has left us. As the great ancestor of Jews, Muslims and Christians, Abram demonstrates a way of living among those who are different from us. Abram deliberately identifies with what is important to those he moves among, identifying himself, his family and his God with what matters to others.

Abram's arrival in an already peopled land, and the way he goes about living in the land that God has promised to him, provide us with a perspective that seems lacking in current debates about the land in Palestine. Would that we had more leaders like Abram to guide us!

More journeys

Abram's journeying has not come to an end once he reaches Canaan. Having got there, he journeys within the land, probably moving as the need arises to find fresh pasture for his livestock. He lives in a tent, but makes for God more permanent places in the form of altars. There is no mention of sacrifice, so it is not clear from the narrative how these altars were used.

When he reaches the Negeb, he encounters a famine (v. 10). This area is a dry region anyway, so in times of drought and famine the situation would have been desperate. Egypt, with its fertile Nile valley, was a refuge for the whole region in times of famine. Abram went to Egypt 'to reside there as an alien', indicating that he may have to spend an extended time there.

PRAYER

You are the God who speaks to your people; speak, our God, to us.
Direct us to your destinations and bless us
so that we may bless others.

DECEPTION & DELIVERANCE

Deception

As Abram is about to enter Egypt, he conspires with Sarai to deceive the Egyptians concerning his relationship with her. This ruse is repeated twice more in Genesis, once again with Abraham and Sarah (20:1–8) and then with Isaac and Rebekah (26:1, 6–11). This tale of trickery was clearly a popular kind of ancestor story!

Knowing that they may have to reside in Egypt for some time, Abram attempts to trick the Egyptians into believing that the attractive Sarai is his sister rather than his wife. He (and perhaps she) is willing to allow the Egyptians to exploit her in order to enhance Abram's chances of living. Refugee families all over the world make similar survival decisions every day. As a refugee, he knows that he has no power or status to prevent those more powerful from taking his wife, should they so desire. What he and Sarai are trying to protect, it would seem, is his life.

Abram's fears prove justified, for the Egyptians respond as he imagined they might. Sarai is 'taken into Pharaoh's house' (v. 15). She becomes his property, in a similar way in which she was Abram's property. She is yet to speak! She is expected to obey her husband, just as Abram was expected to obey God when God told him to 'go'. As Abram had hoped, the sacrifice of Sarai enables 'it to go well' for him (v. 13), for Pharaoh causes him to prosper. Is this what God meant by promising Abram that he would be blessed?

Deliverance

God intervenes. No sooner has Sarai entered Pharaoh's house than God afflicts Pharaoh and his house with 'great plagues' (v. 17)—on behalf of Sarai. Abram looks after himself; God looks after Sarai.

To his credit, Pharaoh acts immediately, summoning Abram to find out what is happening. He clearly recognizes a connection between the presence of Sarai and the plagues. Abram does not even have to explain, so self-evident is the situation to Pharaoh. Ironically, it is Pharaoh who declares Sarai to be Abram's wife. Without even giving Abram a chance to speak—just as Abram did not give Sarai a chance to speak—he expels him from the land of Egypt, although allowing him to take his possessions. In a mocking reminder of God's words to Abram, Pharaoh commands Abram, 'Go' (v. 19).

So, perhaps sooner than he had planned, Abram is back in the Negeb (13:1).

Point of view

How are we to interpret this episode? There is little guidance from the narrator, and we can imagine a number of plausible appropriate interpretations. Is this act a sign of a moral flaw or a lack of faith in Abram? Or is it the act of a desperate husband and wife struggling to survive, whatever it takes? Is it an amusing trickster story in which the weak (Abram and Sarai) deceive the powerful (the Egyptians and Pharaoh), escaping not only with their lives but also with the loot? Or is it a story of God's commitment to the couple, protecting this female body (and its offspring) for a greater purpose? Is it a proto-feminist story of God taking sides with a woman over against men, or is it about God safeguarding marriage, or simply about God's power to intervene? Is God unhappy about Abram being in Egypt, and so acts to have him expelled and returned to Canaan? Or is this story a reading back from a later period of an exodus-type element into the story of Israel's greatest ancestor?

The structure of verse 17 possibly gives us a clue, although it does not give us a full answer to our questions: 'But the Lord afflicted Pharaoh and his house with great plagues because of Sarai, Abram's wife.' The emphasis here (which follows the emphasis in the Hebrew) on Sarai as Abram's wife indicates that God's intervention is about Abram as much as it is about Sarai. But the story is also about God. Just as God is the subject of Abram's call, so here God is the subject of Abram and Sarai's deliverance. Without God's intervention, Abram's ruse would have led to the dissolution of the family of promise.

REFLECTION

What is your interpretation of this episode?

36

ABRAM & LOT SETTLE

Abram now retraces his journey, moving slowly with his household and their livestock from the Negeb back to where his tent had been between Bethel and Ai, and there he worships God at the altar he had built (v. 4). Neither Abram nor any of his descendants worship outside this promised land.

In this third saga or story of the Abram cycle, we are told that Abram was very rich in livestock, in silver and in gold (v. 2). There is no verb in this sentence, although some form of the verb 'to be' is implied. Another translation might be, 'And Abram became very rich…'. It is not clear whether we are meant to understand that Abram gained his wealth in Egypt or whether it was a long process of gradual accrual. From the earlier story, we know that Pharaoh 'dealt well with Abram', which meant that Abram 'had sheep, oxen, male donkeys, male and female slaves, female donkeys, and camels' (12:16). The problem here, however, is that this wealth was obtained through false pretences and trickery. We know that God intervened on behalf of Sarai because she was Abram's wife, but we are not told whether God approves of the wealth that Abram gained through this deception.

The prosperity of nomadic herders like Abram was usually measured in livestock, slaves and tents. Lot, like Abram, has large flocks and herds and tents (v. 5), but Abram has additional wealth in the form of slaves (12:16) and silver and gold (v. 2). Nomads needed a surplus of livestock in order to be able to trade it for slaves or sell it for silver and gold.

Dividing the land

Verse 5 brings us to the focus of this story. The prosperity of Abram and Lot has led to a situation where the land cannot sustain them if they remain together. Before conflict escalates, a solution must be found, but before a solution can be found, the reader needs to be reminded that this is inhabited land (v. 7b). The reminder serves in this instance to indicate the lack of conflict between Abram and his household and those already living in the land, the Canaanites and the Perizzites. The conflict is between Abram's and Lot's households. As in 12:6, here too there is an indication of the time of composition of this text, for we read in both instances that these peoples were 'then' (or, in the NRSV, 'at that time') in the land. Although the original, probably oral, stories about Abram are much older, their current form comes from a time when the presence of the Canaanites and Perizzites in the land is only a memory.

Abram, as the head of the two households, suggests a solution, graciously offering Lot his choice of the available land (v. 9). In what follows, there is an implicit characterization of Lot and a comparison of Lot with Abram. Lot 'lifted up his eyes' and considered the land carefully, and then made an apparently rational choice of land that was well watered, 'like the garden of Yahweh and like the land of Egypt' (v. 10). The allusions to the garden of God in Genesis 2:10–14 and to Egypt conjure up for the attentive reader or hearer not only images of lush plenty but also images of human frailty and failure. These hints are then given full voice by the narrator (or a later editor), who sounds a note of foreboding. Lot has chosen land close to Sodom and Gomorrah, cities which are wicked (v. 13) and which God will destroy (v. 10). Besides these rather cryptic comments, there is no further comment on Lot's choice. Abram simply settles in the other direction, to the west.

God's promises

No sooner has Lot departed than God speaks again to Abram. Now it is Abram's turn to 'lift up' his eyes (v. 14). The land he sees before him —including, it would seem, Lot's chosen land—is now explicitly given to him and his descendants. Not only is he promised this land that he sees; he is also promised descendants like the dust (v. 16). Then God commands him to go and walk through the land, symbolically taking possession of it (v. 17). Whether Abram does this or not is not indicated, but what he does do is to move his household to a new site in the south, at Hebron. As he had done earlier at Shechem (12:6), Abram chooses a site where there is already a Canaanite tree-shrine, but in this place he also builds an altar to Yahweh.

So far in these narratives about the ancestor Abram, there is neither conflict with the local peoples nor any denigration of their religion. Indeed, the early signs are that Abram's worship of Yahweh finds a place alongside, literally, the local religious practices of the Canaanites.

PRAYER

Make us, gracious God, sensitive to the minor conflicts that have the potential to destroy community, and give us the wisdom to find creative and life-giving solutions.

ABRAM *on the* WORLD STAGE

We leave the quiet pastoral life of Abram and enter a world of political and military contestation. Against this vivid backdrop, the narrative itself is quite simple. Lot is taken captive by four kings involved in a campaign, but is rescued by Abram, who drives the armies of the kings off and claims booty. Abram then gives a tithe to Melchizedek, the priest-king of a city named Salem, and keeps nothing for himself.

Pages and pages of commentary have been devoted to trying to sort out the geographical and historical dimensions of this narrative. The principal difficulty is that while it all sounds plausible at first, careful scrutiny reveals geographical inconsistencies and finds almost no historical evidence for any of the major figures. The effect of the narrative, however, is to fill the land with various political entities. This is no empty land, and perhaps that is the story's primary point.

Most of the chapter is taken up with exposition (vv. 1–11), describing the actions and dispositions of the four campaigning kings. Mention is made of Sodom and Gomorrah, whose kings are defeated, but it is only in verse 12 that the story connects with the story of Abram, when Lot, who is identified as 'the son of Abram's brother', is taken captive along with his household.

This inadvertent action draws Abram into the narrative, and he acts decisively, leading his own army against the four kings. In a briefly described military operation (vv. 14–16), in which Abram astutely uses the cover of night to take advantage of the kings' far superior forces, he routs and then pursues the enemy all the way to Hobah, north of Damascus. Although told in hyperbolic terms, the main point is that Abram looks after his own. In addition, Abram is portrayed here as decisive and courageous and extremely wealthy, possessing his own private army.

Abram's integration in Canaan is perhaps the focal point of the narrative. He has allies, we are told (v. 13), and they support his cause (see v. 24). Furthermore, when he returns with Lot, he is welcomed by the king of Sodom and King Melchizedek of Salem. Not only is Abram politically integrated into the region; he is also religiously at home. Melchizedek blesses Abram in the name of El Elyon, God Most High, who is later identified by Abram as his God (v. 22).

Religious matters

Melchizedek is an enigmatic figure, appropriated by the psalmist (Psalm 110) and the author of Hebrews (5:1–10; 7:1–4, 26–28). Here he is priest of El Elyon. Scholars suggest that El is the name of the sky god in the Canaanite religion, and Elyon the name of an associated deity, but they are also two ordinary Hebrew words meaning 'God Most High'. When he speaks to the king of Sodom (v. 22), Abram may be claiming that Melchizedek's god/s is/are actually his God, Yahweh, the God Most High. This could be understood as Abram either claiming that he rather than Melchizedek has the true understanding of the one God, or acknowledging that although their names for God are different, they are worshipping the same God. The latter is more likely, as Abram offers a tenth of his booty to Melchizedek, acknowledging his office as priest of this God Most High. This, then, is a remarkable moment. Abram acknowledges that his God, Yahweh, is known and worshipped, albeit by another name, in Canaan. His response is to bless Melchizedek, fulfilling God's promise that he would be a blessing to others.

The religious embrace between Melchizedek and Abram is contrasted with the tension between Abram and the king of Sodom. The king of Sodom ungraciously demands a portion of the booty that Abram has taken (v. 21). Wiser than his nephew and therefore wary of entering into any alliance with the king of Sodom, Abram hands over all of the remainder of the spoils of war, having given a tenth to Melchizedek. He does, however, insist that his alliance partners take their share.

Characterizing Abram

This strange saga, so different from any of the others, offers us a fairly detailed characterization of Abram. He is secure and settled in the land, and although mainly a man of peace, he will act to protect his family. He is also sensitive to the religious plurality of his context and strives to situate himself alongside the religious beliefs of others and not against them. Finally, Abram is characterized as a 'Hebrew', a word that occurs in Genesis here for the first time. In ancient times, this term was not a national designation, but was used for nomadic peoples (usually of a lower social status). Here it signals Abram as a resident foreigner.

PRAYER

God Most High, may we, like our ancestor Abram, be respectful of the faiths that surround us, forging relationships where appropriate.

ABRAM & GOD TALK (I)

In the previous story, God does not speak, although God is invoked
by both Melchizedek and Abram. This next story begins with God
speaking to Abram in a vision. 'After these things' (v. 1), God came to
Abram. There is a play here on a word in Hebrew that can mean
either 'word' or 'thing': 'After these things/words, a word/thing of
Yahweh came to Abram.' This formula is also reminiscent of the
formula associated with the prophets, linking Abram with those who
came after him and reminding the reader that Abram is the forerunner of the later prophets.

The 'things' that God directly addresses seem to be the unstable
political contexts of the previous saga. God reassures Abram that God
will be his shield, protecting him and prospering him. But these are
not the concerns of Abram. His concern is with his own offspring.
Abram is prosperous and blessed in every respect expect one. He has
no son, so he talks back to God, asking God what is going on (v. 2).
So far, he claims (although the meaning of the Hebrew is unclear), the
only heir he has is a slave in his household, Eliezer of Damascus.
Whether this slave is his child by a woman other than Sarai is not
indicated by the narrative, but it seems unlikely given what follows.

Again (v. 4), in the form of an ongoing conversation, the 'word/
thing' of the Lord comes to Abram, assuring him that his heir will be
one of his own children. In order to make the point, God takes
Abram outside and shows him the stars, telling him that his direct
descendants will be as innumerable as the stars. Though not stated,
it is perhaps implied that God is speaking here specifically of children
from Sarai, given God's earlier concern to safeguard Sarai. The narrator draws the reader into the immediacy and intimacy of God's revelation to Abram by repeatedly using the word 'behold/see' in verses
4, 12 and 17. So verse 4 in the Hebrew reads: 'And behold/see, the
word of Yahweh came to him…'. We experience the vision with
Abram.

The image of descendants as innumerable as the stars forms a nice
combination with the earlier image of descendants as innumerable as
the dust (13:16), for both are images associated with Yahweh (and
El Elyon) as the creator of heaven and earth (14:19, 22) and with the

creation stories in Genesis 1 and 2. The reminder to the reader, and to Abram, is that we are dealing here with God the Creator, for whom descendants are no problem.

Abram believed God

Abram's immediate response is to believe God (v. 6). Much has been and can be made of this simple theological statement (see Romans 4:3). In this story, the effects of Abram's belief are evident in that he does not pursue the matter of descendants with God. He holds what God has said to be true. He embraces, in trust and confidence, what God has declared. The narrator is not finished, however, for he/she continues by expanding the theological reflection (in verse 6b). Abram's belief not only accomplishes something in Abram; it also accomplishes something in God and between God and Abram. God sees Abram in a new way, as righteous or just. Furthermore, there is now reciprocity between God and Abram. Their relationship has deepened.

Covenant

Either the vision continues or there is a second related vision or theophany, in verse 7. Having assured Abram of descendants, God now assures Abram of possession of the land, reminding him that God has brought him a long way already from Ur of the Chaldeans, a journey that his father began (see 11:31). Land is not the primary concern of Abram, but it is certainly a concern, for he immediately asks how he will know that he will possess the land (v. 8). This part of the vision, therefore, follows a similar pattern to the first part. God speaks; Abram questions; God reassures. Instead of showing him the land, as God had earlier showed Abram the stars, God now participates in a ritual act with Abram (vv. 10, 17).

The ritual seems to have signified that whoever failed to fulfil the promise would call down on themselves the fate of the slaughtered animals. Remarkably, the ritual binds God to the fulfilment of the promise. God risks the curse associated with a failed promise.

PRAYER

Thank you, merciful God, for continually communicating with us, your people. Speak, so that we may hear your word.

ABRAM & GOD TALK (II)

Strangely, in the midst of the covenant preparations, as the sun was going down (indicating maybe that God has been communicating with Abram all night and all day), 'a deep sleep fell/came on him, and see, a great and terrible darkness falls/comes over him' (v. 12). The darkness, like the birds of prey swooping down on the cut carcasses (15:11), is full of foreboding. The reader is drawn into the horror of Abram's vision. But it is God who speaks from the midst of this deep sleep and terrible darkness.

Interrupting the promise

In the midst of God's covenant with Abram, we are given a glimpse of what lies in store for Abram's descendants: life as aliens, slavery and oppression (vv. 13–14). This insertion by a later redactor is an attempt to assure the reader that God foresaw the events that were to come and that they in no way compromised the covenant that God was about to enact with Abram. This 'fast-forward' also assures Abram (but really the reader) that the 400-year period of suffering is only a delay and a detour on the path to the fulfilment of God's promise. God is faithful, we are assured.

God, in this parenthesis (vv. 12–16), assures Abram and the reader that Egypt (though it is not named) will be judged by God, that Abram's descendants will return to the land about to be promised to Abram, and that Abram will die of old age and at peace.

The concern of the redactor is that those reading or hearing this story may not appreciate the full force of this promise to Abram, given that it would not be fulfilled for many generations. The answer, says the redactor, is not to be found in a deficiency of God's power. The Egyptian episode, so filled with suffering, was not unforeseen. In God's timetable, 'the iniquity of the Amorites is not yet complete' (v. 16). What seems to be implied here is that the land will, for the foreseeable future, remain in the hands of the Amorites/Canaanites because it is not yet time for God to punish them. So the years that Abram's family will spend in Egypt are part of this waiting period.

Covenant (continued)

Verse 17 returns us to the ritual begun in 15:10, which reaches its culmination in the night, when fire passes between the pieces, signalling the consummation of the covenant. The narrator then explains that this ritual is the making, or literally 'cutting', of a covenant between God and Abram, in which God promised clearly designated land to Abram's descendants—land that already had clearly identifiable geographical boundaries and clearly identifiable inhabitants.

When the promise of God finally does come in verse 18, there is a subtle difference from the similar promises that God has made before (12:1–3, 7; 13:14–17; 15:4–5). For the first time, the divine promise is made with a perfective and not an imperfective verb form. In other words, the promise is made as an action that can be considered already completed. God's promise has become more definite.

At the end of this elaborate and extended ritual, we do wonder why it was necessary for God to go to such lengths to reassure Abram. Earlier, in the same vision, it had been sufficient to show Abram the stars and to make him a promise, and he believed (15:6). Now it seems as if Abram requires something more substantial than God's word. Perhaps, however, this is to place the agency in the wrong place. It is God who initiates in chapter 15, so another way of looking at this ritual of covenant is not to see it as the result of Abram requiring more, but as the desire of God to give more.

Faithful interpretation

The description of the promised land (vv. 18–19) corresponds to the extent of Solomon's kingdom at its greatest (see 1 Kings 4:21), so this too may be a later addition or reworking. Once again we see signs of later communities appropriating and attempting to interpret faithfully what they have received. Since the formation of the canon, believing communities no longer rework the text, but this does not mean that the process of reinterpretation has come to an end—far from it. For us, this process continues in our preaching, teaching and writing.

PRAYER

God of Abram, help us to be faithful interpreters of your word in whatever forms we use to proclaim your word.

SARAI & HAGAR

Women are the focus of this story. Although the story has been included in the cycle of sagas about Abram, he is a secondary character and Sarai and Hagar are in the foreground. When Sarai was first introduced to the reader of Genesis, we were told that she 'was barren; she had no child' (11:30). The second of these phrases is confirmed in 16:1, perhaps suggesting that infertility is not the issue. The reader now knows from the previous story that God has promised that Abram will have his own children as heirs, but whether Sarai or some other woman would bear them has been left open. This ambiguity is sustained in the exposition of this story: Sarai is not incapable of having children, she simply has not yet borne children.

Sarai's proposal

Whether or not Sarai has been party to Abram's conversations with God is not clear. In other words, is she now desperately trying to fulfil God's promise through her proposal (v. 2) or is she merely doing as other women in her situation would do? God is strangely silent in the early stages of this story, so it is difficult to discern the divine perspective. Clearly, however, Sarai believes that her barrenness is an act of God. This may simply be a manner of speech or it may indicate a more deeply held theological conviction. Ten years have passed in the land of promise (v. 3), and Sarai has still not borne a child. In desperation and with a play on words, Sarai says to Abram, 'Go now to my maidservant; perhaps I can build/son a family through her.' What both Sarai and Abram have in mind as they consider this proposal is not just any child, but a son.

Sarai's proposal is that as she has not been able to bear Abram a child, she will give her slave, Hagar, to Abram as a wife to bear children on her behalf. From the stories of Leah and Rachel that follow, this act of a wife giving her servant to her husband as a secondary wife in order to bear children seems to have been a common practice, and remains common in polygamous societies today.

The form of Abram's response, however, suggests that Sarai's proposal is inappropriate. Although he agrees without a murmur, the structure of the narrator's presentation of his response tells another story: 'And Abram listened to the voice of Sarai'. The attentive reader will remember that these exact words were spoken by God to Adam in Genesis 3:17, in the context of judgment: 'Because you have listened to the voice of your wife...'. Sarai and Abram, it would seem, have made a mistake. Unfortunately, the first time that Sarai speaks, she is characterized as doing what Eve did, misleading her husband. The narrative perspective, it would seem, is male. She is also clearly indicated as the agent in 'giving' Hagar to Abram, and here too there may be echoes of Eve 'giving' Adam the forbidden fruit (3:6).

Conflict in the family

Hagar, in contrast to Sarai, conceives immediately (v. 4). As often happens in polygamous families, tensions develop. This is understandable in a culture where children are so important and in which there are hierarchies among the wives. Carrying Abram's child changes Hagar's attitude towards her mistress. Sarai responds to this insolence by remonstrating with Abram, as if somehow he is to blame (v. 5). Abram in turn washes his hands of the matter, and instructs Sarai to deal with her slave (v. 6). It is Genesis 3 all over again!

Hagar is pushed from one power structure in the family to the other. Having been initially under Sarai's authority, she is given by Sarai to Abram. When Sarai remonstrates with Abram, demanding that he exercise his authority to safeguard her legal status as the senior wife, he hands Hagar back to Sarai's authority. In the process, Hagar loses her name, first when Sarai speaks of her after she has conceived and then when Abram speaks of her. Sarai uses her position as the senior wife to treat Hagar harshly, and Hagar runs away.

The language used to describe Sarai's harsh treatment of Hagar is the same language used to describe Israel's condition in Egypt when they were slaves (Exodus 1:11–12). Echoing Exodus again, the language used to describe Hagar's response—'she fled'—is identical to the language used to describe how Israel 'fled' from Egypt (Exodus 14:5). Like Israel, Hagar fled to the wilderness.

REFLECTION

With whom do you identify in this story:
Abram, Sarai or Hagar?

GOD SAVES HAGAR & HER SON

Seeing Hagar exposed and vulnerable in the wilderness, God inter-venes on her behalf, just as God had intervened on behalf of Sarai when she was taken into Pharaoh's harem (12:17). The angel of the Lord seeks and finds Hagar, and then addresses her, first by her name and then by her social location (v. 8). The angel of the Lord asks her two questions, but she only replies to the first, for she has no desti-nation. The angel of the Lord then instructs her to return to her family and to her position in that family. Before she can protest, the angel of the Lord adopts the first-person speech of Yahweh and promises to multiply her offspring (v. 10). The angel of Lord contin-ues, but now shifts to third-person reference to Yahweh (v. 11). Hagar is reassured, firstly, that she shall bear a son. Secondly, she is in-structed to name him with a name that reminds her that 'God hears' (Ishmael). Thirdly and relatedly, she is explicitly told that Yahweh has taken notice of her suffering. And fourthly, the angel of the Lord pro-nounces a blessing on her son (although it is a mixed blessing).

The angel of the Lord

In this instance, the angel of the Lord and Yahweh appear to be the same person. In other cases, this designation, 'the angel of the Lord', can simply be translated as 'the messenger of the Lord'. Here and in many other narratives (Genesis 21:15–21; 22:11–12; 31:11–13; Exodus 3:2–6; Judges 6:11–24) there is ambiguity, for the angel of the Lord is both God and an instrument of God. We should not, however, attempt to do away with this ambiguity, for it captures a profound theological paradox. While Yahweh's presence is affirmed in these encounters, there is also the need to assert that human beings are not able to have an unmediated encounter with God. So Hagar is correct —she has seen God—but the narrator is also correct in asserting that the one who appeared to her was an angel of Yahweh.

The promise

Given the sustained attention given to men in the Genesis narratives, it is easy to overlook the significance of the promise to Hagar. God sees her, when no one else does. To both Sarai and Abram she is simply the vehicle to produce a child. And yet God elevates her, bringing her into the divine view and into ours. As David Cotter has so eloquently put it, 'Like Abram she received a promise of progeny. Like Israel she underwent an Exodus towards freedom. Like Moses she saw God. And why? Because God is justice, and she stands for those for whom God has special concern, the foreigner, the orphan, and the widow.' Indeed, Hagar represents each of these social sectors. As an Egyptian in Abram's household, she represents the alien; as someone who is separated from her own immediate family, she represents the orphan; and as the wife who is abandoned by her husband, she represents the widow. If Abram is the father of promise, then Hagar is the mother of promise.

Naming God

Having been named by God in the form of this mysterious being, 'the angel of the Lord', who is both God and not God, Hagar now names the God she has encountered. The name she gives God can perhaps be translated as 'God who sees me' (v. 13), a most appropriate name. Hagar's place of refuge in the wilderness is also named (but we are not told by whom) in memory of this remarkable encounter, and means something like 'The well of the living one who sees me' (v. 14).

Back home

Hagar, it would appear, does as she is commanded by the angel of the Lord and returns to her social location in Abram's family. In the society of her time, there would have been almost no other viable option. She needed the household of Abram in order to survive and to participate in God's promise.

Hagar is not blessed by Abram. Abram's family has not been a blessing to her, as God had intended it should be (12:3), so God intervenes and does the blessing directly. So begins God's unilateral commitment to the poor, the widow, the orphan, the stranger, the vulnerable and the oppressed.

PRAYER

We remember and heed, God of mercy, your words: 'You shall not wrong or oppress a resident alien, for you were aliens in the land of Egypt. You shall not abuse any widow or orphan. If you do abuse them, when they cry out to me, I will surely heed their cry'
(Exodus 22:21–23).

42 GENESIS 17:1–27 (I)

A NEW COVENANT

In an extensive dialogue between God and Abram/Abraham, in which God is by far the dominant party, the covenant between God and Abram/Abraham's family is sealed in human flesh. The flesh of animals had been used as a sign of the covenant in chapter 15; now human flesh is the sign.

Time has passed, Abram is now 13 years older, Ishmael is a young man, and still there is no sign of Sarai bearing a son. God, under a new name, 'God Almighty' (El Shaddai), again appears to Abram and again promises to make a covenant with him. Again the promise of descendants has priority. This encounter is not merely a repetition of the earlier encounter, although there is substantial repetition, which may indicate that this story comes from another source. There are new elements. First, God is renamed (v. 1), as are Abram and Sarai (vv. 5, 15). Second, Abram is commanded to walk before God and to be blameless (v. 1). Third, Abraham is to be the father of kings (vv. 6, 16). Fourth, the covenant with Abraham is now explicitly extended to include his descendants (v. 7). Fifth, Abraham's family will henceforth be marked in their flesh with a sign of covenant (v. 10). Sixth, the promise of a direct descendant becomes definite and Isaac is named (v. 19). Seventh, the ambiguous place of Ishmael in the family is clarified (vv. 18–20). And eighth, a particular line of the family is designated as the particular bearers of God's covenant—Isaac's line (vv. 19, 21).

New names

The meaning of El Shaddai is not at all certain, but probably means something like 'God Almighty'. The meaning is perhaps not that important; what may be more important is the offering of a new name. God seems to be signalling a new dimension in the relationship with Abram. This is confirmed when Abram and later Sarai are given new and longer names, Abraham and Sarah. The precise significance of these name changes is not clear, for the new names are simply variants of the old ones. But the longer versions of their names may be the primary point. God may be saying, in effect, that the lengthening of their names is a sign of the 'lengthening' ('making great') of their descendants.

Being blameless

God's command to Abram to be blameless (v. 1) introduces a moral dimension into the relationship. The covenant is not just about relationship; it is also about the moral character of those who have entered into the relationship. There are also probably echoes of Noah, who was characterized as 'blameless in his generation' (6:9). Here, however, God seems to be requiring that Abram be blameless in a more absolute sense, not only among his generation but as the founder of the covenant for all generations to come.

Father of kings

In the story told of Abram in chapter 14, Abram was located among the kings of his world, although he was not one of them. He lived on the fringes of the politics of his region, only becoming involved when his family was threatened. Now, it seems, God is telling Abraham that some of his descendants will enter the sphere of politics. This promise prepares the way for the rise of the monarchy in Israel.

Perpetual covenant

What was implicit in the earlier covenant in chapter 15 is now made explicit. God's covenant will be established not only with Abraham but also with his offspring (vv. 7–8, 19–21). It will be a perpetual covenant. The covenant includes not only a promise of the land, but also a promise of ongoing relationship with God (v. 8).

The emphasis in this story is worth noting. God 'establishes' the covenant (v. 7) and humans 'keep' the covenant (v. 10). Circumcision is to be the sign of human commitment to keep the covenant that God has established. A related emphasis is the focus on each and every individual bearing the sign of this commitment. Circumcision is not something that is done representatively; each male must bear the sign. The promise given by God in chapter 12 and the divine commitment given by God to the promise in chapter 15 now demand a response from Abraham.

PRAYER

I hereby respond to your call upon my life, gracious God.
I undertake today to walk before you and to be blameless.

A SIGN *of the* NEW COVENANT

There is to be a human side to this covenant, with a clear sign of commitment (vv. 9–10). That sign is to be circumcision. Adapting a ritual already practised in the region, God invests it with new meaning.

Circumcision as a sign

God demands a sign from Abraham of the covenant relationship, and prescribes what this sign will be and who will bear it (vv. 10–14). Circumcision was clearly known to Abraham, and he needs no instruction on how to perform the rite. Most Semitic peoples (with the exception of the Babylonians and Assyrians) practised it. Local custom is being borrowed, but invested with new meaning. The rite is to be about more than the rite of passage from boy to man; it is to be about belonging to God's people. By instituting the ritual on the eighth day, it is removed from its more usual associations with puberty and marriage.

Although the sign resides in male flesh only—for there is no conception here of so-called female circumcision—the women are included in the covenant, and this is made explicit through God's direct reference to Sarah (v. 15). Women belong to the covenant through their various relationships with men. Although women are discriminated against here, it is important to note that all the males, no matter what their status in the household (v. 12), are to receive the sign. Even slaves in the household were included in the covenant.

The fact that God chose a sign that was restricted to males reflects the patriarchal perspective of these stories. How females felt about it is not easy to ascertain, but we may catch glimpses of their perspective from time to time (not in this story, however). The earlier story of Hagar gives us some insight into the female world, although this world too is constrained by patriarchal concerns. Hagar's forthright refusal to be dominated, even by another woman, is an indication that women were active participants in the world from which these stories come. Unfortunately, however, their stories often only make up the sub-plot of what is primarily a male plot.

Isaac and Ishmael

God's vague promise of direct descendants is now given specificity. Sarah will bear Abraham a son, despite Abraham's amused disbelief (vv. 16–18). Indeed, it is Isaac and not Ishmael, God reveals, whose line will be singled out for the continuation of the covenant (vv. 18–21). Quite what this means is not clear, for all of Abraham's household is to be circumcised, including Ishmael. They are all, therefore, members of God's covenant. Will God's covenant with the other lines be terminated? If so, then this is not much of a 'covenant'.

God does hear Abraham's appeal on behalf of Ishmael, but is unrelenting in terms of prioritizing Isaac over Ishmael. God reaffirms the promise made to Hagar, elaborating it and promising Ishmael numerous and prestigious descendants. Whereas Abraham's line through Isaac will produce kings, however, Abraham's line through Ishmael will produce only princes (v. 20).

Abraham obeys

Once again, Abraham obeys (v. 23), exactly as God had commanded him. Rather pointedly, however, Ishmael is mentioned three times as having been circumcised. Is this the narrator's subtle critique of God's marginalization of Ishmael or simply an indication that Abraham does not quite believe that he will beget a son through Sarah? Or is it a mark of Abraham's longing to have Ishmael, his eldest son, recognized by God?

As in most of the Genesis stories, we find more than one point of view here. The story embodies the different voices of the various communities that have composed and then revised it. The genius of the Bible is its capacity to incorporate multiple voices; the task of the attentive reader is to hear them. In this story, the covenant is limited to one lineage, that of Isaac. But at the same time, every male is made a member of the covenant, undermining the emphasis on only one lineage. So too, although females are ignored by the choice of the sign of covenant, Sarah is singled out for particular attention.

REFLECTION

How do you respond to the sign of the covenant being a sign made in male flesh only, and how do you respond to God's preference for Isaac over Ishmael?

HOSPITALITY & PROMISE

In this story, one of the themes of the preceding story is picked up and developed. God has promised Abraham a son by Sarah (17:16), at which he laughed (17:17). God ignored both Abraham's disbelief and his plea that Ishmael might be considered Abraham's heir (17:18). Abraham and/or the narrator seemed to be making a point at the end of chapter 17 by mentioning the circumcision of Ishmael three times. It is against this background that the next story is set.

God's form

As with the angel of the Lord in chapter 16, it is not clear how God is present here. Is God one of the three men—which would make some sense of the fact that there are only two angels in chapter 19—or is God present in all three men? When Abraham addresses them, he addresses them in the singular (v. 3), yet when they reply, they reply in the plural (v. 5b). Is Abraham addressing one of them when he uses the singular, or is he addressing all three as one? Does Abraham know he is dealing with God or is it only the reader who knows? We can see why the early church used this passage to speak of the Trinity!

There is nothing in Abraham's demeanour to indicate that he is aware that he is entertaining Yahweh. Although he addresses the three in the singular, his use of 'lord' (v. 3) is not a reference to Yahweh but a term of respect to another man. The text appears, then, to be operating on two levels, one the perspective of Abraham and the other the perspective of the reader who knows more than Abraham.

Hospitality

Taking respite from the heat of the day, Abraham sees three men. The reader is drawn into Abraham's experience by the Hebrew construction: 'And he lifted up his eyes, and behold/see, three men...' (v. 2). His immediate reaction is one of welcome and hospitality, inviting these strangers in from the heat and offering them food and refreshment. Although the singular form of address is odd, there is nothing odd about Abraham's response. He is doing what he would normally do for any stranger. He is, indeed, acting out what God had called him to do, namely, being a blessing to others (12:3).

Abraham is humble when talking about his hospitality (vv. 4–5), but generous in the actual practice of it (vv. 6–8). As a good host, he attends his guests while they eat, not joining in the meal with them (v. 8). Abraham stands patiently, in contrast to the impatient reader! We know that something is about to happen, so the courteous welcome, the careful preparations and the meal all generate narrative suspense. Conversation is also a part of hospitality, but Abraham politely waits for them to finish eating. They then initiate the conversation and, rather startlingly, one imagines from Abraham's perspective, ask about Sarah (v. 9).

Promise of a son

Having ascertained that Sarah is nearby, one of the three says that he will return and that when he does, Sarah will have a son. This statement is presented in dramatic terms by the speaker: 'I will return to you in the spring, and behold/see, a son to Sarah your wife' (v. 10). As the speaker perhaps intended, Sarah is listening. But before we hear her reaction, the narrator reminds us of Abraham and Sarah's situation, emphasizing that Sarah has already entered menopause (v. 11). This interruption of the narrative by the narrator is an indication that this story had an independent existence before being included in the Abraham cycle of sagas.

Finally we hear Sarah's reaction. She laughs to herself and bluntly dismisses the man's words, recognizing that she is worn out and that her husband is old, and so how can she still have sexual pleasure (v. 12)? It is worth noting that although the talk is all about childbearing, Sarah associates it with sexual pleasure. The sensuality and sexuality of Genesis 2:23–25 remains a part of what it means to be human.

The visitor now reveals 'his' true identity, and so Yahweh speaks (v. 13). Yahweh paraphrases what Sarah has said, politely omitting the reference to sensual pleasure. Sarah had thought she was alone and so had laughed and mocked her own situation. She becomes embarrassed and afraid at having her offstage comments overheard, and so denies them. But her reaction turns out not to be that important, for, as God says, 'Is anything too wonderful for the Lord? At the set time I will return to you, in due season, and Sarah shall have a son' (v. 14). Neither Abraham's nor Sarah's disbelieving laughter can prevent God's promise.

PRAYER

Restore in us, generous Lord, the gift of hospitality that our ancestors in the faith practised with such generosity.

NEGOTIATING *with* GOD

It is not easy to determine whether 18:1 is the end of the story in chapter 17 or the beginning of chapter 18. So, too, here it is difficult to decide whether verse 16 is the conclusion to the visit of God to Abraham's tent or the beginning of the story about Sodom.

Like a good host, Abraham sees his guests on their way, with little sign that he is saying farewell to Yahweh. Somehow the narrative manages to allow the mundane and the divine to exist side by side.

God's dilemma

In verse 17, we are clearly being given narrative access to Yahweh's thoughts. If we read verse 16 as the introduction to the story of Sodom, then it is as if God has second thoughts as 'he' (in the guise of the visitors) leaves Abraham's presence. Having revealed rather than hidden what will happen to Sarah, God now enters into an interior dialogue about whether to hide or reveal what is about to be done to Sodom. Only twice before in Genesis have we been granted access to God's interior monologues, in 6:5–7 and 11:6–7, and both were about judgment.

The first reason God gives for not hiding what is about to happen has to do with Abraham's role in God's plan to bless all others. Abraham needs to understand how God sees things. This becomes clearer when we come to the second reason God gives, which is that God has an intimate relationship with Abraham—he 'knows' him (v. 19 in the Hebrew, rather than the NRSV's 'chosen'). The third reason given is that Abraham will need to teach his children to practise God's ways of righteousness and justice, so Abraham himself needs to be taught the principles by which God works.

God speaks

The mind of God having been made up, Yahweh (identified as such by the narrator) speaks to Abraham (v. 20). What God says is significant, given the interior monologue. At the very centre of God's concern for the world—a world to which Abraham must be a blessing—is the cry for justice. The Hebrew word used here, David Cotter informs us, 'is a technical legal term and designates the cry for help which one who suffers a great injustice screams'. God is attentive to this kind of cry, and so sets off to investigate (v. 21).

Negotiation

The ambiguity of the divine identity continues in verse 22, where it is not clear exactly who goes down to Sodom. It appears that two of the men go down to Sodom, while one of the men—Yahweh—remains with Abraham (although chapter 19 complicates the matter).

In verse 23, Abraham draws near to the divine presence and dares to discuss the situation in the plain below. God has said nothing about what will happen to Sodom (and Gomorrah), but Abraham has discerned that there is just cause for the cry that has come from there, and so anticipates God's judgment. Abraham's intervention is motivated by what God will do if the judicial investigation presently underway proves to be ambiguous. Perhaps Abraham is drawing on the lesson of the rite of circumcision in chapter 17, namely that each individual is required to make a commitment to God's covenant. Abraham seems to be asking whether God is going to judge collectively or individually. 'Will you indeed sweep away the righteous with the wicked?'

In order to understand God's thinking on this matter, Abraham poses, in quite strident language initially, a number of related scenarios, pushing God to weigh the individual against the collective. When God takes his argument seriously, Abraham pushes to see where God's boundaries are, although he does this more cautiously (vv. 27, 30, 31). It is not clear why Abraham stops at ten, but this is perhaps because he recognizes that the basic unit in society is the extended family and that to focus on the individual (in our modern sense) is to abrogate basic human connectedness. The basic building block of society, Abraham seems to imply, is the family and not the individual. So if one family is righteous, then there is potential for the larger society to be redeemed. Perhaps too, in the back of his mind, he is wondering about Lot and his family.

PRAYER

Thank you, our God, for texts like this, which remind us
that you invite us to communicate directly with you
and that we can 'talk back' to you.

HOSPITALITY & SODOM'S SIN

Down below in the plain of Sodom, where Lot has located his household (13:11–13), the two companions of Yahweh continue with their mission and enter Sodom. Their identity shifts: they are now called 'messengers' and are clearly distinguished from Yahweh, who it seems will not enter Sodom. Having been with Abraham in the heat of the day (18:1), the two messengers of Yahweh arrive in Sodom in the evening.

Hospitality

In a scene that mirrors the meeting at Abraham's tent, Lot sits in the gateway of Sodom, much as Abraham sat in the entrance of his tent. Like his uncle Abraham, Lot's immediate response on seeing the two strangers is to offer them hospitality (v. 2). With night drawing near, Lot's offer of hospitality is more than an offer of food and refreshment; it is also an offer of safety. Given that their task is to assess the sin and injustice of Sodom, the messengers refuse, opting to spend the night in the public square. Lot persists, knowing full well that the streets of Sodom are not safe at night. The messengers relent and join him in his home, where he provides them with a generous meal.

The fact that we find Lot seated in the gate of the city indicates that he has prospered, like his uncle, and is now a leader in the city. That he is the only one among the many men who must have gathered at the city gate to offer hospitality foreshadows what is to come.

Domination

No sooner have Lot's guests eaten than 'the men of Sodom' arrive to assert their dominance and power over these visitors (v. 4). What the men of Sodom want to do is to rape the strangers in order to demonstrate their dominance. This was and remains a common practice in many societies, and was particularly evident in the context of war, when the victors raped the vanquished (both male and female), or in contexts of confinement, such as in prison. The man who did the penetrating showed his superior status and power over the man or woman penetrated. The men of Sodom are not at all interested in Lot's daughters—a clear indication that their actions have nothing to do with lust or sex. They want to dominate and humiliate the strangers. This is the injustice that has come before God. God has heard the cries of the vulnerable. This assessment is supported by other biblical texts in which Sodom is characterized by a disdain for the poor, the vulnerable and the marginalized (Isaiah 1:10; 3:9; Ezekiel 16:49). This text says nothing at all about homosexuality. It is about male rape of males.

Preventing rape

Lot, to his credit, intervenes, making himself vulnerable by leaving his house to try to dissuade his 'brothers' (v. 7). With delightful attention to detail, at this point the narrator tells us that Lot 'shut the door after him' (v. 6). The guests are safe for the moment, behind the closed door, but Lot is now exposed among his male compatriots. Foolishly, and misunderstanding the desire of the mob for domination, Lot offers his daughters to them (v. 8). While Lot's offer affirms the sanctity of his hospitality to his guests and is to be commended, his disregard for his daughters is difficult to comprehend.

Provoked rather than persuaded by Lot's intervention, the men of Sodom remind him of his outsider status and then threaten to teach him the lesson they intended to teach the strangers (v. 9). The lesson is that they are in control and that they are dominant. As the mob presses Lot up against his closed door, it is now the turn of the messengers of Yahweh to intervene, saving Lot from the gang rape initially intended for them (v. 10). Again the door is shut, separating Lot from his fellow male Sodomites. Lot has chosen to stand with the vulnerable and this choice has broken his ties with his community.

The messengers then reveal their divine authority and identity, striking the men of Sodom with blindness. The references to both the old and young men of Sodom being involved (v. 4) and to both the small and great being struck with blindness (v. 11) is further evidence of the nature of Sodom's sin. The only way that the different sectors of Sodom's male society can all assert their superiority is to pick on strangers. Among themselves there are clearly defined relationships and lines of authority, regulating to some extent the desire for power and dominance. Judges 19:16–30 tells a similar story, although the outcome there is even more horrific.

PRAYER

Forgive us, particularly us men, merciful God, for our lust for power and our desire to dominate others.

JUDGMENT *on* SODOM

While the men of Sodom blindly grope for the door to Lot's home, the messengers prepare Lot's family for departure. Their investigation is concluded, all of the men of Sodom except Lot having demonstrated their depravity. It is now time to leave them to God's judgment. There is an urgency in the messengers' tone as they ask Lot to identify his family and then go on to explain their mission and its outcome.

Deliverance

Having witnessed the unrighteous behaviour of his fellow citizens, Lot does not argue. He again makes himself vulnerable by leaving the safety of his home (v. 14) in order to urge his sons-in-law to leave the city. Once again he tries to identify with the male Sodomites among whom he has made his home, but once again he is rebuffed. His sons-in-law, like Sarah on the hills overlooking Sodom (18:12), laugh. There it was a divine promise of grace and blessing, here judgment, but in both instances the hearers were unable to receive the message, for it seemed so ridiculous.

The preparations for departure take place that very night, and as the new day dawns Lot is urged by the divine messengers to take his wife and daughters (leaving the disbelieving sons-in-law) and flee the city. Lot hesitates, for things tend to look more hopeful in the light of day than they do in the darkness. He seems to be having second thoughts, so the messengers, agents of a merciful God (v. 16b), grab hold of him and forcefully remove him from the city.

The mention of 'the Lord/Yahweh' in verse 16 causes an identity shift again, for in the next verse there is a shift from the plural 'they' to the singular 'he' in the Hebrew. By verse 21 the transition has been made and we find a first-person singular pronoun. This may indicate that the compositional history of the story includes a number of related stories being combined. The narrative effect is of God's increasing participation in the story as the destruction of Sodom draws nigh.

Pointed by the messenger(s) in the direction of the hill country from which he originally set out when he left Abraham (13:10), Lot begs to be allowed to remain in the plain. Quite what he fears is not clear, although it seems to be the considerable distance that he must travel to reach the hill country. Lot is understandably jumpy, and he may be worrying about how he will be treated on the long road, himself now a stranger. The messenger (singular) permits him to settle in Zoar, a nearby city (v. 21), promising that it will be spared the destruction about to descend on Sodom and its environs. Like his uncle Abraham, Lot has negotiated with the divine and been heard.

Destruction

As day dawns, sulphur and fire rain down on Sodom and Gomorrah (the latter now being associated with Sodom) from heaven. Now Yahweh is directly involved. The destruction is complete. There were not ten righteous people to save the city (18:32). The intended effect of God's judgment and the reason it was disclosed to Abraham are evident in the way Sodom and Gomorrah (though the latter is hardly mentioned in our narrative) have become vivid symbols of divine judgment on an entire society (see Deuteronomy 29:23; Isaiah 1:9; 13:19; Jeremiah 49:18; 50:40; Ezekiel 16:46; Hosea 11:8; Amos 4:11; Zephaniah 2:9; Psalm 11:6; Lamentations 4:6).

The totality of the destruction is emphasized by two final descriptions. The first is the fate of Lot's wife, who strangely 'becomes a pillar of salt' (v. 26). There appears to be no direct divine act here; it is almost as if, in looking back, she has taken on the destruction behind her. Although we may speculate about this enigmatic mention of Lot's wife, the text does not, but moves on to a second description of the complete judgment on Sodom. From the plain, the eye of the reader is directed to see the destruction from above, from Abraham's perspective (v. 27).

In the early hours of the morning, Abraham returns to the place where he stood with God and where he now bears witness to what happens when the cry of injustice comes before God. Fire sealed the covenant between God and Abraham (15:17) and fire now seals God's judgment.

Lot's family had not been a specific part of the negotiation between God and Abraham the day before (18:23–32), but in God's mercy and because of the commitment to Abraham, Lot is spared. From the viewpoint of the narrative, everyone else was wicked (18:25).

PRAYER

God who watched over Lot and his family, watch over all those who have to flee their homes.

SURVIVAL, INCEST & ANCESTORS

The final story about Lot is a strange one. After this, Lot disappears from the stories of Abraham. Whether or not Abraham should have taken Lot with him when he left Haran is left up to the reader to decide (see 12:1). What to make of this story is also left up to the reader, for there is little indication of the narrator's perspective. This reticence on the part of the narrator is itself strange, given the subject matter of the story.

Resettling

Having begged to be allowed to settle in Zoar, Lot is now on the move again. Initially reluctant to travel all the way to the hill country, he now undertakes that journey, fearful of the fate that fell upon the plain. He now wants to get as far away from the site of God's judgment as he can, even if it involves living in a cave (v. 30). The prosperous nephew of Abraham (13:5) has lost everything except his two daughters. He seems also to have lost the will to act, for it is his daughters who take the initiative in order to survive. The assumption implicit in this account is the necessity to secure descendants, preferably male descendants, who will continue the lineage.

Incest

The older daughter's assessment of their situation seems odd. She claims that 'there is no man on the earth/area to come in to us as is the custom of all of the earth/area' (v. 31). This statement can perhaps be understood in two ways. The claim of the older daughter may be that there are literally no other (male) survivors in the area. There may even be an allusion here to the wickedness of all the males of Sodom (19:4), an emphasis of the previous story. All the males have been judged as wicked and destroyed. The only male left is the righteous Lot. This claim seems rather exaggerated, but hyperbole is often a feature of the saga genre.

A second interpretation of the statement involves a recognition on the part of the older daughter that there are no *suitable* males in the area. Either the males that are available will not countenance entering into a relationship with this alien and destitute family, or Lot's older daughter will not consider entering into a relationship with those among whom they find themselves.

However we understand the statement, the result is the same. The two daughters devise a strategy by which they will be impregnated by their father. Their desire, they state, is that they may 'preserve offspring through our father' (v. 32). Without these acts, there will be no more descendants of Lot.

The daughters use wine so that their father will not 'know' who he is having sex with. The implication is that Lot would not willingly impregnate his daughters. They have taken matters into their own hands. Their strategy is successful and they both bear sons. The irony is that although they do preserve their father's lineage, this is the last we hear of Lot.

Point of view

Remarkably, the tale is told in a detached manner. There is almost no indication of a narrative point of view. But we can reconstruct a number of plausible social locations for the story. One possible interpretation is that it was a derogatory story told by Israelites about the origins of the Moabites and the Ammonites (vv. 37–38), their occasional enemies. In this instance, the story has a mocking humorous tone and is told about the Moabites and Ammonites rather than by them. Another possible interpretation is that the story was told with pride by Moabites and Ammonites, as a celebration of the determination and initiative of their ancestral mothers, and there is no sense of shame in it. A third interpretation is that the story provides the reason why Lot disappears from the family tree of Abraham. In this case, the reference to Moabites and Ammonites serves to indicate that Lot's family is now a different lineage, one that has been severed from the lineage that will become Israelite.

REFLECTION

The preservation of this story is a graphic reminder of two features of the book of Genesis. It illustrates how reluctant the compilers of Genesis were to discard any story that had any association with the major characters and main plot of the narrative. Every morsel is collected, cherished and inserted into the larger narrative. It also demonstrates the multiple voices and points of view that reside side-by-side in Genesis.

DECEPTION *in* GERAR

Abraham's story continues after an interlude in which he has been peripheral to the main action. Once again he moves towards the region of the Negeb (see 12:9), and once again he enters into a form of deception that involves Sarah.

We are not given any reasons for Abraham to move from his settled location at the oaks of Mamre. Perhaps, like Lot (19:30), Abraham wants to get as far away from the destroyed site of Sodom as he can. Whatever the reason, Abraham moves south and settles between two places that we have already been introduced to, Kadesh (14:7) and Shur (16:7). He travels far enough from his previous settlement to be considered an alien, which the text emphasizes with a play on words. The verb that the NRSV translates as 'residing… as an alien' is similar to the place name 'Gerar' (v. 1).

Without any discussion between Abraham and Sarah (as there had been in 12:11–13), Abraham declares Sarah to be his sister. This time we are given no reason why Abraham chooses to take this course of action. As on the previous occasion, the separation of Sarah from Abraham leads to Sarah being taken into a harem, this time the harem of King Abimelech. Just as this narrative is more direct than the earlier similar story of deception, so God is more direct, intervening directly by addressing King Abimelech in a dream. The story is narrated from God's and not Abraham's point of view.

Negotiation

Within the dream, God (Elohim) and King Abimelech negotiate. Perhaps this is why the story has been inserted at this point in the narrative: it reveals God's judgment and mercy, just as the story of Sodom did. God begins dramatically by informing Abimelech, in the words of the RSV, 'Behold, you are a dead man…' (v. 3). The reason is clear: he has taken a woman who is married. Echoing the words of Abraham in 18:23, Abimelech presumes God's justice and so asserts his innocence (v. 4). He recounts the conversation he had with both Abraham and Sarah, in which they deliberately misled him. We now learn that Sarah did go along with Abraham's deception. Abimelech proclaims that he has acted with 'integrity' in the innermost part of his being, his 'heart'

(v. 5). The Hebrew word for 'integrity' here is the same word that God used to demand this quality of Abraham in 17:1 ('blameless'). Ironically, it is not Abraham but Abimelech who possesses this characteristic, as God affirms in verse 6. While acknowledging Abimelech's integrity, God makes it clear that Sarah has been protected by divine intervention.

God once again intervenes on the part of a vulnerable woman. God had earlier intervened on behalf of Sarah, Hagar and possibly on behalf Lot's daughters by allowing them to bear children.

It is not enough, strangely, for Abimelech to protest his innocence and integrity: he must also make reparations, including submitting himself to Abraham's intercession (v. 7).

Reparation

Abimelech responds as soon as it is light, informing his attendants, who are justifiably afraid when they discover how close to death they have come (v. 8). Abimelech then has an extended conversation with Abraham, just as he had had an extended conversation with God the night before. Now it is Abimelech who takes on the role of chastiser. He gives Abraham 'a good talking to'.

Abraham's response (vv. 11–13) is cast in a rather negative way by the narrative. First, Abraham's claim that he believed that there 'is no fear of God at all in this place', has proved to be unfounded, given the character of Abimelech and given the character of God. Second, his rationalization about his genealogical relationship with Sarah fails to recognize that, in portraying her as his sister, he has denied his primary relationship with her, namely that she is his wife. Third, Abraham even resorts to blaming God, for it is God who has caused him to wander (v. 13), and so forced him to act in this way!

Abimelech does not even bother to respond to Abraham. Instead, he responds to God's word, by fulfilling and going beyond what God required of him. Remarkably, he addresses Sarah directly, affirming and publically declaring her honour (v. 16).

The threat that hovered over the household of Abimelech is lifted by God. Abraham is blessed by Abimelech, although he has not been a blessing to Abimelech.

PRAYER

Forgive us, merciful God, for taking your grace for granted when we betray those with whom we are in relationship.

SARAH SENDS HAGAR AWAY

The connection with the previous story seems to be the power of God to open and close the female womb. Having restored the fertility of Abimelech's household, God now opens Sarah's womb, as had been promised (18:10). The anomaly between a Sarah who is seen as desirable by King Abimelech (20:2) and a Sarah who is well past her childbearing years (18:12) is not a serious concern for this chain of sagas. These previously independent sagas have been connected in this way for other reasons. Among those reasons is the emphasis on God's power and promise, specifically on God's promise of progeny. The age of Abraham is emphasized in this story (vv. 2, 5), and we already know that Sarah considers herself too old to bear a child (18:12). Without any fanfare, at the appropriate time (v. 2b; see 18:10, 14), Sarah bears a son. Abraham obeys each of God's earlier instructions, naming the boy Isaac (17:19) and circumcising him on the eighth day (17:12).

A new laugh

Delightfully, the narrative moves from description to dialogue. We are allowed to share something of Sarah's joy. Sarah's expression of joy induces a chuckle from the reader of the Hebrew text, for it plays with Isaac's name, which means 'he laughs'. The name reminds her (and us) of her earlier laugh of disbelief (18:12). She now has a new laugh, a laugh of joy and amazement. We, like her, might have wondered what had happened to God's promise of a son, but the delay of three chapters only serves to prolong the dramatic tension.

Separation in the family

Unfortunately, the joy is relatively short-lived. About three years later, after Isaac is weaned and therefore less dependent on his mother, Sarah sees Hagar's son playing with Isaac. The Septuagint, which the NRSV follows, is quite specific here, describing Ishmael (who is unnamed at this point) as 'the son of Hagar the Egyptian, whom she had borne to Abraham' and describing Isaac (who is named) as 'her son' (v. 9). The Hebrew text simply has, 'But Sarah saw the son of Hagar the Egyptian, whom she had borne to Abraham, laughing'. This allusion to Isaac's name in the Hebrew text indicates that there is something in Ishmael's laughter that worries Sarah.

The sight of Ishmael, either on his own or with Isaac, causes Sarah to worry about the future family tensions that may arise within this polygamous marriage. She is the senior wife, but Hagar has the eldest son, so Sarah becomes fearful for her son's inheritance. Once again Sarah goes to Abraham and asks him to send Hagar and her son away. Understandably, Abraham is deeply distressed by this request. He is being asked to abandon his eldest son, the one whom he begged God to recognize (17:18). Sarah may no longer see Ishmael as her son, but this is not the case with Abraham. It takes intervention from God to persuade Abraham to follow Sarah's request. God, it would seem, does not heed Abraham's pain as a father, deflecting attention away from the father–son relationship to God's larger purpose (v. 12) and assuring Abraham that Ishmael will not be abandoned by God (v. 13).

From what we know of Abraham's relationship with Ishmael, the parting must have torn him apart. Abraham is trapped between his wife's and God's desires. He gives in and sends Hagar and their son away with meagre provisions. The narrator empathizes with Abraham's pain, referring to Ishmael not by his name but as 'the child' (v. 14).

God's intervention (again)

As on the previous occasion (16:7), God intervenes in the form of an angel. Hagar has given up on life. Having been cast out by her husband, she now separates herself from her son, unable to watch him die of thirst. But God is attentive to the cries of the destitute and vulnerable, and so responds to 'the voice of the boy' (v. 17). Interestingly, it is not Hagar's weeping that attracts God's attention but the sounds of her dying son.

While God desires to separate Ishmael from Abraham, God does not desire to see Ishmael separated from Hagar. Once again, Hagar receives a divine promise that Ishmael will become a great nation (v. 18; 16:10), and she and Ishmael are provided with the resources they need to survive. The story then fast-forwards, affirming God's ongoing presence with Ishmael (vv. 20–21).

PRAYER

Thank you, God of the vulnerable, for hearing the cry
of the marginalized.

ABRAHAM SETTLES *in* BEER-SHEBA

The story of the expulsion of Hagar in chapter 16 was followed by God establishing a covenant with Abraham, in which God made it quite clear that the covenant would follow Isaac's and not Ishmael's line. After the second and final expulsion of Hagar in chapter 21, Abimelech makes a covenant with Abraham. Having bound himself to God's covenant in chapter 17 through circumcision, Abraham now binds himself to Abimelech through an oath (v. 24). The mention of Phicol, the commander of Abimelech's army (v. 22), perhaps indicates that there was an element of coercion in Abimelech's dealings with Abraham. Whether Abraham enters into a formal relationship of fealty with Abimelech freely or through coercion is not clear. The fact that Abimelech modifies his earlier offer (20:15), requiring formal allegiance, is perhaps an indication of Abraham's growing prosperity and so potential threat. Abimelech, we know (20:3), is acutely aware of the power of Abraham's God, and so seeks to obtain an assurance from Abraham that he will 'not deal falsely' with him (v. 23).

This covenant might be an indication of Abraham's (and God's) commitment to those outside the covenant family. Abraham, as we have come to expect, relates well with the indigenous inhabitants of the land.

Conflict and covenant

Verse 25 shifts the perspective from Abimelech to Abraham. Abimelech is the initiator of the covenant in verses 22–24, and Abraham is the initiator of the covenant in verses 25–30. This second perspective makes it fairly clear that a formal agreement is necessary between Abraham and Abimelech to avoid conflict. Just as the potential for conflict around limited resources led Abraham and Lot to divide their households (13:6–7), so too here the conflict over access to water for their livestock requires a formal agreement. Through the ritual exchange of seven ewe lambs, Abraham secures title to the well that he has dug. The name 'Beer-sheba' captures both the oath (meaning 'well of oath') and the covenant ritual (meaning 'well of seven').

With the covenant concluded, Abimelech and his army commander (who has been hovering ominously in the background) depart for 'the land of the Philistines' (v. 32). This reference, and the later one that 'Abraham resided as an alien many days in the land of the Philistines' (v. 34), is anachronistic. At the time portrayed in these ancestral narratives, the Philistines were not yet settled in Gerar; this only happened much later. There is also some confusion about whether Abraham resides inside or outside the borders of 'the land of the Philistines'. In verse 32, Abimelech leaves Abraham to return to the land of the Philistines, and yet in verse 34 we are told that Abraham resides within the land of the Philistines. The numerous redactions of these narratives probably account for the discrepancy.

Abraham settled (again)

Although he is an alien, Abraham is once again settled. Ironically, he has settled in the same area as Hagar and Ishmael (21:14). Perhaps his move to Beer-sheba was deliberate. Perhaps Abraham moved north from the immediate vicinity of Abimelech (20:1) to be closer to his eldest son.

Like the indigenous inhabitants of the land, Abraham planted a sacred tree (12:6; 13:18), 'and called there on the name of the Lord, the Everlasting God' (v. 33). This name for God, El Olam, was probably a local name for a local deity, whom Abraham associates with Yahweh. Abraham is here appropriating a relevant local designation for his God. Remarkably, these ancestral narratives see no conflict between different names for and understandings of God. Abraham adopts the local practices of worship, integrating them with his own understanding of God. Furthermore, Abraham even learns more about his God from the religion of others. Although Abraham's family has been singled out for a particular relationship with God, this does not exclude others. Indeed, the narratives continually portray the presence of God outside of the family of promise.

PRAYER

Allow us, Everlasting God, to live in harmony with our neighbours, whatever their culture or creed.

The BINDING of ISAAC (I)

In the Jewish tradition, this story is known as 'the *Akedah*', the binding of Isaac, and it is recited daily as part of the morning service. For Christians, too, this story is significant, remembered in its own right and as part of the Easter Vigil. It is also retold in the book of Hebrews (11:17–19). It is a deceptively simple story in terms of its language and its plot. Abraham hears the divine voice, which instructs him to take his son Isaac and offer him as a burnt offering. Without a murmur, Abraham obeys, but is stopped by the angel of the Lord at the last moment, when it is clear that Abraham fears God.

Yet this is an immensely difficult story to interpret, allowing as it does for a number of different appropriations. Generations of ordinary readers of the Bible, scholars, artists and poets have struggled to 'hear' this text. Is it a story about the evil in the heart of God, or a story about God's need to know that we are willing to sacrifice absolutely anything in order to be obedient, or a story about the divine rejection of child sacrifice, or a story about the sacrifice of human desire?

The frame

This story as we now have it in the book of Genesis has at least two frames. The first is the narrative framework of the Abraham sagas. Within this framework, the story locates itself within the larger story of Abraham's longing for a son, the birth of Ishmael, and the 'sacrifice' or expulsion of Ishmael (21:14). Because of tensions within the family, Abraham 'sacrifices' the son whom he loves (17:18), Ishmael. This 'sacrifice' is made on behalf of Sarah and 'her son' (21:9, 10), Isaac. It is also a 'sacrifice' that God has commanded (21:12).

The second frame is the immediate narrative frame of the story (v. 1a). Whether this comment by the narrator, namely that 'God tested Abraham', was initially part of the saga or not is impossible to determine. Without it, the reader is left floundering, and so it may well have been there from the beginning. The notion of God testing Abraham, explicit here for the first time, may also be implicit in several of the earlier stories. Indeed, some have seen this test as the culmination of a series of tests that God has set before Abraham, beginning with the command in 12:1 to leave his father's household, a test that Abraham only partially passes. Even knowing that this is a test, however, does not prevent the reader from wondering what kind of God would set such a test.

The journey

After the narrative introduction informing us that it is a test, the divine voice calls Abraham's name and he answers, immediately. Without any preamble or explanation, God then instructs Abraham to do three things. First, he must take his son (for Isaac is no longer only Sarah's son), the only son he now has left (for Ishmael has been sent away), the son whom he loves (for he has come to love this son in the same way as he loved Ishmael). Second, he must journey to 'the land of Moriah' (v. 2). So far, so good. The idea of a father taking his son on a journey is one we can comprehend. It is the third command that causes consternation: 'offer him there as a burnt offering'. While the reader reels, even though we know it is a test, Abraham does not flinch. Just as he 'rose early in the morning' to 'sacrifice' Ishmael (21:14), so too he now 'rose early in the morning' to obey God once again.

The preparations are described in agonizing detail (v. 3). In contrast, the destination is left vague and we are given no details of the inner turmoil that must have been consuming Abraham. Three long dialogue-free days pass. Perhaps Abraham was unable to speak. When at last he does speak, he is unable to name his son, speaking of him only in the way that God spoke of Ishmael, as 'the boy/lad' (v. 5; see 21:12, 17, 20).

Abraham's instructions to his two servants reveal several important things. First, Abraham makes it clear that he and Isaac will do the final part of the journey on their own. Here the full dread of what Abraham has been commanded to do can be felt. Abraham can do what God has commanded in the sight of God alone; he cannot do it in the sight of other humans. Second, the detached way in which Abraham speaks of Isaac indicates how difficult it is for him to do what God demands. Third, in what Abraham says there is a sign of hope: 'we will worship, and then we will come back to you' (v. 5).

PRAYER

Our Father, do not bring us to the time of testing
(Matthew 6:13; Luke 11:4).

The BINDING *of* ISAAC (II)

After Abraham has given his instructions to his two servants (22:5), he and Isaac take the last few terrible steps of the journey alone.

Isaac speaks

Neither of Abraham's sons has yet spoken. We have heard Ishmael laughing (21:9, in the Hebrew) and crying (21:17, through God's ears). Finally, a son speaks, and when he does, the terrible silence of the journey is ripped apart by the obvious question: 'Where is the lamb for a burnt offering?' (v. 7). Just as God has called Abraham by name (22:1), so too Isaac calls Abraham by the only name he knows for him: 'Father!' The question is made all the more poignant by the immediacy of Abraham's response to his son's voice. Just as Abraham responded immediately to the call of God, in like manner he responds to the voice of his son, naming him for the first time as 'my son' (v. 8).

Abraham's answer to his son's question reveals little. What does he believe at this point? If he believes God, then Isaac is 'the lamb' (22:2), and yet his instructions to his two servants hold out the hope that God will provide another 'lamb'. The framing of Isaac's question and Abraham's response by the repetition of the phrase 'So the two of them walked on together' (vv. 6, 8) forces us to imagine what might be going on within and between them.

The offering

Finally they reach their destination. Once again, the narrative pace is slowed down by the careful description of the preparations. Among the preparations is that Abraham 'bound his son Isaac' (v. 9). Surely things have gone too far, the reader protests! But no, the narrative is relentless and the reader, like Abraham, is not spared. Having earlier 'laid' the wood for the fire on his son Isaac to carry (v. 6), Abraham now 'laid' his son Isaac on the wood (v. 9). The final horrible sentence echoes Hagar's 'casting' of Ishmael under one of the bushes in the wilderness to die (21:15), for the same Hebrew word is used as Abraham now 'cast/reached out his hand and took the knife to kill/slaughter his son' (v. 10).

But just as God intervened to save Hagar and her son, now God intervenes to save Abraham and his son. The angel of Lord 'cried out' (v. 11) to Abraham, by name, twice, making absolutely sure that Abraham heard. The terrible act is countermanded. God is satisfied with Abraham's obedience. The shifting identity of 'the angel of the Lord' of earlier narratives (see 16:10; 21:17)—speaking initially in the third person of God and then in the first person as God—is encountered here. God is both indirectly and directly present. The divine voice is followed, as in the case of Hagar and Ishmael (21:19), by the granting of new sight. Hagar '*saw* a well of water' and Abraham '*saw* a ram, caught in a thicket by its horns' (v. 13). In the case of Abraham, the Hebrew is more dramatic, inviting the relieved reader to share Abraham's sight: 'And Abraham lifted his eyes and he saw, and behold/see, a ram…'.

Abraham sacrifices the ram 'instead' of his son (v. 13). He does this instinctively, receiving no divine order except to desist from sacrificing his son. A burnt offering is made—the first of many within Abraham's family—but it is an animal, not a human, that is slaughtered. Was the ram there from the beginning? (In the case of Hagar, was the well there from the beginning?) If so, what prevented Abraham from seeing it? Does only complete obedience to the divine open up our human sight?

God is satisfied. Abraham has passed the test; he fears God. But what of Abraham and Isaac? How do they cope with the aftermath of these events? The narrative is uninterested in these questions, but they have plagued readers for generations.

Blessing

The narrative does not delve into the minds of Abraham or Isaac (or Sarah, the mother who is left behind), although there is enough in the narrative to draw us imaginatively into the depths of its possibilities. The narrative moves quickly into a conclusion, wrenching the reader from his or her speculations. Abraham is blessed for his obedience (v. 17). After this blessing, however, God and Abraham never again speak to each other. Perhaps this test was more than their relationship could bear.

TASK

Try to find a number of different interpretations of this story, whether from other commentaries or art or poetry. Which of them articulates elements of your own understanding of the narrative?

The DEATH & BURIAL of SARAH

A genealogical note

After the emotionally draining story of the binding of Isaac, there is a short transitional genealogical note (22:20–24). The inclusion of this genealogy here may seem a little clumsy, but it does serve a number of narrative functions. First, although Abraham has left his father's household, he is kept informed about them. The ties of the extended family are strong. Second, in contrast to the struggle that Abraham and Sarah have had in bearing children, Abraham's brother Nahor has fathered twelve sons. This foreshadows the twelve sons of Ishmael (25:13–16) and Jacob/Israel (35:22–26). Third, the genealogy introduces the reader to the family of Rebekah, the future wife of Isaac, preparing the way for the second generation. And fourth, the shift in genre allows readers and hearers to regain their composure after the emotional demands of the previous story.

The death of Sarah

Although interrupted by the genealogical note, the death of Sarah does come immediately after the story of the binding of Isaac, raising the question of a possible connection. Do we have here a subtle indication from the narrator of the damage done by this incident to Sarah? Many Jewish commentators over the ages have seen a connection and have speculated on how Sarah might have responded. The narrative as we have it only hints, however; it does not reveal.

Strangely, Sarah dies in Hebron, while, according to the narrative, Abraham has been in Beer-sheba (21:33). Although we must not rely too much on the shifts in setting, given the complex compositional history of these texts, the Hebrew text supports the geographical separation between Abraham and Sarah by saying that Abraham 'came' to mourn Sarah (23:2). The narrative does not delve into the question of why they were apart. Perhaps Sarah refused to live with Abraham after he took 'her son' (21:10) to sacrifice.

The Hebrew text of 23:1 is clearly in the form of a genealogy: 'And Sarah's life was a hundred years and twenty years and seven years, the years of Sarah.' The use of this form of death notice is significant.

First, Sarah is the only woman in the Bible whose lifespan is recorded, emphasizing her importance among the ancestors. Second, the use of a genealogical formula similar to that found later in the death notices of Abraham (25:7) and Ishmael (25:17) explains, perhaps, why the genealogy about Abraham's brother was inserted at this juncture.

A burial site

The concern of the narrative shifts to the question of proper burial. This is the first time in Abraham's family, according to the narrative, that they have had to bury a prominent member of the family. Traditionally, an important family member would be buried in the family homestead, but Abraham has left that far behind. So he enters into negotiations with the local indigenous population about securing property for a burial site.

The reader is reminded, by this protracted but polite negotiation, how little Abraham actually has. After all this time and despite God's repeated promises, Abraham possesses no land. He is still an alien. As we were reminded in chapter 14, the incident reminds us that Abraham lives in an inhabited land.

The negotiations between Abraham and the indigenous Hittites (23:4–16) is a wonderful example of ancient Near Eastern rhetoric, as they politely circle and then settle the matter in question.

Land at last

So Abraham possesses a piece of the land of Canaan at last. The death of the woman who has journeyed with him from the beginning is the occasion for the acquisition of the first piece of God's promised land. Significantly, the land is formally and legally acquired from its indigenous inhabitants; it is not wrested from them through war or divine agency. The importance of this first piece of land is underscored in 23:17–20, where its location and legal possession are carefully noted.

PRAYER

We remember today, God of our foremothers, those women who have gone before us in the faith. We thank you for their lives and witness.

A WIFE *for* ISAAC

The death of his wife prompts Abraham to consider the needs of the next generation. He has a responsibility to see to it that Isaac obtains a wife. Three things become immediately clear. First, Abraham seeks out the most trustworthy of his servants as a confidant and executor of his requirements (v. 2). Second, Abraham is determined that Isaac must make an endogamous marriage within the clan. This seems a little strange, given that Abraham has been commanded to leave his father's household (12:1), but Abraham is adamant. Third, Isaac himself is to remain in Canaan, for Canaan is the land of promise and Isaac is the vehicle of God's promise (17:21).

The story is told in detail and at a leisurely pace. This appears to have been a much-loved story, remembered for its role in the establishment of the second generation of promise and for its romance.

The oath

Summoning his most trusted servant, Abraham instructs him to find a wife for Isaac, binding the servant with a solemn oath. This form of oath, swearing by the genital organs (v. 9; see also 47:29), appears to have been an ancient custom. Abraham sets the parameters and assures the servant of God's guidance in this matter.

The journey

Like so much of Abraham's life, the securing of Isaac's future involves a journey, although it is one that Abraham himself is too old to take. Instead, we journey with his resourceful servant to the north-east. The servant is well provisioned, including 'all kinds of choice gifts' to form part of a dowry. The journey, though long, is over quickly and the servant arrives at his destination, the place of Nahor, Abraham's brother (v. 10).

The sign

Using his common sense and asking for God's guidance, the resourceful servant attempts to identify a suitable bride for Isaac. The task required of the appropriate woman is a fairly onerous one, drawing water to quench the thirst of ten camels (vv. 12–14). It is worth noting that the servant does not expect God to intervene in a direct way, as the previous sagas might lead us to expect. Like the Joseph story (chs. 37—50), this second longest story in the book of Genesis assumes God's presence and activity, but they are 'behind the scenes'. This may indicate that this short story, like the Joseph novella, comes from a common source of stories about the ancestors in which there is a more restrained theology of God's presence.

Because God is active in the very fabric of life, 'before he had finished speaking, there was Rebekah...' (v. 15). She is of the right lineage, she is beautiful and she is a virgin. There is a moment's suspense as we wonder whether she will meet the last remaining requirement, providing generous service to the stranger and his camels. And she does. The servant, of course, knows less than the reader, for we have been informed about Rebekah by the narrator. The servant must wait and see how she acts and who she is (v. 21).

The negotiation

Having got through the first round of the servant's selection process, Rebekah is now investigated further. The servant probes her family and again tests her hospitality (v. 23). He discovers that she is not only generous and hospitable but that she is also kin to Abraham (v. 24). God, he now knows, has guided him.

Caught up in the excitement and romance of the moment, Rebekah rushes home to her mother's household to share and show what has happened, bearing as she does the gifts of a gold nose-ring and bracelets, given to her by the mysterious stranger (vv. 22, 30). Her brother, Laban, now takes charge, the energy shifting from the female to the male domain (vv. 30—32). Again, Abraham's servant is treated with impeccable hospitality, but, having taken care of his animals, the servant refuses to satisfy his own needs until he has fulfilled his mission (v. 33).

PRAYER

Thank you, our Father, for those who put the needs of others before their own needs, faithfully fulfilling your purposes.

A LOVE STORY

Realizing that the servant will not eat until the purpose of his visit is communicated and concluded, Laban instructs him to 'tell' (24:33). The servant faithfully repeats the words of Abraham to him and recounts in detail what happened at the well and his own thought processes, slowing the pace of the narrative and heightening the dramatic tension (vv. 34–48). The servant misses nothing, not even his conviction that God is at work (v. 48). Laban and his family show no signs of being offended by the servant's presumption, for when the key question is posed (v. 49), finally, it is quickly answered (vv. 50–51). Laban, like the servant, is overawed by God's guidance in this matter, and so the betrothal is confirmed. Once again the servant bows before God (v. 52). To seal the marriage arrangement, gifts are exchanged and food and drink shared (vv. 53–54).

God may not be an overt presence in this narrative, but God is seldom far from the action. The servant, although taking his own initiative, brings God into all his deliberations and acknowledges God in all his behaviour. He remains a remarkable testimony to what it means to walk with God.

True to his task, the servant seeks to leave forthwith the following day (v. 54b), having completed the task assigned to him by Abraham. True to his character, as we will see in his dealings with Jacob, Laban tries to delay the departure of Rebekah (v. 55). The servant insists, however, again invoking God (v. 56) and reminding them that he is on a mission for his master, Abraham.

Somewhat surprisingly, Rebekah is given the final say (v. 57). In societies like this, both then and now, marriage was a formal arrangement between families. But, both then and now, even in such a context, the consent of the woman (and the man) involved was usually sought, for without it the marriage might do more harm than good to the families concerned. Rebekah readily consents, confirming the agreement. We can only imagine what was going through the mind of this young woman as she contemplated leaving her family and heading off with a stranger to start a new life. But as her earlier excitement indicates (24:28), romance has a way of making us do what we would not ordinarily contemplate! She is sent off, both with her nurse as a companion and chaperone and with the blessing of her family (vv. 59–60). Romance carries Rebekah from her home to the home of one who is a relative, but at the same a stranger.

The statement in verse 59 that 'they sent away their sister' and the reference in the blessing (v. 60) to 'our sister' suggests that Rebekah was sent off, as is common in such societies, by the women of the community.

The consummation

The return journey is narrated briefly, until it is time for the bride and groom to meet, at which point the narrative pace slows again as the reader is allowed to savour the moment of meeting and the consummation that follows. This is another indication that the story is about more than a marriage alliance between two parts of a family. The reader is allowed to watch as the young couple see each other for the first time. Romance is in the air!

As in countless romances since, in the evening Isaac 'lifted up his eyes and he saw, and behold/see' the woman destined for him was coming towards him from the distance (v. 63). She in turn sees him, dismounts (or, literally, 'falls' from her camel!), demurely veils herself, and they walk towards each other. His task complete, the reliable servant—perhaps Eliezer of Damascus, who would have inherited had Isaac not been born (15:2)—gives his report and then leaves the lovers to consummate the marriage that has already been legally established. So ends this beautifully told ancient love story. Even the mention of Isaac's loss of his mother is subordinated to his newfound love (v. 67).

We are explicitly told that Isaac 'loved her'; this is the first of only two references to marital love in the Bible (see also 29:18). So it is not inappropriate to interpret this story as a love story. Sexuality, we have seen (2:23–25; 18:12), has its place in marriage; so too, this story tells, do love and romance.

REFLECTION

What are the similarities and differences between this story and modern love stories?

ABRAHAM & ISHMAEL DIE

Following on from the previous long, slow-paced love story are a number of linked, short postscripts.

Keturah's sons

The first, verses 1–6, deals with another wife of Abraham. Although the passage is located here after the death of Sarah, it is unlikely that this indicates a chronological framework. Keturah bears Abraham six sons, and, even if she was a young woman, it is improbable that all of them were born after Sarah's death, considering Abraham's age. The overall narrative purpose in locating this fragment here is to be as comprehensive as possible about Abraham's life. Why Keturah and her sons (and daughters) do not feature more centrally in the narrative is not clear. The most likely explanation is that she and her offspring were not considered significant enough to generate stories. Hagar, although a secondary wife, does play a quite central role in the story of Abraham (and she is mentioned again later in this chapter). Keturah is at least mentioned by name, indicating that she was remembered by some. The use of the plural in verse 6 may indicate that there were also other secondary wives (what the NRSV calls 'concubines'), although the plural may simply refer to Keturah and Hagar.

After the naming of the males, a distinction is made between them and Isaac. Everything substantial that Abraham had was given to Isaac (v. 5), but his other sons were not left totally bereft, for they were given gifts. We are also told that Abraham made a decision to separate these sons from Isaac, although this seems to have been far less stressful than the sending away of Ishmael (21:9–21). Abraham, it appears, realized that the conflicts within a polygamous family often demanded the separation of the sons by different mothers.

Abraham's death

The next fragment deals with Abraham's death (vv. 7–11). After a long and full life, Abraham died 'and was gathered to his people'. This phrase articulates rather well the belief in many societies that those who die after a full and productive life go to be with the other ancestors of the community. Abraham has gone to join the ancestors, and as such will be invoked by those who come after him.

Wonderfully, the two sons closest to him come together to bury him (v. 9). Again, this is common practice in polygamous societies; whatever the tensions in life, death unites the family. Abraham is buried with Sarah in the land he purchased for the purpose.

Abraham does not explicitly bless his son(s). The blessing of the next generation will become an important feature of the stories that follow, but in this cycle of sagas Abraham does not bestow a blessing. Instead, the narrator informs us (v. 11), it is God who blesses Isaac.

Isaac, we already know, has chosen to remain in the area of his mother's tent (24:62, 67), at Beer-lahai-roi. Whether this is another indication of possible estrangement from his father after his aborted sacrifice, we are not told.

Ishmael's death

The third of these fragments (vv. 12–18) collected at the end of the story of Abraham concerns the death of Ishmael. It is almost as if the redactor is tidying things up so that we can concentrate on the stories of Isaac. Ishmael, the death notice states, is first and foremost 'Abraham's son' (v. 12). The priority given to this relationship is profound, indicating as it does the enduring nature of their bond. We know of Abraham's feelings for Ishmael (17:18; 21:11–12). The compiler of this death notice gives Ishmael his rightful place in Abraham's family.

As God promised (17:20), Ishmael became the father of twelve princes, and a revered ancestor, being gathered to his people (v. 17), just like his father.

The second generation

With the passing of Sarah and Abraham, the first generation has completed its purposes. With the passing of Ishmael, the focus can now comfortably shift to Isaac, the second son. The narrative stage is now set for the stories of the next generation.

REFLECTION

When we reflect on our lives, we are perhaps tempted to tell the grand narrative, the narrative that seems to flow and form a coherent picture. But what stories are told by the fragments in or postscripts to our lives?

ISAAC'S SONS

The stories of Isaac begin with the story of the birth of his sons, Esau and Jacob. Like her mother-in-law Sarah, Rebekah has trouble conceiving. During their 20 years of childlessness, Isaac prayed to God 'for his wife, because she was barren' (v. 21). Isaac surely knew the stories of how God had given Sarah a son in her old age and how God had prevented the women of Abimelech's household from conceiving (20:17–18).

Rebekah conceives, but, uniquely in the Bible, she has a difficult pregnancy. Now she is driven to prayer. Her cry in verse 22 mirrors her distress, for the Hebrew sentence is itself almost unintelligible. She receives an oracle in which God interprets the distress in her womb. Her difficult pregnancy is a sign of things to come. She will bear twins, another unusual event in the Bible, and the twins will represent two nations. The oracle goes on to say that there will be a reversal of the natural order of things, for 'the elder shall serve the younger' (v. 23). This notion of reversal is key to many of the Isaac stories. Indeed, in some respects Isaac himself may be said to have usurped the position of his elder brother, Ishmael.

Esau and Jacob

Rebekah endures her troublesome pregnancy and gives birth to twin boys, each of whom is named according to a particular feature of their birth. Esau is named after his ruddy and hairy appearance; Jacob is named after his hold on his brother's heel (vv. 25–26). Although it is common to name children in this way in many societies, the links are not as clear as is implied by the narrative. The Hebrew word translated 'red' by the NRSV is a play on the name Edom, and the Hebrew word translated 'hairy mantle' by the NRSV is a play on Seir, the country of the Edomites (see 36:8). And yet the child is not given either of these names, but is named 'Esau', the derivation of which is not clear. Similarly, although the text associates the name 'Jacob' with the event of the younger son grasping the heel of the elder, the name does not have this association. It is more likely that the name 'Jacob' means 'may God protect', although the story does not appear to know this meaning. What appears to have happened is that there has been an attempt by a later redactor to invest these ancient names with new meanings that would resonate with a later audience who already knew something of the story of these two boys. Esau (Hairy) and Jacob (Heel) have become caricatures in this story.

Two types

The attempt to see Esau and Jacob as types rather than individuals continues in the next section, verses 27–28, in which each is characterized by their preferred occupations. Esau is the hunter and Jacob is the shepherd. The separation and delineation of the differences between Esau and Jacob is extended to their parents, Isaac loving Esau and Rebekah loving Jacob. No reason is given for Rebekah's love for Jacob, which lends it significance, while the reason given for Jacob's love for Esau (v. 28) seems to trivialize his 'love'.

Lentil soup

The potential conflict that we have encountered so far in the Abraham sagas has come about because members of the household (for example, Lot) or community (for example, Abimelech) share the same way of life. Now we are introduced to a new problem (but see 4:2): the conflict between two different modes of production.

Esau the hunter is dependent on what he can find in the field on any given day, so he has times of plenty and of want. Jacob the shepherd, in contrast, has a more settled lifestyle. In verses 29–34, this difference becomes the pivot on which the story turns. Like the two sections to which it is linked, this part of their story takes on representational proportions. Esau is again caricatured, this time given a new name, Edom, because of his reference to the 'red stuff' that Jacob is cooking. Jacob too lives up to the purported meaning of his name, taking hold not of his brother's heel but of his brother's birthright. In melodramatic fashion, Esau, who is 'about to die' (v. 32), exchanges his birthright for a bowl of lentil soup (v. 34).

It is not difficult to see the humour in this collection of anecdotes about Esau and Jacob. There is much here that is the stuff of comedy, and we can imagine howls of laughter around the fires as it was told and retold.

REFLECTION

How does Hebrews 12:16–17 characterize Esau?

ISAAC *in* GERAR

This story begins with an overt reference to the stories about Abraham. The reader will be forgiven for wondering whether this story is not really a retelling of a now-familiar story about Abraham (12:10–20; 20:1–18). But no, the narrator assures us, this is a different famine and a different ancestor. Famine is, after all, a perennial problem in the region, so it is not surprising that Isaac must follow in his father's footsteps to survive. What is surprising is that he uses his father's rather unsuccessful form of deception.

The promise

The reference to famine (v. 1) implies that Isaac will journey to Egypt, as Abraham had done (12:10). When he gets to Gerar, though, his journey is interrupted by an oracle from God. He is instructed not to go to Egypt but to stay where he is, for this is the land that God will give to him. The promises made to Abraham are now passed on personally to Isaac, but God makes it clear that this is by virtue of Abraham's obedience. This is a new theological development in the larger narrative of the ancestors. Isaac inherits the promise because of the merit of his father (vv. 2–5).

Having received the promise, Isaac takes matters into his own hands, like his father before him, seeming not to trust God's promise. This time, however, God does not need to intervene, for neither Abimelech nor any of his people attempt to take Rebekah, as Isaac has feared. Abimelech, it would seem, has learned his lesson. But when he sees Isaac 'fondling' Rebekah, he immediately confronts him (v. 9), angry that Isaac has once again placed him and his people in jeopardy. Although God is not mentioned, the weight of God's presence in the two previous stories is felt here too. Abimelech takes on God's role (20:7), promising death to any of his people who 'touches this man or his wife' (v. 11).

Prosperity and conflict

Isaac's prosperity is not a direct result of the ruse, as it was in the case of Abraham. It is not Abimelech who compensates him, but he himself who works for his wealth. Over the many years that he is in Gerar (v. 8), Isaac engages in agriculture and livestock farming, and God causes him to prosper. Prosperity, as we have noted, brings tensions as competition increases for limited resources, particularly water.

Inevitably, matters come to a head. The wells that his father had dug have been stopped up by the Philistines (v. 15), and Abimelech himself tells Isaac to leave. The geographical details of Isaac's subsequent movements are not clear. Isaac opens old wells and digs new wells, some of which generate conflict with the local inhabitants, and so he keeps moving until he eventually finds uncontested water in a place that he calls Rehoboth, designating that he has now found 'room' (v. 22). The semi-nomadic lifestyle of Abraham and Isaac mean that they are constantly in search of room enough to settle for a period.

It is not until he comes to Beer-sheba, the place where Abimelech and Abraham concluded their covenant (21:32), that God reaffirms the promise (v. 24). Having found space, Isaac's first priority is to build an altar and to worship. He then pitches his tent and establishes his household.

Renewal of covenant

In a repetition of his visit to Abraham (21:25–34), Abimelech and his adviser and his military commander visit Isaac (v. 26). Isaac is clearly now far enough away not to be an imminent threat, but close enough to warrant some form of alliance. After some frank talking, and an acknowledgment from Abimelech that Isaac is now 'the blessed of the Lord' (v. 29), they share hospitality and exchange oaths. The repetition of the phrase 'in peace' (*shalom*, vv. 29, 31) is another reminder that Isaac's family, like his father's, are generally at peace with the peoples of the land in which they are aliens. Furthermore, in this story Abimelech speaks of God not as Elohim, as previously (21:22), but as Yahweh (v. 29). Yahweh is known and acknowledged outside the covenant family.

Fragmentary ends

The very day the covenant is concluded, water is struck—a sign of blessing. The well is given two names, one of them being Beer-sheba, a name purportedly given to this place by Abraham (21:31), but here apparently named by Isaac.

PRAYER

We remember this day, gracious God, those who have no room in this world, no place to call home.

FRATERNAL STRIFE (I)

The genealogical fragment (26:34–35) probably belongs to the narrative that follows it, for it provides, together with 27:46 and 28:6–9, the frame for this story and the next. In 26:34–35 Esau marries into the local population, in 27:46 Rebekah laments the Hittite women in general and perhaps Esau's Hittite wives in particular, and in 28:6–9 Esau marries a Ishmaelite rather than a Canaanite/Hittite wife. Although there is no overt condemnation of Esau's marriage to women from outside his family, we are told that Esau's Hittite wives 'made life bitter for Isaac and Rebekah' (26:35), and so Rebekah is determined that Jacob will not marry 'one of the women of the land' (27:46). In an attempt to please his parents, Esau marries from within the family in 28:6–9. Between these framing fragments are two related stories, both orchestrated by Rebekah.

Contending favourites

True to the little we know of him, in his old age Isaac summons his elder son, the one whom he loved 'because he was fond of game' (25:28), and asks him to prepare his favourite dish as a prelude to the passing on of his blessing. True to the little we know of her so far, Rebekah intervenes on behalf of the son she loves, Jacob. The division in the family is reiterated by the reference to Esau as Isaac's son (27:1) and Jacob as Rebekah's son (27:6).

In what follows, the male characters are rather flat and predictable, while Rebekah emerges as a character with initiative and purpose. Overhearing her husband's conversation with Esau (27:5), she formulates a plan and acts. Jacob is found to be a willing accomplice, although he does worry about the consequences if the plan does not work. Rebekah dismisses his concern and tells him to do as she has instructed.

Again, there is a comical element to Rebekah's preparations. Jacob is worried that his father will 'feel' him (27:12) and so detect, despite his poor eyesight, that he is not Esau. While it is hard to imagine Isaac not being able to tell the difference between his two so very different sons, Rebekah's ruse of using animal skins to simulate Esau's hairiness pushes our credulity too far, and we are forced to smile. Is Isaac truly so senile that this rather crude trick will work?

Isaac and Jacob

The encounter between Isaac and Jacob (as Esau) is delightfully told. Jacob is forced to think on his feet, for Isaac asks a question not anticipated (27:20). Jacob boldly and blasphemously invokes God's name. Isaac appears perplexed and so wants to confirm that this is indeed Esau, resulting in the 'feel' that both Jacob and Rebekah had anticipated. Remarkably, although Isaac realizes that the voice is Jacob's, he concludes that the hands are Esau's! Disorientated, he asks for assurance, so Jacob once again declares that he is Esau (27:19, 24). Apparently satisfied, Isaac eats and drinks. But there is one final test, one that Rebekah has anticipated, for Isaac summons Jacob to kiss him. It is only when he smells Esau's smell in the garments Jacob is wearing that he sighs and begins his blessing.

Isaac's blessing is sevenfold. It is a beautiful poetic blessing, capturing the characteristics of the man whom Isaac imagines he is blessing, and is quite different from the patriarchal blessings we have encountered so far (12:1–3; 13:14–16; 22:17; 26:24), omitting any mention of progeny and the possession of the land in which they sojourn.

Esau and Jacob

As in any good drama, no sooner has Jacob left the stage than Esau enters. Once again Isaac asks, 'Who are you?', omitting the phrase 'my son' (compare 27:18 and 32). Esau answers as Jacob had, although his emphasis is on his position in the family rather than on his name (v. 32). Jacob, it appears, had sufficient shame to use the reverse order (v. 19).

Isaac's response is violent, but there remains an element of comedy, for he asks, 'Who was it then that... I have blessed?' (27:33). Surely he now knows that he has been duped? Esau is understandably distressed and full of bitterness, begging his father to bless him also. Isaac finally sees what has happened and whom it is that he has blessed, but refuses to retract the blessing, adamant that it has already been enacted (27:37). Esau is distraught, for, like the reader, he cannot imagine why Isaac cannot bless him too (27:38). But according to his understanding of the bestowal of blessing, Isaac knows he can do no more. When he does eventually 'bless' Esau, it comes out as a curse (vv. 39–40).

PRAYER

Give us your wisdom, Lord, as we strive to bring up our children and to prepare them for life.

FRATERNAL STRIFE (II)

The way in which the male and female characters are characterized in the previous part of the narrative has led some scholars to speculate that this story may have been told by women. The male characters are rather one-dimensional and none of them really understands what is going on. The underlying comic tone is also suggestive of the kind of story women tell to gently mock their men—men who like to imagine they are in control but who are actually controlled by their women.

Esau hated Jacob

Deception has its consequences, which will govern the shape of the family story for many years to come. In 27:36 we heard Esau's own voice as he lamented the manipulation of his brother. His brother has 'taken away' both his birthright and his blessing. In verse 41 we hear what he says 'in his heart' (as it says in the Hebrew) as he contemplates the killing of his brother.

It is not clear what the relationship is between Esau's 'selling' of his birthright to Jacob for the bowl of lentil soup (25:33) and Isaac's blessing of the firstborn. If Esau has already given up his birthright (under only mild duress), then why is he complaining? He has already exchanged his position as firstborn with Jacob. Jacob's claim to be Esau (27:19) is a lie, but his claim to be the firstborn in the same sentence is not. Or is it? Esau clearly sees the 'taking' of his birthright as separable from his right to his father's blessing as the firstborn (27:36).

Equally puzzling is the apparent inability of Isaac to retract his blessing. All performative utterances—those that accomplish what they claim in their very utterance—such as blessings, require certain conditions to hold for them to have effect. Obviously it is not just anyone who can bless anyone else. Isaac, as the patriarchal figure, has the appropriate position to bestow a blessing, but does it count if the object that he blesses is fraudulent? He appears to think so. He does not consider Jacob to be the appropriate recipient of blessing (27:35), and yet the blessing retains its force.

In the midst of this muddle, Esau can only hate and plot his vengeance. He will not make his move while Isaac is alive, perhaps out of respect for his father or perhaps because he fears how his father will react, even though he is (or was) his father's favourite.

Rebekah intervenes again

Given that Esau's words are spoken 'to himself' (literally, 'in his heart'), it is not apparent how anyone could have conveyed his words to Rebekah. Perhaps the look on his face when he watched Jacob was enough to make it clear what he intended. However Rebekah came to discern his murderous intentions, the fact is that Rebekah does know, once again indicating that she is the key protagonist in these stories. She immediately acts, devising a plan that will send Jacob away to her brother 'for a while' (v. 44, literally, 'a few days'). She does not want to lose both her sons, one through murder and the other through having to flee as a fratricide (v. 45). Rebekah, it turns out, knows her elder son well, for in the end his rage will cool and he will forgive his brother, but she underestimates how long Jacob will be away. It will not be 'a few days' but 20 years, and she will never see him again.

In order to implement her plan to separate her sons, she requires the support of her husband, so once again she manipulates him, complaining about the Hittite women in general (v. 46) and perhaps Esau's wives in particular (see 26:35). In words reminiscent of her difficult pregnancy (25:22), Rebekah laments the possibility of her favourite marrying a Hittite woman. On cue, Isaac summons Jacob and sends him to the house of Rebekah's brother, Laban, where he is to take a wife (28:1). Ironically, Isaac sends Jacob on a journey that he himself was forbidden to take (24:6). Although Jacob has received his father's blessing as the firstborn and now receives a blessing of progeny and land (28:3–4), he is in fact being sent out of the land.

Esau's wives

Having followed his father's dealings with Jacob, Esau tries to comply with what appear to be Isaac's wishes. Perhaps he is trying to win the affection of his mother and father by taking a wife from within the family (28:8–9), Ishmael's daughter. There is no further comment on Esau's initiative. The story now shifts to follow Jacob.

PRAYER

Make us mindful, loving God, of the preciousness and fragility of our family relationships.

JACOB'S DREAM

The Bible almost never recounts the details of journeys, but the story of Jacob is an exception, for on his journey to his uncle Laban, Jacob encounters God. The overt presence of God in this story is a change from the stories that precede it, in which God's presence is more subdued. Some scholars suggest that the more overt presence of God is associated with the theological perspective of the Yahwist, and the use of the name Yahweh for God in this story would tend to support that position.

Jacob, it appears, is alone. All the things that make for life in his world are absent. This is surprising, for when Abraham sent his trusted servant to seek a bride for Isaac, he provisioned him generously (24:10). Perhaps Jacob's situation stems from the urgency with which his mother despatched him (27:43). So, separated from his family, he heads east from Beer-sheba towards Haran, without even a bedding roll for his head (v. 11).

Jacob is, of course, retracing his grandfather's journey, the first of his family to do so. The significance of the journey becomes clear when Jacob encounters God in a dream.

Jacob's ladder

Asleep with his head on a stone—the first of three occasions in which stones appear in Jacob's story—Jacob sees a ladder between earth and heaven, with the angels of God ascending and descending. The reader is drawn into the dream from Jacob's perspective by the use of the Hebrew particle, 'behold/see' (twice in verse 12).

Commentators have speculated on the two-way movement of the angels, wondering what it signifies. The final word in verse 12 in the Hebrew might offer a clue, for although it is normally translated 'on it' (as in the NRSV), it can also be translated 'for him'. The latter translation may indicate that the angels have come to see Jacob, the vehicle of God's future purposes. This understanding is appropriated by John's Gospel, where Jesus tells Nathanael that he will see 'heaven opened and the angels of God ascending and descending upon the Son of Man' (John 1:51).

'And behold/see', God takes up a position 'beside' Jacob, indicating support (v. 13). Jacob is not really alone. And then God speaks. God is identified by the name Yahweh and by being the God of Abraham and Isaac. In this statement we move from the first, through the second, to the third generation of promise. The promises are the same as those we have become familiar with: a promise of land and progeny, a promise that he will be a blessing to others, and that God will be with him. There is also a promise that God will bring Jacob back to the land he is about to leave (v. 15).

Jacob's pillar

When Jacob awakes, he is awestruck. His response indicates a belief, apparently common in the ancient Near East, that God/gods inhabited particular places. Such is the sense of God's presence that Jacob feels he must be in 'the house of God' (v. 17). Having set up and anointed his sleeping-stone as a memorial pillar, Jacob names the place 'Bethel' ('house of God'). This is the same area in which his grandfather Abraham built an altar (12:8), and the reference to Bethel by name in that story is a further indication of the complex compositional history of these stories. Abraham built an altar in the area, and Jacob now sets up a religious memorial column or *massebah*, a common religious practice in the region.

Jacob's promise

Jacob's response to God's promise is unlike any other that we have encountered, for the entire commitment of Jacob is framed by the conditional, 'If... then' (vv. 20–21). If God will be with him, if God will guide him, if God will feed and clothe him, so that he will return to his father's home in peace, then Yahweh will be his God. Jacob's bargain with God does not end there, however, for he goes on to say that if all transpires as God has promised and as Jacob has now reformulated, then Jacob will establish Bethel as a site of worship— and, what is more, he will give God a tenth of all that God gives him. Here certainly is a new generation!

PRAYER

Thank you, God of Jacob, for your presence in the day and the night, particularly for those moments when we are awestruck by your presence. May we remember them, establishing them as memorials for lonelier times.

JACOB, RACHEL & LEAH

After his encounter with God, Jacob continues his journey and eventually arrives in the region that is his destination. His first impression is favourable, for 'behold/see' (twice in verse 2) a substantial well and large flocks. Jacob, as we will come to realize, knows something about shepherding and he is clearly impressed by what he sees here. The well is carefully maintained and protected by a large stone, and there is also a clear system in place to water the flocks (vv. 2–3). The detail in this opening scene suggests prosperity and careful management.

Jacob engages the local shepherds in conversation, establishing that he is indeed in the right place. Providentially, it is precisely at this moment that Rachel, Laban's daughter, arrives (v. 9). There are echoes here of the similar scene so many years before, when Abraham's servant met Rebekah, Jacob's mother, at a well—perhaps this very well (24:15–21).

Jacob among family

In a reversal of what happened with his mother (see 24:19–20), when Rachel arrives, Jacob waters the flock belonging to her and Laban. Verses 9–11 are full of family references. Every person, and even the flock, is linked to 'his mother's brother Laban'. Jacob is overcome with emotion as he finds himself once again among family. The Hebrew text captures this rather nicely. In verse 1 Jacob 'lifted up his feet and went'; in verse 11 he 'lifted up his voice and wept'. His journey has come, for the moment, to an end. Both Rachel and Laban are clearly delighted by his arrival. Family relationships are again emphasized: Jacob is 'her father's kinsman', 'Rebekah's son', and Laban's 'sister's son'. He is indeed 'bone and flesh' of this family (v. 14).

Jacob the worker

Jacob remains with Laban's family for a month before there is a shift in the relationship. Jacob is not simply here to visit, and Laban, like the reader, is well aware of this. Jacob will have to work for what he wants.

In a gracious manner, Laban as head of the household broaches the subject of Jacob's future, saying that he cannot expect Jacob to work for nothing. He thereby gives Jacob the opportunity to propose a betrothal. Before Jacob is able to speak, however, the narrator informs us that Laban has two daughters, both of whom are appealing (v. 17). We sense a complication here, but it is not developed at this point, for we are immediately told that Jacob loves Rachel. Jacob then does speak, proposing to work seven years for Rachel. This is acceptable to Laban and the time quickly passes (v. 20).

At the completion of the contracted time, Jacob initiates the marriage, and Laban appears to comply. He deceives Jacob, however, bringing him his elder daughter, Leah, instead of Jacob's love, Rachel. Laban's desire to see his elder daughter married before the younger is understandable, for it is the custom in many societies to secure the marriage of the eldest daughter first. What is unexpected is the deceitful way in which Laban handles the matter. Ironically, Jacob the deceiver is now deceived.

Jacob the deceived

The irony of Jacob being duped is not lost on the reader. There is even a comic moment in which Jacob discovers that it is Leah and not Rachel with whom he has consummated the marriage: 'And when it was morning, behold/see she was Leah!' (v. 25). Jacob's father Isaac was unable to detect the deceit, failing to recognize which son he was blessing; so too, Jacob is unable to detect the deceit by failing to recognize the woman he 'went in to'.

Understandably upset, Jacob confronts Laban about the deceit. Laban calls on local custom to explain his actions, but immediately goes on to propose a way forward. Jacob must fulfil the required full marriage week with Leah, after which he can marry Rachel. By offering Rachel immediately, Laban prevents Jacob from doing anything rash, retaining his services for another seven years. Laban, it would appear, is a smooth operator. The narrative does not linger over the incident, and within a few short sentences Jacob has married both Leah and Rachel. The mention of Zilpah (v. 24) and Bilhah (v. 29), the maid servants of Leah and Rachel respectively, indicates that the married life of Jacob will become more complicated, as does the statement that he loved Rachel more than Leah.

REFLECTION

Given the marriage stories we have read so far, what do they tell us about marriage in this society?

JACOB'S FOUR WIVES & THEIR SONS

This section is immensely important for much of the remainder of the book of Genesis, particularly the story of Jacob and Joseph in chapters 37—50. From now on, the story focuses on one father, Jacob, but there is the constant presence of four wives/mothers in the background.

Leah

Leah has been only briefly characterized so far as having 'lovely' eyes (29:17). Unfortunately, the Hebrew word here is uncertain in its meaning and some have translated it as 'weak', trying to account, no doubt, for why Leah remained unmarried. Whatever its meaning, God is particularly predisposed towards her—as God was to Sarah in the harems of Egypt or Gerar, or Hagar in the wilderness. God takes the side of the vulnerable, and in this patriarchal world women are particularly vulnerable. God sees Leah's lack of love and so compensates by making her especially fertile. Leah is unloved but fertile, while Rachel is loved but barren (v. 31).

Leah bears a son and names him Reuben, which means 'See, a son'. She knows that God has seen her situation, but she yearns for her husband to see her with love. She hopes that, by bearing him a son, she will persuade him to love her. The situation seems unchanged when her second son, Simeon (meaning something like 'Hearing'), is born. God has heard that she is hated. By the time her third son is born, Levi (meaning something like 'Joining'), she believes that Jacob must change towards her, for she has now borne him three sons. But there is no sign in the narrative that Jacob has come to love her. She goes on to bear a fourth son, Judah (meaning something like 'Giving thanks').

Rachel and Bilhah

The focus now shifts to Rachel. The barren Rachel envies her sister and, as often happens in cases like this, the marriage comes under pressure. Rachel blames Jacob and Jacob blames God (vv. 1–2). Long years of infertility finally force Rachel to opt for a surrogate, and so, like Sarah before her (16:2), Rachel asks Jacob to father children on her behalf through Bilhah her servant. Bilhah becomes Jacob's wife (v. 4) and bears Jacob and Rachel a son. Rachel sees this son as an indication that God has heard her yearning for a child and has granted her justice. She names him Dan (meaning something like 'He has done justice'). Rachel's response to Bilhah's second son, Naphtali (meaning something like 'My struggle'), is a clear indication that Rachel considers herself to be in a childbearing contest with her sister.

Leah and Zilpah

Not to be outdone, Leah too offers her servant, Zilpah, to Jacob to bear children on her behalf. Jacob now has four wives. Zilpah bears two sons, and Leah names them Gad (meaning something like 'Fortune') and Asher (meaning something like 'Happiness').

As so often happens in polygamous families, petty squabbles escalate into major family conflicts. This seems to be what happens in the incident with the mandrakes. Mandrakes were considered to be aphrodisiacs, so both Leah and Rachel covet them. Rachel grants Leah a night with Jacob in exchange for the mandrakes that Reuben has found. It appears that Jacob has given up sex with Leah since she has become less fertile, but that he sleeps with Rachel on a regular basis. Rachel, we can assume, covets the mandrakes because they enhance the sexual intercourse that is still a feature of their love-marriage. She yearns to bear a child, but even while she cannot, she still enjoys sex with Jacob. As they negotiate about the mandrakes (vv. 14–15), harsh words are exchanged between the two women—the only conversation between women in the book of Genesis.

Jacob seems a rather passive figure in all this, but perhaps he is simply trying to keep the peace among his wives by going along with their agreement. As a result of their intercourse that night, Leah conceives and bears another son, Issachar (meaning something like 'There is hire'). Seeing that Leah is still fertile, Jacob must have continued to have at least intermittent sex with her after this, for she bears yet another son, Zebulun (meaning something like 'Prince'). Significantly, in most of Leah's reactions to the birth of her sons, God is acknowledged in some way. In a devastating commentary on the relative importance of sons and daughters, Leah's daughter Dinah is included in the list of offspring, but without any comment on her name.

PRAYER

Help us, gracious God, to see the needs of those around us and to minister to them rather than to exploit them for our own gain.

LABAN & JACOB NEGOTIATE

Rachel

Having dealt with each of the wives of Jacob and their mainly male offspring, the focus finally comes to Rachel, the loved but barren wife. Finally God remembers Rachel and she gives birth to a son, Joseph (meaning something like 'Add'). Perhaps God remembers her plight when she remembers her sister's plight. She gives Leah what she desires; now God gives her her desire.

Jacob prepares to leave

Motivated, it would seem, by the birth of a son to his favourite wife, Jacob is ready to return home. He approaches Laban and asks for permission to leave. Three times (two of which are evident in the NRSV translation) he reminds Laban of his service (v. 26). Laban's response reveals that he is reluctant to let Jacob go, for Jacob has caused him to prosper. What follows is a complex and difficult-to-follow negotiation of a semi-legal nature. While Jacob is kin, he is nevertheless a dependant of Laban, and in order to extricate himself from his legal obligations to Laban he needs to have his wits about him. Here we see two smooth operators squaring off! This scene shares similarities with that in which Abraham negotiates for land in which to bury Sarah (23:3–16).

The negotiation

Jacob's initial claim is that all he wants are his wives and children (v. 26a), but he makes it clear that he expects more, for he reminds Laban of the service he has given him (v. 26b). Laban responds by acknowledging that he does indeed know—through divination, he claims—that God has blessed him on account of Jacob, and that therefore it is reasonable that Jacob should benefit by sharing in Laban's good fortune. Jacob does not come immediately to the point, for it would be impolite to do so. Instead, he confirms what Laban has said, namely that God has blessed Laban on account of him. He then comes to his key concern, his need to provide for his family. Leaving with his wives and children is impossible unless he has means of supporting them (v. 30), and that involves livestock. Laban responds positively, so Jacob continues, offering Laban what he knows Laban wants in return, namely further service (v. 31). In exchange for his additional service, although the period is not specified, Jacob asks for the marked animals in Laban's flocks. By this means, Jacob's flocks will be distinguishable from Laban's. Laban agrees, and the deal is concluded (v. 34).

In order to retain Jacob's services for longer, however (and to keep his daughters and his many grandsons within his homestead), Laban removes the marked males and females from his livestock, reducing the chances of marked offspring being born (v. 35). He separates these animals from the rest of the flock and gives them to his sons to shepherd, sending them to pastures three days' journey away.

Jacob's strategy

Having been tricked (again), Jacob responds with a strategy of his own. Jacob's strategy is a combination of sympathetic magic and careful flock management. The peeled, stripped rods that he wants his flock to mimic in their offspring are set up in the area where the flocks most frequently copulate (vv. 37–39). He then carefully manages the operation, separating the marked livestock from the unmarked, thereby increasing his chances of producing marked livestock (v. 40), and selecting wherever possible the more vigorous of the livestock, ensuring that his flock retains good breeding stock (vv. 41–42). The unmarked and feebler stock are given to Laban. Combining magic and natural selection, Jacob establishes large flocks, and enough surplus wealth to enable him to purchase slaves, donkeys and camels. He is now fully equipped for his return journey.

The role of God

God is invoked by both Laban (v. 27) and Jacob (v. 30), but is otherwise in the background of this story. In the next set of linked stories, we find a much more theological interpretation of Jacob's wealth.

PRAYER

God of all, thank you for the abilities you have given us, and thank you for the work in which we can express those abilities. We ask that all may find fulfilling work.

JACOB LEAVES LABAN (I)

Jacob's increasing wealth is met with resentment by Laban's sons. They are correct in saying that Jacob 'has gained all his wealth from what belonged to our father' (v. 1). What they will not acknowledge is the hard work and ingenuity of Jacob. As long as Jacob remained with them, his wealth did not matter, but the prospect of his leaving generates resentment. Laban too, we are told, is affected (v. 2). Into this context of family tension God speaks, commanding Jacob to return to the land of his ancestors and his kin. God promises to go with him.

Jacob persuades Leah and Rachel

Jacob must now persuade his primary wives, Leah and Rachel, to leave their father's household. This is more than an emotional issue; it is also a legal issue. He begins by stating what everyone probably knows, that there is tension between his father-in-law and himself (v. 5). The God of his father has enabled him to endure, he says, and he has served their father with all his strength, despite the fact that their father has repeatedly tried to cheat him. It is God, he asserts, who has brought him prosperity, giving him the flocks that he and Laban agreed would be his. Jacob does not want his wives to blame him for the growing estrangement. Jacob then explains in more detail, attributing the growth of his marked flock to God's intervention (v. 9). God has brought Jacob justice (v. 12). He tells them that God has reminded him of their encounter at Bethel and commanded him to leave Laban's land and return to his own land (v. 13).

Rachel and Leah respond by sharing their perspective, which is equally bleak. They feel that they have been 'sold' by their father. Instead of retaining their bride-price and passing it on to them, as it is implied he should have done, he has squandered it (v. 15). They are regarded, emotionally and legally, as foreigners. They therefore see no future in remaining in their father's household. They confirm that they too recognize God's hand in matters and affirm that the wealth that they now have is rightfully theirs and their children's. Speaking with one voice, the two wives are united in this, and so they give their support to Jacob (v. 16).

Jacob prepares to leave

Having secured the support of his wives, Jacob then secures his live-stock by driving them off Laban's land (v. 18). In a rather awkward series of sentences, an indication perhaps that a number of previously independent stories have been combined, we learn that Laban is away when Jacob prepares to leave, and that Rachel has stolen her father's household gods (v. 19). Now it becomes apparent that Jacob is not simply leaving; he is fleeing (v. 21).

The household gods that Rachel takes will have been her father's teraphim, small images of the deities who were the protectors of Laban's household. We are not told why she took them. She may have wanted to make her father's household vulnerable by depriving it of divine protection. If this is the case, then Rachel's resentment of the way in which her father has treated her must have run deep. She may, however, have simply wanted to take these familiar deities with her on the long journey to a strange land with strange gods. Indeed, it may well have been her husband's mention of 'the God of Bethel' that prompted Rachel to take with her the gods of her home. She knows the gods of her home, but she does not know this God of Bethel who encountered her husband with such power (28:12–16). She inhabits a world in which deities are attached to particular places and in which the concept of a God who transcends localities is only just beginning to emerge.

Jacob has chosen an appropriate time to go, for the shearing season was usually a busy one, consuming the attention and energy of those involved. With his face set for home, Jacob leaves.

PRAYER

Forgive us, God who transcends all names and places, for our limited understanding and our attempts to hold on to particular representations of you. Fill us with a deeper knowledge of yourself.

JACOB LEAVES LABAN (II)

Jacob has chosen his timing well, for it is only three days later that Laban learns of Jacob's departure and sets off after him—but not before God intervenes on behalf of Jacob (v. 24). The geographical details are unclear, but after seven days Laban overtakes the fleeing family somewhere in the hill country. Laban upbraids Jacob, using language that emphasizes the underhanded way in which he feels Jacob has dealt with him (vv. 26–28). He has been deprived of bidding farewell to his family in the fitting manner. In the midst of this reasonable response, there hovers a threat of harm (v. 29), but Laban quickly assures Jacob that any harm he had intended him has been preempted by God. Laban's catalogue of complaints against Jacob is not finished, however, for although he gives Jacob the benefit of the doubt over his hasty departure, he accuses Jacob of taking his household gods.

Jacob tells the truth, namely that he was afraid that Laban would not let his daughters depart (v. 31). He then quickly adds that if Laban can find his gods, or indeed anything that belongs to Laban, he can take them. Moreover, he condemns to death whoever may have taken Laban's household gods, being completely unaware that his beloved wife Rachel is the culprit (v. 32).

Repressed anger

Rachel has hidden the teraphim beneath her, and rather cheekily begs her father's pardon for not rising, claiming that she is menstruating (v. 35). Even if Laban suspects that Rachel is hiding them, he will have considered them polluted by contact with a menstruating woman. So Laban does not push the matter and does not find them. Jacob, of course, assumes that this was just another trick of Laban's and rounds on him angrily. What follows is 20 years' worth of repressed anger (vv. 36–42). He begins with a set of angry questions, but quickly moves on to a series of statements that describe in detail his service over the past 20 years. The image he presents is of someone who has done more than was required of him. Prudently, he does not publically accuse Laban of mistreating or cheating him (as he had done in 31:7 to his wives), although right at the end he does mention that Laban changed his wages ten times. It is God, he finally claims, who has caused him to prosper.

Making peace

In acknowledging God's role in his prosperity, Jacob refers to God in a number of different ways: God of my father, God of Abraham, and the Fear of Isaac (v. 42). The last of these is unusual but probably signifies the deity feared and worshipped by Isaac. Here we see how God was referred to by multiple names, each name designating a different aspect of God's apprehension by particular people.

After hearing this tirade, Laban tries a different tack, and while he claims that everything Jacob has is his, he acknowledges that there is not much he can do about his daughters' decision to leave with Jacob (v. 43). He pointedly does not mention the flocks, wondering perhaps how he might appropriate them. But in the end Laban does nothing about the flocks either. Recognizing that he must make the best of the situation, he enters into a covenant with Jacob (v. 44).

Once again, as he had done at Bethel (28:18), Jacob erects a stone pillar and together with his kinsfolk—for they are now his kin—he assembles a cairn (v. 46). The text is unclear here, probably because of the attempts of a number of different editors to name the site. It is also not clear who set up and/or named the pillar/cairn. The purpose of the covenant is clear, however: it asks God (in the rather lovely language of the NRSV) to 'watch between you and me, when we are absent one from the other' and it stands as a witness to the proper treatment of Laban's daughters. The memorials also serve to keep the two families apart if the reason for passing them is to cause harm (v. 52). These are worthy commitments and a good end to the relationship between Jacob and Laban.

All that remains is for the two families to feast together and then to take their leave. Laban finally gets to do what he said he wanted to do (v. 28), which is to kiss his daughters and grandchildren and to bless them. He leaves to return home, but Jacob still has some way to go before he is home.

PRAYER

Help us, loving God, to build memorials in our lives which will remind us to care for those who are under our protection.

JACOB PREPARES *to* MEET ESAU

No sooner is Jacob on his own than 'the angels of God met him' (v. 1). No words are exchanged; it seems as if the angels are content merely to see him, as was the case in Bethel (28:12). This very brief fragment is probably included here to signal Jacob's new beginning. The angels came to see Jacob as he set out on his journey and now they come to meet him on his way home. Quite what the name Mahanaim means is not clear, although it appears to have something to do with the notion of 'God's camp' and may mean 'Two camps' or simply 'Camp'.

Preparing to meet

Twenty years have not dulled Jacob's memory of the hatred he saw in Esau's eyes and of Esau's threat to kill him (27:41), so he sends messengers ahead of him (v. 3). We learn from the narrator that Esau is in the land of Seir (meaning 'Hairy'), the country of Edom (meaning 'Red'). The narrator seems to be indicating that Esau has established himself so well in the intervening years that the very place in which he lives is named after him (see 25:25). He is at home in the world.

The instructions that Jacob gives to his messengers are carefully formulated (vv. 4–5). First, Esau is to be addressed as 'my lord'. Second, Jacob is to be designated as his 'servant'. The relationship between them, Jacob claims, is a reversal of the blessings that both he and Esau received from their father (27:29, 40). Indeed, it is a reversal of what God told Rebekah about the babies in her womb (25:23). In a way, Jacob is trying to restore the blessing to what it ought to have been, had the deception not taken place. Third, it must be made clear that Jacob has been an alien all these years, even though he has been staying with family. Jacob wants Esau to know that life has not been easy. Fourth, Jacob has acquired possessions. Here, Jacob is indicating that he has the means to make compensation. Fifth and finally, Jacob wants it emphasized that he yearns to 'find favour' in Esau's eyes, not hatred.

Dramatic tension builds, for when the messengers return it is with a partial and unsatisfactory reply. Esau is coming to meet Jacob, but what his demeanour is, we are not told. We are also not told what, if anything, Esau said in response to Jacob's careful message. The fact that Esau has four hundred men with him sounds ominous, so Jacob's reaction is understandable: 'Jacob was greatly afraid and distressed' (v. 7). He immediately makes defensive plans, hoping to save his household from total destruction.

Jacob's prayer

Having done what he humanly can, Jacob turns to God in prayer (vv. 9–12). Jacob begins by acknowledging God as the God of his fathers. He then calls God by name, Yahweh, reminding God of the divine call to return to his land and kin, and reminding God of the promise to be with him (31:3). For the first time in his life, Jacob asks for help from God. For the first time, Jacob calls himself a servant of God. Jacob has indeed come a long way! Having served Laban for 20 years, he is now willing to serve Esau and God.

There is no immediate answer from God, so Jacob does what he can. He prepares a lavish gift of livestock and strategically positions the animals in such a way that Esau will encounter wave after wave of gifts (v. 16). When Esau does finally get to him, Jacob hopes that he will be predisposed to receive him. The Hebrew text of verse 20 is more vivid, and can be literally translated as follows: 'For he said to himself: "Let me cover up his face with the gift before my face; afterwards I shall see his face; perhaps he will lift up my face." The gift passed on before his face.' The many repetitions of 'face' make it abundantly clear how Jacob both yearns and fears to see Esau face to face.

Jacob gives the livestock a whole day's head start (v. 21). While he waits for his gift to make its way towards Esau, he puts the final part of his plan into action. During the night, he takes his most precious possessions, his wives and children (although it appears that only the male children are counted), and moves them across the Jabbok river. Now everything he has is between him and Esau. He remains on the other side of the river—which will become the boundary of his descendants' land (Numbers 21:24; Deuteronomy 2:37; 3:16; Joshua 12:2; Judges 11:13, 22). He is where he began, alone.

PRAYER

Help us, loving God, to repair our damaged relationships.

JACOB MEETS GOD

Having prepared as thoroughly as he can to meet Esau face to face, Jacob first meets God face to face. The encounter is a mysterious one, in which God is both intimate and remote. God is intimate in that there is a bodily encounter; God is remote in that God never declares a particular identity. It is left to Jacob to declare that he has 'seen God face to face' (v. 30).

The man

Without any preamble other than that Jacob was left alone, the main protagonist of this story is introduced, not by his identity but by his act: 'a man wrestled with Jacob' (v. 24). The narrator seems to conflate his/her perspective with that of Jacob's. The narrator does not know anything that Jacob does not know, and as far as Jacob is concerned, he is being wrestled by a man.

The only other thing we are told about this strange encounter is its duration. It lasts until the morning. Whether Jacob is asleep or awake is not clear. The one who initiated the struggle does not prevail; he is unable to subdue Jacob. What does this mean? Is it some kind of psychological comment on Jacob's inner self or is it a comment on his physical prowess, or both? Is Jacob wrestling with himself or another? The story captures our imagination, provoking all kinds of possibilities.

Finally, unable to subdue Jacob, the man strikes or touches (depending on the translation) Jacob's hip, dislocating it (v. 25). If we translate the verb as 'struck' (with the NRSV), then it is through a violent act that Jacob's hip is pulled out of joint; if we translate the verb as 'touched', then the act retains a mystical spiritual quality.

The story becomes even more strange when the man commands Jacob to release him, for apparently the dislocation of his hip has not caused Jacob to relax his grip on his assailant. But it is not the command to release him that is strange; it is the reason: 'for the day is breaking' (v. 26). It would seem as if the person wrestling Jacob is some kind of spirit or being who has form during the night but must disappear before dawn breaks. Most cultures have beliefs like this. It is remarkable that this story has remained unedited: there is no attempt to modify it or to defend God from this kind of characterization.

The name

When Jacob hears the reason for the command to release the man, he correctly assumes that this is no ordinary being. Grasping the opportunity, he refuses to let him go unless this being blesses him. The man responds, asking Jacob for his name, as if he does not know who he is. Again, stories in which one is warned not to reveal one's name, especially to dark forces at night, abound in most cultures. Perhaps that is behind the request for Jacob's name. But Jacob, who was afraid of Esau by day (32:11), is unafraid to reveal his name to this mysterious supernatural being by night. The man blesses Jacob by giving him a new name (v. 28). Something has happened to Jacob, of which this encounter is the culminating moment. He is now one who 'has struggled with divine and human beings' and who 'has prevailed/ overcome/has been able' (v. 28). The name given to represent his new status is Israel, which means something like 'The one who strives with God' or 'God strives'.

Jacob still refuses to release his grip, demanding to know his assailant's name. But the being deflects his request with a question— 'Why do you ask my name?'—implying perhaps that Jacob/Israel should know by now with whom he has been wrestling. Before Jacob can respond, the man blesses him. It is at this point, apparently, that Jacob releases the enigmatic figure of the night. In memorial of his encounter, Jacob (still so named) names the place 'Peniel' ('the face of God'), as the full import of what has happened during the night strikes him: 'For I have seen God face to face, and yet my life is preserved' (v. 30). Dawn finds Jacob limping past 'Penuel', a variant of 'Peniel', bearing in his body the mark of his encounter with God.

Dietary comment

The awesomeness of this encounter is somewhat spoiled by an insertion by an editor who sees some link between a dietary taboo and this incident (v. 32). Although clumsy, this editor's comment reminds us again that these texts were constantly reinterpreted by successive generations, all of whom venerated Jacob as one of their great ancestors.

PRAYER

May we, like Jacob, encounter you, our God,
when we least expect it.

JACOB MEETS ESAU

Limping into the dawn, Jacob 'lifted up his eyes and saw, and behold/see, Esau was coming, and with him four hundred men' (v. 1). This is an ominous sight indeed, and Jacob quickly springs to action, deploying his immediate family into three groups, in order of his preference. This preferential ordering of his family will shape almost everything that happens in the family for ever. Here we note it; later we will need to examine it in more detail and study its effects.

Placing his secondary wives, Zilpah and Bilhah, and their children at the front, Leah and her children behind them, and then Rachel, his favourite, and her son at the rear, Jacob (for so he is still named) moves ahead of them all to confront Esau. Having met with God, he is now ready to face his brother. But there is no fight in Jacob, only submission. He bows seven times before Esau, as contemporary court ritual prescribed for a supplicant coming before his lord (v. 3). Esau's party is indeed an impressive one, four hundred strong. When we remember that Abraham was able to muster only 318 men when he went to rescue Lot (14:14), we realize how well Esau has done. He has made a place for himself in the world, despite the lack of his father's blessing.

The meeting

The emotional and narrative tension is broken as Esau breaks away from his retainers and runs to meet Jacob, clutching him in an emotional embrace (v. 4). Esau immediately takes control, asking about the women and children. Still in shock, Jacob responds formally, acknowledging God's role in his family and referring to himself as Esau's servant (v. 5). Taking their cue from Jacob, each set of Jacob's family bows to Esau. Trying to overcome the awkwardness of the meeting, Esau asks Jacob what he intended by the droves of livestock he has encountered (v. 8). Jacob is honest, and admits that he sought to find favour in his lord's eyes. Esau responds, calling Jacob his brother, and saying that this gift is not necessary, that he has plenty and that Jacob must keep what he has for himself. Jacob insists, and for the first time some warmth of emotion begins to break through his formal demeanour (vv. 10–11). He is clearly overcome by Esau's gracious reception, likening it to seeing the face of God. The comparison with his night of wrestling shows just how emotionally draining Jacob found this meeting with his brother. His fear has turned to relief and to genuine joy. The gifts he sent to placate his brother are now genuine gifts of gratitude, to God and to Esau for his warm welcome.

Settling down

Esau continues to keep the conversation going, suggesting that they travel together (v. 12). Still unable to relax fully, addressing Esau as his lord, Jacob dissuades him, claiming that he will need to travel very slowly so as to allow his livestock opportunity to graze and so as not to overtax his children (v. 13). In other words, he does not want to delay Esau. Or perhaps he is not yet ready for sustained interaction with his brother.

Esau offers to leave some of his men with Jacob, which Jacob appears to refuse, again referring to Esau as his lord (v. 15). Esau's 'kindness' after Jacob's deception is more than Jacob can bear. They agree to meet in Seir, but Jacob moves in the opposite direction. Jacob breaks his journey at Succoth, named after the temporary booths that Jacob built there, and then finally settles at Shechem, where he purchases land and builds an altar named after his 'God, the God of Israel' (v. 20).

Reconciliation?

Jacob and Esau meet, but their meeting is not really substantial enough to speak of reconciliation. Of the two, Esau appears to make the more effort to restore the relationship. Jacob's fear of Esau, which must have grown to epic proportions in the 20 years they were apart, proves too potent for Esau to overcome easily. He chooses instead to avoid his brother. They will not meet again until their father's burial.

PRAYER

Most merciful God, thank you for the opportunities you give us to reconcile with those we have wronged. Enable us to be gracious to those who seek to be reconciled to us.

RAPE, LOVE, DECEIT & DEATH

Dinah, the forgotten daughter of Jacob (32:22), but one of the few remembered and named daughters in the whole of Genesis, is the subject of this story. In each of the generations so far, those of Abraham and Isaac, God has intervened on behalf of vulnerable women. God does not intervene in this story to save Dinah from rape, but her brothers do wreak a terrible vengeance on her behalf.

We know very little about Dinah, other than that she was Leah's daughter. While we are told the meaning of each of her brothers' names (29:31—30:24), the meaning of her name is not mentioned. And when we encounter her in this story, we learn little more about her. Her ordeal begins as most rapes do—rather innocuously. She 'went out to see the daughters of the land' (literally) in the area where her father had settled (v. 1). A woman visiting other women, particular women similar to her, is a normal occurrence and does not require a chaperone. She should have been safe. Nevertheless, this has not prevented male commentators from constructing a reason why she was at fault, why she was 'asking for it'. They point to the similar language used when her mother, Leah, 'went out' to Jacob in the field to ask him to sleep with her (30:16). The same phrase is used here as Dinah 'went out' to visit the women of the region. What these male commentators miss, of course, is that Leah was doing nothing inappropriate; and neither was Dinah.

Rape of Dinah

Rape is a male problem, and this is clearly the case in this story. Unable to control himself—or unwilling to control himself, for he was a prince who was used to getting what he wanted—Shechem 'saw her... seized/took her and lay with her and debased her' (v. 2, in the Hebrew). There is little ambiguity here: this is rape. Some scholars have suggested, however, that the final verb in the sequence could be translated as 'humiliated', indicating that there may have been some other aspect of the relationship between Dinah and Shechem that offended her brothers.

What is strange is that Shechem does not immediately cast her out after he has raped her (see 2 Samuel 13:15–18). Because rape is an act of violence, those who perpetrate it do not usually react as Shechem does. Shechem's response is therefore unexpected. Instead of reviling her, 'his very self clung to Dinah, daughter of Jacob, and he loved the young woman and spoke to the heart of the young woman' (v. 3). Shechem is clearly a damaged person, someone who can shift from violent assault to tenderness within moments. The thought of being married to him must have further traumatized Dinah, but she has no voice in this transaction. Shechem demands that his father 'take/seize' this woman to be his wife, and the verb used here is the same verb as was used to describe his brutal assault on Dinah.

Her brothers' response

The story now shifts from Dinah's ordeal to Jacob's response. Jacob is the first to hear of it, but we do not know how he reacts. We have to wait until his sons return from the field to find a reaction, and even then it is the sons who react, not Jacob. In fact, Jacob says nothing at all about the rape of his daughter, although he must have communicated the incident to his sons, for they were unlikely to have heard this version from Hamor, Shechem's father. Confronted with two stories, one related to them by their father and the other by Hamor, the sons are outraged by this totally unacceptable crime.

Seeing their reaction, Hamor begins to negotiate with them, first appealing to them by saying that his son's 'heart is set' (literally) on Dinah (v. 8). To this initial appeal he adds a wider incentive, that of marriage between their clans. Third, he offers them a place in his land, subtly threatening them to comply or else lose access to the land, opportunity to trade and the possibility of acquiring property. Finally, Shechem himself intervenes, and indicates that he will provide whatever dowry they demand (v. 12). During all this male negotiation, we do not know where Dinah is, but presumably she is still in Hamor's city, waiting to discover her fate.

Hamor and Shechem are in a position of power. But Jacob's sons put forward a difficult demand that appears to indicate a willingness to agree to the marriage, while safeguarding their commitment to marriage within the family. Hamor and his family must become their family through the ritual of circumcision; then the marriage can take place (v. 15).

PRAYER

Help us men, God of Dinah, to control our desire
for power over women.

REVENGE *on* SHECHEM

The solution that Jacob's sons appear to offer King Hamor and Prince Shechem is a fascinating one. They seem to be offering them a way of becoming 'family'. All that is required, it would seem, is circumcision. Yet the narrator has warned us that the sons of Jacob are being deceitful (34:13), so we should not take their offer at face value. And anyway, it seems strange that King Hamor and his city could so easily shed the 'disgrace' (v. 14) associated with a marriage alliance with Jacob's family. After all, circumcision on its own is simply the removal of a small piece of male flesh.

Having heard what sounds like a very strange demand, we as readers are perhaps a little surprised to find that the words of Jacob's sons 'pleased' Hamor and Shechem (v. 18). Remarkably, they agree and persuade the males in their city to comply. Their power must have been immense! It is one matter to circumcise oneself for 'love'; it is quite another to get a city full of other men to follow suit. The long description of Hamor and Shechem's discussion with the leaders of the city at the gate, the traditional site for such political discussion, is perhaps an indication that it took some persuasion.

The deceitful, revengeful plan

In fact, there never was any intention on the part of Jacob's sons to enter into any alliance with the man who had raped their sister. Their plan now becomes apparent. The circumcision solution is simply a ruse, albeit a very clever one. Circumcision will debilitate the males of the city, leaving them vulnerable to attack. What is more, this way of 'emasculating' them carries with it a poetically appropriate form of retribution for the crime of rape.

Knowing all about the circumcision process, two of Jacob's sons, Levi and Simeon, both sons of Leah and therefore directly related to Dinah, wait until the males of Hamor's city are at their most incapacitated, then they sneak into the city and kill them all. They also take Dinah—she is 'taken' for the third time—from the city (v. 26). With Dinah safely out of the city and the males dead, the other sons then enter the city to plunder it. As Shechem had 'taken/seized' their sister, they now 'take/seize' everything, including the wives and children of the slain (vv. 27–29). Vengeance and violence on a scale that Lamech would have been proud of (4:23–24) is visited on the city and all its inhabitants.

Jacob speaks

At last Jacob speaks (v. 30), and when he does, it is to rebuke Simeon and Levi for what they have done in alienating his family from the local inhabitants of the land. Jacob is understandably fearful of their vulnerability, but he must take some of the blame, for he said and did nothing in response to the rape of his daughter, thereby allowing violence to fester in the hearts and imaginations of his sons. God too says and does nothing. Simeon and Levi are unrepentant, believing that they have restored their sister's honour and rescued her from ongoing abuse. In their minds, marriage was never an option.

Jacob's reaction does indicate how precarious life for his family was in a land in which they were always strangers and sojourners. Some kind of alliance with the local peoples was necessary for survival, and this was the argument put forward by King Hamor. But by raping Dinah, Prince Shechem ruptured any chance there might have been of an alliance of any kind. Tragically, the very men who abhorred the rape of their sister almost certainly perpetrated the same form of violence on the women of the city, for 'every child of theirs and their women they carried off and they plundered' (v. 29). Like the men of Sodom, they used rape to assert their dominance over those who were vulnerable.

Dinah's story?

What Dinah would have had to say on any of this, we will never know. As it turns out, this is not her story but the story of males and male violence. The tension between those living with their livestock on the land and those living in the city may explain the viciousness and violence in the story. As we have seen, conflict between the people of the land and ruling élites who lived in the cities characterized the ancient Near East for centuries. Perhaps this story reflects something of that conflict, although we should not for a moment allow this to deflect our gaze from its focus on the rape of Dinah.

REFLECTION

Retell this story from Dinah's perspective. If she had kept a diary, what would she have written in it?

JOURNEYS *to* & *from* BETHEL

This chapter contains a number of loosely connected stories about journeys. Once again, as we approach the end of the stories of Jacob, we come across all those fragments that various redactors did not want to lose and so attached here. They do not add much to what we know about Jacob; indeed, Jacob has been rather quiet since he met Esau, and we already see signs that the larger story is beginning to shift to the fourth generation.

To Bethel

God's silence during the rape of Dinah is broken. God instructs Jacob to return to Bethel, where he met with God so many years before (28:10–22). Jacob had promised that if God would guide and sustain him on his journey, then Yahweh would be his God (28:21). God has clearly done this, but what has not been fulfilled is Jacob's request that God return him to his father's house in peace. Jacob has found a measure of peace with Esau, but he has yet to return to his father's house and find peace there. The first leg of the journey home begins with a return to Bethel. Earlier, in a dream, God had appeared to Jacob as 'the God of Bethel' (31:13), so Bethel is clearly a significant place in the relationship between God and Jacob.

Knowing that he is going to a place with which he identifies his God, Jacob collects all the other family gods and leaves them in Shechem, lest they offend the God of Bethel (v. 2). Interestingly, these other gods are not destroyed, merely hidden, much as Rachel hid the gods of her father Laban (31:34). Even the place where they are hidden, 'the oak that was near Shechem' (v. 4), is a sacred site (see 12:6). Out of respect for the God of Bethel, Yahweh, these gods are left behind.

As they journey, 'a terror from God' (v. 5) prevents any of the cities they pass from interfering with them. Perhaps the story of what was done to Hamor's city played some part in this. Jacob thus returns to Bethel safely. God has been faithful. In the midst of his return and his settlement, there is a touching mention of the death of Rebekah's nurse, Deborah (v. 8). She is buried in a place that became known as

'Oak of weeping'. This note reminds us that these stories are real stories about a real family.

Verses 9–13 are also linked to Bethel, but it is not clear how they fit into the journey. This is either another version of Jacob's change of name (see 32:28) or a reconfirmation of the name change. The reference to Jacob having come from Paddan-aram, which is where he lived with Laban, seems to suggest that it is an alternative tradition. On his journey from Paddan-aram, this tradition tells us, God appeared to Jacob, blessed him, changed his name (as he had changed Abram's name), and passed on to him the promises made to Abraham and Isaac (see 17:5; 26:3).

What we have, then, are two accounts of the changing of Jacob's name and the naming of Bethel. This account confirms that Jacob is to be the primary line of God's covenant with his family.

To Ephrath

If we attempt to read these fragments as a connected journey, then Jacob is being disobedient to God's command to settle in Bethel (v. 1). More probably, the short fragment in verses 16–20 is a previously independent piece of tradition that has been inserted here because it relates to Bethel. In this fragment, Jacob leaves Bethel for Ephrath, travelling south. On this journey, Rachel bears a second son. Although the barren Rachel (29:31) must have been overjoyed at the prospect of this her second son, his birth costs her her life. The son is given two names, one by his mother (which means something like 'Son of my sorrow') and one by his father (which means something like 'Son of the right hand' or 'Son of the south', v. 18). The naming of the son is followed without any comment by the death and burial of Rachel, the beloved wife. Unfortunately, we do not have a full narrative recounting her death; instead we have a fragment without much emotional content.

But she is well remembered, the town of Bethlehem being linked to her resting place. Jacob too remembers her by erecting yet another stone memorial pillar (see 28:18; 31:45).

PRAYER

We are reminded, most merciful God, that you call us to make many journeys in our lives. Enable us to see your purpose for us in each of them.

JOURNEYS & FAMILY MATTERS

A record of some of Jacob's journey continues, although the links to Bethel are not as clear as in the earlier fragments. Linked to these journeys, journeys that eventually return Jacob to his father's home, are a number of genealogical lists. As the life of Isaac comes to an end, and as the stories of Jacob come to an end, family matters are concluded.

To Eder

In a very brief fragment we are told that Jacob/Israel journeyed to a place known as Migdal Eder (in the Hebrew), which means a 'cattle/flock tower'. This place is associated with an act of incest between Reuben and Bilhah (35:22). The note that 'Israel heard of it' is all the comment there is, although whether it refers to Israel the nation (in which case it is an indication of condemnation: see 34:7) or Israel/Jacob the father and husband (in which case it may be an indication of Jacob's lack of action: see 34:5) is not clear.

To Hebron

Just before the fragment that recounts Jacob's return to his father's home, there is a brief genealogical note (35:23–26) recounting Jacob's sons, prompted perhaps by the mention of Reuben (who is specifically designated as 'Jacob's firstborn') and the impending death of Isaac. Jacob returns home, at last. The narrator's comment is a bleak one, reminding the reader that Abraham and Isaac (and Jacob) are still aliens in the land (35:27). Isaac dies and is gathered to the ancestors, having lived a full and long life. Reunited at long last, Esau and Jacob bury him (35:29). Before the reader can ask the many questions that this family reunion brings to mind, the text moves on. There is no pause to consider whether or not Jacob found peace with his father as he had hoped when he fled his home so many years before (28:21).

Esau's family

Just as Ishmael's genealogy appears in Genesis 25, so too Esau's appears here. In both cases, the intention seems to be to sum up the life and inheritance of the eldest son, but in both cases this is also the son who is not the chosen line of God's covenant.

The very inclusion of Esau's line raises doubts about the notion of a particular line of covenant. Although we have been told that 'the elder shall serve the younger' (25:23), there are no signs of this at all. In fact, God's declaration to Rebekah and Isaac's blessing of Jacob above Esau (27:29) seem to have had little effect.

There is a series of lists of Esau's descendants, some of them overlapping. However, they differ from the data given to us in 26:34 and 28:9. The first list (36:1–8) begins with Esau's Canaanite wives and then goes on to recount how Esau apparently left the land of Canaan to settle in a land to the south-east, so as not to drain the scarce resources of the land.

In the next passage (36:9–14), there is a list of Esau's sons, overlapping with the list above it, but including also Esau's grandsons. These grandsons are also included in the third list (vv. 15–19), although there they are called (in Hebrew) 'chiefs of the sons of Esau'. This list emphasizes the political rather than the familial dimensions of Esau's line.

The fourth list (36:20–28) is a genealogy of 'Seir the Horite', one of the indigenous ancestors of the region in which Esau eventually settled. It is included here because the two families intermarried. For example, Anah's daughter Oholibamah is specifically mentioned in amongst the male descendants (36:25), when daughters are hardly ever mentioned in genealogical lists, because she became one of Esau's wives (36:2). Timna, another daughter, is also listed (36:22), for she was one of the secondary wives of Eliphaz, one of Esau's sons (36:12). Following this genealogy is a list of the chiefs of the Horites (36:29–30).

The king list in 36:31–39 is repeated in 1 Chronicles 1:43–50, and is similar in form to the king lists found in 1 Kings 16:22; 2 Kings 1:17; 8:15; 12:21; and 13:24.

It is almost impossible to reconstruct the history that lies behind these lists, although the challenge has been taken up by many commentators. From a narrative perspective, the accumulation of genealogies at this point emphasizes the importance of Esau in the family, even though he is not the designated line. God, it would seem, has more than one plan.

PRAYER

*Thank you, gracious God, that you usually have
more than one plan for us.*

JACOB & JOSEPH: *an* OVERVIEW

We move quite abruptly from the genealogy of Esau into one of the most carefully constructed and memorable stories in the Bible—the story of Joseph. Even among those for whom the Bible is an unread text, the Joseph story lingers in the memory. Sunday schools, Andrew Lloyd Webber's musical *Joseph and the Amazing Technicolour Dreamcoat*, and African woodcuts have all celebrated this remarkable story.

As we study the story together, the source of its power will become apparent. Not only is the narrative itself wonderfully constructed, but the themes it takes up touch our lives. Here is a story of a large and complex family, full of the tensions that all families embody. Here is a story of betrayal and of hope. Here is a story of slavery and political power. Here is a human story with which we can each identify.

History and story

All readers of this story, even scholars, agree that it is a finely crafted, complex and extended narrative. Although there are occasional interruptions (the most obvious example being chapter 38), the story flows smoothly from scene to scene, drawing the reader into the narrative and maintaining our attention throughout. Here is an excellent example of the biblical author as creator.

Although scholars have postulated that there may have been more than one version of the Joseph story, which have been combined in this narrative, there is general agreement that an author has taken the existing stories and thoroughly reworked them to form one integrated literary product. We may still find the odd reminder of the earlier Joseph stories from which this one has been constructed but, on the whole, what we have before us is the fruit of a single creative author.

It is immediately apparent, however, that the Joseph story has been embedded within the larger narrative of the ancestors of Israel. Chapter 36 is the genealogy of Esau, listing rather than narrating his descendants and their clans. As we might expect, chapter 37 then begins with the genealogy of Jacob. But this genealogy is immediately interrupted by the lengthy literary work that is the story of Joseph. We move abruptly from a genealogical list to a complex narrative. It appears, then, that at some stage in the composition of the book of

Genesis, the story of Joseph was inserted into the genealogy of Jacob. This is, after all, an appropriate place for it. Joseph was one of the sons of Jacob. Indeed, he was the eldest son of Jacob's favourite wife, Rachel. Jacob's genealogy is not forgotten, but it is subsumed by the Joseph narrative.

As with the other ancestor stories, Joseph is almost certainly a real, historical ancestor, about whom stories were told and retold. And as we have already seen with the other ancestor stories, here too the emphasis is not so much on what life *was* like (in historical detail) but on what life *is* like (with its patterns and rhythms). The Joseph story is definitely more complex than the ancestor sagas we have come across so far, but, like them, it has shed its historical detail with its constant retellings, so it is very difficult to locate this story in its historical setting. While its literary setting is clear—moving between Canaan and Egypt—the historical setting is more elusive.

Is the story based on historical fact? This is difficult to determine because so little historical, geographical or political detail remains. Those scholars who have attempted to ascertain whether and to what extent there is a match between the literary setting and the available historical record have found few resources with which to work. This does not mean that Joseph's story 'did not happen as it says'. What it does mean is that we cannot, with any certainty, make historical claims about the narrative. The fact that it is history-like is clear, but the kind of detail we need to determine its historical reliability is simply absent.

The absence of this kind of detail is itself a significant clue to the central concern of the story. The primary focus of the Joseph story is what life is like, both life in the past and life in the present. It is a human story, a story about a family and a community. It is also a theological story, a story that attempts to discern God's presence in life. That is why so many generations of readers have been captivated by this remarkable story.

REFLECTION

Before reading this story in detail, what are the things
that you remember about the Joseph story? What do you think
the story is about?

TENSION *in the* FAMILY

The genealogy of Esau in chapter 36 is followed by the genealogy of Jacob in chapter 37. No sooner has the genealogy begun, however, identifying Jacob as the descendant of the ancestors that have gone before him and locating him in the land of Canaan, than it is interrupted. It is interrupted in two ways: first, by a shift in literary genre from genealogy to narrative; and second, with a shift in focus from Jacob to Joseph.

Beginning in Canaan

Verse 1, however, does do important work: it locates the story in Canaan. The literary setting is significant in that it provides a claim to the designated land. This great ancestor, it is affirmed, resided in the land of Canaan. It is important to make this assertion at this point because, at various times in their history, the people of Israel/Jacob would find themselves in other lands. More specifically, the Joseph story will take Jacob and all his family to Egypt. This verse provides the starting point—in Canaan.

The word 'resided' in the paragraph above is a reasonable translation for the Hebrew word translated in the NRSV by 'had lived as an alien'. There seems to be a contrast here between Jacob, who 'settled in the land', and his father, who had 'lived as an alien' in the land. It is clear from verse 1 that neither Jacob nor his father are indigenous to the land. They are first sojourners and then settlers. There is some ambiguity, then, at the very beginning of this story, about land and belonging.

Father and mothers

Verse 2 begins with Jacob, but abruptly shifts to Joseph. In the Hebrew there is no grammatical transition, not even a conjunction. 'These are the genealogies of Jacob' is what the Hebrew says, followed immediately by 'Joseph...' So it does appear as if the Joseph narrative has been inserted into the genealogy of Jacob at this point, interrupting it.

Again, we see the tendency both to collect and to create. The story of Joseph is an important one that must be included in the story of the great ancestors. Here is a reasonably appropriate place to insert it. The fact that it interrupts the genealogy was not, clearly, considered to be a problem by the redactor who did it. This redactor was primarily a collector. His central concern was to incorporate an important tradition.

This was not the case with the author of the Joseph story. Here we have an author who is prepared to rework previously existing narratives about Joseph into one coherent and complex account. We see evidence of his attention to detail immediately. The genealogy foregrounds Jacob, the father, but the author of the Joseph story draws attention to the mothers. Readers already know that this family has one father and four mothers. We are expected to know this by the author of the story that begins in the second part of verse 2.

Joseph is introduced as a young man doing what young men in his society did: he was 'shepherding the flock with his brothers'. What we need to know, however, is that the brothers with whom he is shepherding are particular brothers. They are the brothers of his father's secondary wives, Bilhah and Zilpah. These women are the female servants who were given by Laban to Rachel (29:29) and Leah (29:24) respectively.

Family conflict

These particular sons are mentioned, it seems, because they are sons of the secondary wives, while Joseph is the son of one of the primary wives, Rachel. In polygamous families, there is often tension between the children of senior and junior wives. Here it is no different. Joseph, we are told, was 'shepherding with his brothers'. While this is almost certainly the correct translation, the text could also be translated to say that Joseph was 'shepherding his brothers'. This ambiguity signals the first of many possible causes for the tension that exists. Did Joseph see himself as superior to his brothers? Had his father asked him to 'keep an eye on' them? We can only guess. What is clear from verse 2 is that Joseph brings 'a bad report of them to their father'. Again, however, there is ambiguity. Is the report about the brothers' bad behaviour, or is the report itself bad, either because Joseph should not have been reporting on his brothers ('telling tales') or because Joseph has fabricated his report? To find answers to these questions, we must read on.

PRAYER

Gracious God, thank you for our families—
for each member of them.

FATHER & SONS

Verse 3 begins with a name change. The Jacob of 37:1–2 is now called Israel. Scholars have usually explained this shift as evidence of different sources. There were at least two versions, it is argued, of the Joseph story, one referring to Joseph's father as Jacob and the other as Israel. The Joseph story as we now have it, though one story, still bears the marks of its sources.

Favouritism

This verse also provides another reason for tension within the family. Joseph, we are told, is his father's favourite. The reason given is that Joseph is the son of his father's old age. The attentive reader, being alerted to the presence of multiple wives, may also detect an implied reference to Rachel. Rachel, we know, was Jacob's favourite. As in most polygamous families, the first wife married is married for family or clan reasons. In many societies, as in this one (29:26), the younger sister may not marry until her older sister has married. In such circumstances, the second or third wife is often the favourite or 'loved wife' (as the Zulu people in South Africa express it).

Israel (as he is referred to here) clearly makes no attempt to hide his favouritism. Indeed, he flaunts it by making Joseph a very special robe. While it is not clear precisely what this robe looked like, it is a luxurious item, associated with royalty in 2 Samuel 13:18. The King James translation uses the phrase 'a coat of many colours', which has caught the popular imagination and been taken up in the musical on Joseph's life created by Rice and Lloyd Webber. Such an extravagant gift generates jealousy, particularly in a polygamous family, so it is no surprise when we read that Joseph's brothers resented him because of it.

The text does not differentiate between the sons of the various mothers at this point, indicating that it was most probably all of Joseph's brothers who resented him. His father's favouritism has aligned them all against him. The Hebrew phrase that expresses this is not easy to translate, but the NRSV captures the gist of it (v. 4). His brothers are unable to speak to him without becoming resentful and angry. It is important to note, however, that the brothers do not hate

Joseph because of his luxurious coat. Verse 4 is clear: they hate him because the coat is a visible sign of their father's preferential love.

The dreamer

So far, there are at least two related causes for the conflict that is about to consume this family. First, there is the animosity between sons of different mothers. Second, there is a father's favouritism towards one of his sons. These two reasons are related in that both have their origin in the dynamics and realities of the polygamous family.

Verse 5 provides yet another reason for family tension. Joseph, we are told, dreams a dream. To an African reader, this is significant in itself. Dreams are a form of connection and communication between the living and the 'living dead' (the ancestors). The young are often the vehicle for this communication, being closest to those who have departed. So it is no surprise that Joseph dreams dreams. What is significant, though, is that Joseph tells the dream to his brothers.

We have already been told that Joseph and his brothers were not able to talk without tension. So why does Joseph talk to them about his dreams? Is he just thoughtless, or is he trying to provoke them? Is Joseph the kind of character who needs to be the centre of attraction? Fortunately, because this is a complex narrative and not a simple saga, we will discern more about Joseph's character as we read on. At this point, the narrator tells us just enough to keep us reading. Suspense is generated as we are told of the effect of Joseph's dream on his brothers before we even know what it is about. Such is the artistry of this narrative. We must read on! As we will see in the next verse, it is also the content of the dream that generates tension.

PRAYER

*Make us mindful, gracious God, of our roles in generating
conflict in our families and communities. Forgive us
for our insensitivity to the feelings and perspectives of others
in our families and communities.*

JOSEPH'S DREAMS

Having told us of the dream's impact on Joseph's brothers, the narrator now tells us the content of the dream. The repetition in verse 6 further delays the actual content of the dream, increasing our suspense.

Joseph and his brothers are the main characters in his dream, and in it they are doing things that are fairly normal in such a society. Just as we first met Joseph and his brothers shepherding, so we now see them binding the fruits of the harvest. These activities tell us something about the kind of community from which the Joseph stories arose—a settled agrarian society—but the detail is not specific enough for us to use these details to date the text to a particular period.

Interpreting the dreams

Significantly, Joseph does not interpret his dream. He is the dreamer here, not the interpreter. It is his brothers who interpret the dream (v. 8), and, as we might expect, they interpret it in line with the tension between Joseph and themselves. They see the dream as just one more example of Joseph's lording it over them.

The tone in which Joseph recounts his dream contributes to the hostile interpretation that his brothers give to the dream. The NRSV does not convey the tone as clearly as it might. In addition to the use of the imperative 'Listen now!' the Hebrew uses two interjections in verse 7, which can be translated as 'Now, see/behold': 'Now see/behold, when we were binding…' and 'And now see/behold, my sheaf stood and…'. The effect of these interjections is to summon the hearer to pay attention and to see things as Joseph sees them. Joseph, it seems, is demanding that his brothers pay attention to his dream. Again, either Joseph is just naive or he is deliberately provoking his brothers. This is why the text says that the brothers 'hated him even more because of his dreams and his words' (v. 8). It is not just what he says that upsets them; it is also how he says it.

The brothers are alarmed by the possibility that Joseph either imagines himself reigning over them or, worse, that the dream is a sign that Joseph will in the future 'really reign' (v. 8 in the Hebrew) over them.

The tension then escalates with a second dream in verse 9. Without a pause, the narrative continues, building momentum and tension. Again, Joseph chooses to tell his brothers, and again, the language and tone are the same as in the first dream: 'Now see/behold, I dreamed a dream again, and see/behold...'. The content is different, but the central image of 'bowing' is present in both.

This time, however, it is not the brothers who interpret the dream, but their father. We are not told of the brothers' reaction, but their silence is only a prelude to our hearing the voice of his father. We learn now, in verse 10, that when Joseph tells his brothers this second dream, his father is also present. Once again, Joseph does not interpret his own dream; his father does. But before we hear the interpretation, we are told that his father rebukes him, questioning what kind of dream it is. Even his father is worried that Joseph may be dreaming dreams from his own ambitions.

Israel's interpretation is similar to that of the brothers: he assumes that the dream is about the whole family bowing before Joseph. He is clearly disturbed by this interpretation, inverting as it does the usual order of the family. It is worth noting that although she is apparently not present, Israel includes Joseph's mother in his interpretation (v. 10). They are not always prominent, but women do play an important role in this patriarchal story.

Two responses

We already know of the brothers' response. They hate Joseph, and now in verse 11 we are told that they are jealous of him. Jealousy has not yet been named as a cause of tension in this family; now it is named. In the verses that follow, we will see its outworking. For now, however, the reader is left neither with the brothers' jealousy nor with the father's initial outrage, but with the image of a more reflective father. Israel ponders on what he has heard. He does not allow his initial concern to exclude further reflection.

As he pauses to reflect, so too must the reader, for in the next verse there is a shift in scene.

REFLECTION

Like Jacob, O God, help us not only to react but also to reflect on what we hear from others, no matter how disturbing it may sound.

The PLOT *against* JOSEPH

The intensity of the family conflict is lifted slightly at the beginning of this next section. We return to normal family life, with the brothers shepherding. Significantly, Joseph is not with them, as he was in 37:2. Has Israel kept Joseph at home in order to relieve the tension among the brothers? If so, why does he then send Joseph out to check up on them (vv 13–14)? Surely this would exacerbate the tension?

Place names

We are told in verse 14 that Israel is living in the valley of Hebron. The brothers, Israel believes, are near Shechem, but they have actually moved on to Dothan (v. 17). Further on, we read that there is a caravan of traders on its way from Gilead to Egypt, carrying the kind of goods that were used in Egypt for embalming and medicinal purposes (v. 25). It is this kind of detail that gives the story its history-like feel. Archaeological research has located these sites, and they are plausible locations for the activities that are described here.

Lost and found

Why the narrator has chosen to include the incident about Joseph's being found by a stranger (v. 15) is not clear. Is there a symbolic message here? Are we being told that it is Joseph who is 'lost' and not his brothers, or are we being told that Joseph will always be 'found' and guided by God? What this incident definitely does is to slow the action of the narrative, building suspense as we wait to see what will happen when Joseph at last finds his brothers.

The narrator's artistry is again evident in the two perspectives offered in verses 17–18. In verse 17 we approach Dothan and the brothers from Joseph's perspective. In verse 18, we look out from Dothan, with his brothers, and enter into their perspective.

Death, rescue and slavery

We are told in blunt terms that as the brothers watch him walking towards them in the distance, they plot to kill him (v. 18). The general plan seems to have been to kill Joseph and then throw him into a pit or dry water cistern. From verse 21, however, it appears that Reuben was not in on the initial plan, so when he hears of it, he counters by modifying it. The narrator takes us into the mind of Reuben, thereby informing us that Reuben proposed this alternative because he intended to rescue Joseph later (v. 22). Reuben, it seems, feels responsible, and intends to return Joseph to his father. Reuben's response makes sense when we remember that he is the eldest son of the first wife, Leah (29:32). Not only are Reuben's mother and Joseph's mother sisters, but Joseph is also the eldest son of Rachel. Once again we see the dynamics of the polygamous family at work.

Being the eldest of all the brothers, Reuben clearly carries authority, for we read that the other brothers follow his plan. We are specifically informed that Joseph is stripped of his beautiful robe. This sign of Israel's favouritism is shortly to become a sign of betrayal and death. We are also specifically told that the pit is empty (v. 24), reminding the reader of the possibility of rescue.

As the brothers sit, however, callously eating while their brother languishes in the pit, Judah comes up with another plan. Judah too is a son of the first wife, Leah (29:35), so perhaps he too feels some sense of responsibility to his aunt's son. Although this may be part of the reason for the change of plan, Judah's overt motive is profit. He sees the Ishmaelite traders as a way of avoiding direct responsibility for Joseph's death and of benefiting in financial terms. Like Reuben, he persuades the other brothers by arguing that Joseph is indeed their own flesh and blood, and so they should avoid being directly responsible for his death (vv. 26–27).

Destroying the dream

All of the brothers, except perhaps Reuben, desire to destroy not so much Joseph as his dream. This is evident in verses 19–20. These verses pose the question of whether Joseph's dream will be fulfilled or not. Joseph's dream seemed to suggest that his brothers would bow before him. By killing him, they would ensure that the dream could not be fulfilled. However, although they think selling him into slavery will serve a similar purpose—terminating the interpretation of the dream that they fear—their act of mercy keeps the possibility of fulfilment open.

PRAYER

Deliver us, our God, from acts of vengeance. May we be merciful, as you are merciful to us.

SOLD *into* SLAVERY

Having agreed to sell Joseph to the Ishmaelite traders, who are on their way to Egypt, the brothers watch the caravan approach, just as they had earlier watched Joseph approach. The story becomes a little confusing at this point, however, for in verse 28 we suddenly find that it is Midianite traders who arrive, not Ishmaelite.

Ishmaelites and Midianites

There are a number of possible readings of this verse. First, it could be that Midianite traders, unobserved by the brothers, find Joseph in the pit, pull him out, and then sell him to the Ishmaelite traders who are also in the area. This is what the NRSV translation suggests. Second, it could be that it is the brothers who pull Joseph out of the pit and sell him to the traders. This second option fits better with the narrative so far, but we then have to account for the confusion between Midianites and Ishmaelites.

Some scholars argue that these different names can be used to refer to the same people, and so might be used interchangeably (see also 37:36 and 39:1). Others see evidence here of the different sources the author has used to compose the story, with one source referring to Ishmaelite traders and another referring to Midianite traders. Those who take this line argue that it is the Yahwist source that uses the term 'Ishmaelite' and the Elohist source that uses the term 'Midianite'.

The first option makes the brothers slightly less culpable than the second, although the difference is not great. They are responsible.

Reuben's grief

Again it appears as if Reuben has not been with the brothers as they have discussed Judah's compromise plan, for he returns in verse 29 to rescue Joseph, as the narrator had indicated he intended to do (37:22). Reuben, it seems, is genuinely grieved to find Joseph gone, but this time he is too late. He tears his clothes in grief—a common custom in this culture—as his father shortly will also do. He knows that he will be held responsible for his younger brother's fate, and so he does not know what to do (v. 30).

The cover-up

In order to hide their crime, the brothers, including Reuben, decide on a cover-up. The take the sign of favouritism and make it instead a sign of deception and betrayal. Reuben, the eldest brother, is now reduced to silence, and it will be a long time before he speaks again. Instead of taking responsibility as he did earlier, he gives in and joins the group. The solidarity of the group is regained. The crime is concealed. The brothers now act as one, slaughtering a goat to cover their crime.

Deception and despair

The brothers do not tell their father a fabricated story. Instead, they allow him to construct his own interpretation of what might have happened, from the bloodstained robe. Here, and later in the narrative (39:16–18), clothing is used to tell a false tale. The brothers are passive: they do not even bring the bloody robe to their father. Literally, the Hebrew text says that they 'caused it to come' to their father (v. 32). Then, in front of their father they speak with one voice, as a collective. They do not lie, but they allow the blood-soaked robe to tell the lie. Worse, they allow their father to draw his own false conclusions from the faked evidence.

The effect on Jacob (note that the name has reverted to Jacob) is devastating. His uncontrollable grief is vividly described. He refuses to be comforted, even by his daughters, who are mentioned here for the first time. He sees no way back from his grief. His favourite son is dead, violently killed. The imagined death is worse than any reality, and there is not even a body to bury, to bring closure. Indeed, Jacob foresees no closure, ever. His only release is weeping.

This chapter comes to an end where it began, with no *shalom*. Earlier, the brothers could not speak to each other with *shalom*, peace (37:4). Joseph and Jacob perhaps played their own parts in contributing to the lack of *shalom*. Now the brothers have played their parts. *Shalom* is shattered.

PRAYER

*Father, forgive us for our failures to accept responsibility
for our actions.*

DESPAIR & HOPE

The inconsolable grief of Jacob is not the final word in the chapter, although it is the final word on his family in Hebron. In order to find a word of hope, we have to leave Jacob with his grief. We have to leave the fractured and hurt family that we have begun to know. The daughters have been explicitly drawn into the narrative, albeit belatedly, and so have the wives to Jacob and the mothers to their sons. The whole family is profoundly not at peace. There is no *shalom*.

The narrator, however, provides a glimmer of hope by shifting the scene. We leave Jacob and his family in their despair in order to follow Joseph. With one word in the English translation ('Meanwhile…') and a simple conjunction in the Hebrew ('and'), we are transported from Canaan to Egypt.

Midianites and Medanites

To add to the textual confusion of 37:28, verse 36 of the Hebrew text compounds the problem by saying that it is 'Medanites' who sell Joseph in Egypt. However, it is only the Masoretic text that has this reading. The Samaritan Pentateuch, the Septuagint, the Vulgate and the Syriac all have 'Midianites', which is why the NRSV uses this term. The textual confusion does indicate that various redactors and scribes over the ages have struggled, as we have, to make sense of the available text. Fortunately, the confusion does not detract from the power of the narrative.

From Canaan to Egypt

A child of Israel/Jacob is now in Egypt. Soon his whole family and their descendants will be there too. Indeed, it is in Egypt that God will hear the cry of slaves and send Moses to deliver them. The journey from Canaan to Egypt begins here, with Joseph as a slave. Having been sold into slavery by his brothers (whether directly or indirectly, depending on how we read 37:28), Joseph is now resold to new masters.

From a son to a slave

This story assumes a trade in human beings, but as this unfortunate phenomenon has been a part of human history for so long, it does not help us very much to locate our text historically. Slavery is simply a part of the story's world. It is no wonder that generations of Africans and African Americans have been drawn to this story. They know the reality of being a son or daughter one day and a slave the next.

For the sake of profit, the Midianites, like Judah and his brothers, sell Joseph in the slave markets of Egypt. Perhaps because of his relatively good physical condition, having been the pampered favourite son of a reasonably prosperous family, Joseph catches the eye of Potiphar, one of Pharaoh's senior officials. Joseph has a new master.

Interruption

We as readers now have to wait a while before we can continue with Joseph's story, for the narrative is interrupted by a story about Judah. As we will see, this story of Judah has its own integrity and does not fit very well here. Nevertheless, some redactor chose to insert it here so that it would be preserved. This is the impulse of a collector.

In some respects, this is not an inappropriate place to locate the story of Judah. There is no separate series of sagas (as with Abraham, Isaac and Jacob), nor is there an extended narrative account (as with Joseph) about Judah. This lone story therefore needed to be placed somewhere, and this is a reasonable place. The Joseph story is interrupted after its opening act, the suspense is prolonged, and Judah has been introduced as a character in the Joseph story. Furthermore, inserting the story of Judah here makes chronological sense in that it accounts for the 20 years (see 37:2 and 41:46, 53–54) between Joseph's being sold into slavery and the brothers' arrival in Egypt to buy grain.

Yet, as we will see, the story of Judah is somewhat out of place here. It has been made to fit, but the fit is not a comfortable one.

REFLECTION

Why do you think the story of Judah is inserted at this place in the story of Joseph? What are the connections?

TAMAR & JUDAH (I)

While the story of Tamar and Judah clearly interrupts the Joseph story, it is not entirely out of place. First, we have already been introduced to Judah in chapter 37, and this story develops his character and perhaps provides us with an indication of why he intervenes to save Joseph and later Benjamin. Second, the Judah and Tamar story fits the chronology of the Joseph story, filling the gap between the sale of Joseph and the encounter between the brothers in Egypt. Third, this story underlines the interest of Genesis in alternative lines of descendants. David will be the descendant of Perez, who is mentioned in 38:29. Within a story about Joseph, we are reminded of the line of Judah. Fourth, there are specific thematic links with Genesis 37, including the recognition and interpretation of objects associated with a particular person, the use of a goat, and the betrayal of a brother.

Judah's marriage and sons

The story begins with a vague reference to time and place. These details are not important. The phrase that Judah 'went down' (v. 1) will, however, be echoed by 39:1, where we read that Joseph was 'taken down' to Egypt. The same verb is used, suggesting parallels between these two brothers who are separated from the rest of the family. The crucial difference, of course, is that Judah's journey was a choice, whereas Joseph's was forced upon him.

Like his uncle Esau, Judah disregards the family custom of marrying within the clan and 'takes/marries' a Canaanite woman. The language is similar to that used in the story of Dinah, except that this woman is not even named. Judah 'saw her and came in to her' (v. 2; compare 34:2). He names the first of their sons and she names the next two, which perhaps indicates that he was losing interest in the marriage or that they had never married in any formal sense. The mention of Chezib as the place where he was when his third son was born may also be significant, for it means 'Falsehood' (v. 5).

Tamar and Onan

Tamar is introduced to us simply as the wife of Judah's eldest son, Er. Er, we are told, was wicked and so was killed by God (v. 7). Judah then instructs his second son to father children on behalf of the deceased brother. This was a common practice, known as levirate marriage, but Onan is unwilling to comply, for he knows that these children will be considered the children of his elder brother, and therefore in line to inherit ahead of his own children. He does not deny himself the pleasure of sexual intercourse with Tamar, but by withdrawing as he is about to ejaculate, he denies her the possibility of impregnation. For failing in his duty, God also puts him to death.

Tamar sent home

Because Judah fears for his youngest son's life, imagining perhaps that Tamar is somehow responsible for the deaths of his two sons, he sends her (using the imperative form of the verb) to her father's home, claiming that his youngest son is too young to undertake levirate marriage just yet. This would have brought great shame to Tamar and her family and may even have resulted in their having to return the dowry that they had received. Her own situation was also ambiguous, for she could not remarry while she remained contractually tied to her father-in-law. The apparent promise of a levirate marriage to Judah's son Shelah keeps her trapped as a perpetual widow.

Tamar abandoned

'After many days' we perhaps expect to read that a levirate marriage eventually does take place, but instead we read that Judah's wife dies. 'When he was comforted' (a Hebrew phrase referring to the period of mourning), he immediately leaves his home and goes off to visit his sheepshearers with his friend (v. 12). Whether Judah was relieved to be rid of his wife and so immediately went 'off with the boys', or whether he needed to throw himself into work in order to cope with his grief, we can only speculate. Whatever his motives, he leaves, thereby abandoning Tamar to her fate. When Tamar hears that he has left, however, she now knows where she stands, and she decides to do something about it. Instead of waiting to be summoned from her father's house, she sets out to take control of her own future, within the constraints of her context.

PRAYER

Remember those, God of love, who struggle in loveless marriages.

TAMAR & JUDAH (II)

Tamar discards her widow's habit and locates herself in a public thoroughfare, the entrance to Enaim (which means something like 'Opening of the eyes' or perhaps 'Twin wells'), a place where married or widowed women would not sit. By sitting here, she notices and is noticed. What she intends to do, we do not know, but she is clearly waiting to confront Judah when he returns from Timnah. When Judah and his son come into view, she notices that Shelah has indeed now grown up, and yet she has not been given in marriage to him. At the same moment she is noticed by Judah, who mistakes her for a prostitute (v. 15).

Seizing the moment, she plays the role, negotiating with him when he propositions her rather crudely. Either she has planned this deception in detail or she is thinking on her feet, for she obtains not only a payment for her body but also a pledge to ensure that she will get her fee. Once the transaction is concluded, Judah wastes neither time nor his seed: 'He went into her, and she conceived by him' (v. 18). Having acted outside any of the roles prescribed for her by her father's or her husband's family, Tamar now returns to 'the garments of her widowhood' (v. 19).

Searching for Tamar

Judah remains true to his promise of payment. Yet when his friend goes to pay on his behalf, for Jacob is probably embarrassed to return to the woman he paid for sex, the woman cannot be found. Interestingly, Jacob's friend asks where 'the cult/temple prostitute' is, and not 'the prostitute' as she was earlier referred to by Jacob (using a quite different Hebrew word). Hirah the Adullamite perhaps assumed that she was a prostitute associated with a sacred site, perhaps that of the goddess Astarte, the goddess of love. The townspeople he asks, however, inform him that there is no shrine prostitute in this area. When he reports this to Judah, Judah decides not to pursue the matter, lest he be laughed at (v. 23).

When three months have passed, her ever-vigilant family, we must assume, inform Judah that Tamar must have been having sex outside of her marriage/widowhood, for she is pregnant. It is unlikely that

Tamar had been having other relationships, so the statement that 'she has played the whore' is somewhat overstated, but a typically harsh societal judgment on a woman like her who is found to be with child. Judah shows no mercy and does not even bother to hear from her. She has no voice in matters such as this. 'Bring her out, and let her be burned' is his response (v. 24).

Tamar breaks her silence

For the second time, Tamar acts outside of societal norms: she sends a message to her father-in-law. And yet she does not expose Judah in public manner; she has no wish to humiliate him, merely to inform him. Relinquishing the objects that link her pregnancy to Judah, she risks all, for Judah could reclaim his belongings and then deny her interpretation. Clothing, as we have seen, can be used to deceive (37:32).

Judah immediately takes responsibility (as he will do again in 44:16–34). Judah's absolving of her actions is stated using a comparative: 'She is more in the right than I am.' What does Judah mean by declaring her 'righteous'? Perhaps he recognizes that she has made the right decisions, strange as this may appear to us, or perhaps he finally recognizes that she is not responsible for the death of his sons. God alone is responsible for that.

Tamar's child

This strange story comes to an end with another set of twins. Like Jacob's mother, Tamar bears two boys who change places. The one who pushes himself out first is called Perez (meaning something like 'Breach') and the one with the crimson thread is called Zerah (meaning something like 'Brightness', perhaps alluding to the crimson thread).

In this story we encounter a remarkable woman who dares to step outside the bounds of her world and, in so doing, is declared righteous. In the whole book of Genesis, only two people are called 'righteous': they are Abraham (15:6) and Tamar (v. 26).

PRAYER

Thank you, gracious God, for Tamar, our mother in the faith, who acted in a manner that we find difficult to comprehend and yet is declared to be righteous.

JOSEPH *in* EGYPT

There is some repetition at the beginning of chapter 39 as we take up the story of Joseph where we left it in chapter 37. A redactor, realizing that the story of Judah and Tamar has disrupted the Joseph story, reminds the reader of the closing verses of chapter 37 by summarizing them in 39:1. But whereas chapter 37 concluded with Joseph being sold by the Midianites (or Medanites), chapter 39 has Joseph being sold by the Ishmaelites. The confusion of chapter 37 in this respect is carried over into chapter 39. Some scholars, as has been indicated, see these names as interchangeable, in which case the difference is of no consequence. Others, however, see the shift between these different names as a remnant of the two sources that have been used to construct the current story of Joseph. The tendency to collect is present even among those who compose. The composer of the form of the Joseph story we have in our Bibles is reluctant, it would seem, to tamper too much with the sources he is drawing on.

The presence of the Lord

While chapter 39 clearly continues the Joseph story, it does present us for the first time with a new perspective—the perspective of God. The first new thing we learn in verse 2 is that the Lord (Yahweh) is with Joseph. So far, God has been 'behind the scenes', and the reader has had to infer, for example, whether God is involved in Joseph's dreams in chapter 37. Here the presence of God is explicit. The narrator wants the reader to know that God is present in the drama that is unfolding.

Perhaps the narrative needs to be overt about the presence of God at this point because Joseph is now among foreigners, people who worship other gods. Perhaps, too, God's presence becomes more obvious now that Joseph is alone and separated from his family. Verse 2 implies also that it is God's presence with Joseph that causes him to prosper. This becomes explicit in verse 3, where we learn that even his Egyptian master is able to see God's presence with Joseph. Furthermore, Potiphar recognizes that it is God who causes whatever Joseph does to prosper. The particular formulation of the NRSV here is important to note: 'the Lord caused all that he did to prosper in his hands'. This is a fairly literal translation of the Hebrew, and it is fortunate that the NRSV follows the Hebrew quite literally here, for in the next section (39:8–9) there is some debate about just what Potiphar has placed in Joseph's hands! The attentive reader is meant to see the connection between that discussion and this description.

In this section, however, the emphasis is abundantly clear. God's presence with Joseph is recognized by Potiphar, who gives him more and more responsibility in his household. First he is taken into Potiphar's own house (v. 2), then he becomes Potiphar's attendant (v. 4), then Potiphar puts him in charge of his household, and then Potiphar entrusts him with everything he owns (v. 4). In a few short verses, Joseph rises a long way. The rapidity of the narration here conveys the almost breathless pace of Joseph's journey from the pit in the desert to being in charge of Potiphar's house. The message is clear: it is God who has done this.

To drive home the message, verse 5 reiterates it by giving the reader a sense of time elapsed. Although narrated briefly, considerable time has passed. The point being made is that over a period of time and many tasks, God has been faithfully present with Joseph, causing all that he does to prosper. More importantly, for there is a missiological element here, God's presence with Joseph impacts on those associated with Joseph. Potiphar and his house are blessed by association. What God intended Abraham to be (12:3), so Joseph is in Potiphar's home.

The emphasis in this section is on the agency of God and, to some extent, Potiphar. Joseph is passive, the recipient of their actions. We know, of course, that Joseph has done many things, but we do not see Joseph acting. Potiphar acts, but even his actions are determined by God's actions. God is the primary actor in this early part of Joseph's new life in Egypt. In the next section, however, Joseph will have to act, and how he acts will tell us a great deal about him. For now, the focus is not on Joseph but on God.

PRAYER

Fill our lives, loving God, with your presence; bless the work of our hands and our relationships.

JOSEPH ABUSED

In this scene, Joseph both acts and is acted upon. Verse 6 again reminds us that Joseph is in charge of everything in Potiphar's household. There is an added piece of information, however, which is that Potiphar did not concern himself with anything in the household except what he ate. So this first part of verse 6 tells us not only about Joseph but also about Potiphar. Joseph is capable and trustworthy. Potiphar, the story perhaps implies, has so entrusted the well-being of his household to Joseph that he has become neglectful of everything in it, including his wife.

The second half of verse 6 follows without a pause, suggesting some connection between the first and second parts of the verse. Joseph, we are told, is handsome. This comment is left to hang for a while, allowing the reader to wonder why the information is being given. Time passes, as the first part of verse 7 indicates, and then someone else acts—Potiphar's wife. Before she acts, it is made absolutely clear who she is: she is 'the wife of his master'. What she does is twofold. First, and the Hebrew is rather poetic here, 'she lifted up her eyes to Joseph'. Second, this action is immediately followed by speech in the imperative mode. She instructs him to lie with her.

Who she is and how she talks to Joseph indicate quite clearly the power relations in this encounter. She is the one with power. Some scholars have felt uncomfortable with this, suspecting that here is just one more story in which the woman is blamed for sexual promiscuity. But those who have experience of the slavery and domestic work in the homes of the powerful know that both women and men are the victims of predatory sexual abuse from their masters and madams. Potiphar's wife is the madam who sexually harasses her servant. She may not have much power in the patriarchal world of her time, but she certainly has power over a foreign slave.

For the first time in a long time, Joseph acts (vv. 8–9). His first response is to say no, to refuse. His second response is to explain his position. Joseph does not want to lose his job, so he tries to reason with her. Speaking at length, he makes it clear that although he is in charge of 'everything', this explicitly excludes her, precisely because she is the wife of his master. Of course, he is also reminding her that she is married! His next sentence shows that Joseph is thinking not only strategically, but also theologically. Committing adultery, which is what this act would be, is immoral and sinful in the sight of Joseph's God. Having invoked Potiphar's name, Joseph now invokes God's name.

Harassment in the home

The sexual harassment of Joseph continues (v. 10), as it generally does in situations of unequal power, but Joseph is steadfast in his refusal, refusing not only to have sex with her but even to be with her. The home has become an unsafe place.

In verse 11, there is an ominous shift. Time has passed, but now our attention is focused on one particular day. The reader knows what is about to happen. The house is suddenly empty of servants; the scene has been set. Refusing to be refused, Potiphar's wife takes a further step in her sexual abuse of Joseph. She physically takes hold of him, and once more commands him. Fortunately, Joseph is physically strong enough to break her hold, and, forsaking his garment, he flees. The garment he leaves behind is probably the undergarment worn beneath the outer cloak. As a servant, Joseph would have been wearing this undergarment as his working clothes. If this is the case, when he fled, he would have fled naked out of the house. The house is no longer a safe place, and so Joseph has had to leave it. We must try to imagine the enormous pressure there must have been on him simply to give in to this sexual abuse. How does one place at risk a comfortable and secure job by refusing those with power? And yet Joseph does just this.

The consequences of this final act of refusal are swift. Potiphar's wife marshals the other servants and begins to construct her deceitful story. She lashes out at her neglectful husband, blaming him for bringing 'a Hebrew' (v. 14) into the household. She hopes that her discriminatory designation of Joseph as 'a Hebrew' will do its work among the other, presumably Egyptian, servants. She then situates herself as the victim, using Joseph's garment as proof. Once again a garment is used to deceive. Joseph's beautiful robe was used by his brothers to deceive his father, and now his undergarment is used to deceive the other servants and later Potiphar.

PRAYER

We remember, our God, those like Joseph and David's daughter Tamar (2 Samuel 13) who are victims and survivors of sexual abuse. Watch over and protect them.

JOSEPH *in* JAIL

As readers, we know that the first time Joseph's clothing was used to deceive, the deception was successful. We wait now to see what will happen. Joseph seems changed from the spoiled and insensitive favourite whom we initially encountered in chapter 37. God is now with him, and he has prospered. Surely God cannot allow such a miscarriage of justice? But the ruse works again.

Deception in the home

Potiphar's wife keeps Joseph's garment close at hand, waiting for her husband's return. When he does return, she repeats the story she told to the servants, but in a carefully constructed form. She says, literally, 'He came to me, the Hebrew slave whom you brought among us, to make sport of me' (v. 17). She begins by making Joseph the perpetrator. She follows this with her derogatory designation of Joseph as 'a Hebrew'. She then blames her husband, implying that he intended it to happen. This is followed by her portrayal of herself as the resisting victim. Finally, she gives her false explanation of how she has come to hold Joseph's undergarment.

The effect of her carefully constructed story and the 'evidence' of Joseph's garment have their intended effect. Potiphar's 'anger burned' (v. 19). Joseph, as a slave, is not given any opportunity to give his side of the story. Instead he is immediately taken, by Potiphar himself, and put in prison. The threefold repetition in verse 20 emphasizes the brute fact of Joseph's imprisonment. He is back in the pit—or, as the Hebrew text puts it, he is in the 'house of the prison'. Joseph has fled from and then been cast out of the 'house' of Potiphar; his new 'house' is a prison.

The pattern

The reader is meant to see an emerging pattern. Joseph was his father's favourite, but ended up in a pit. Then he prospered in the house of Potiphar, but ended up in prison. But this is not the end of the pattern or of the story, for we read in verse 21 that 'the Lord was with Joseph' even here (see also v. 23). Once again, God is with him, showing him kindness and favour in the eyes of others, and so causing him to prosper.

The result is exactly the same. The chief jailer does just as Potiphar had done (vv. 22–23). The cycle continues. What will the end result be? For how long will this pattern be repeated? The possibilities are apparent. Although he is in prison, Joseph is in contact with potentially powerful people, for he is in 'the place where the king's prisoners were confined' (v. 20). These are no ordinary prisoners, and Joseph, we know, is no ordinary slave.

The Hebrew

In the eyes of Potiphar's wife, Joseph was nothing but an object to exploit for her own purposes. Perhaps Joseph was also no more than a valuable commodity in the eyes of Potiphar, and now the chief jailer. The fact that God was with him only made him more valuable. But God's obvious presence with him probably also protected him, for why else did Potiphar not deal with him more harshly?

It may be significant that God's overt presence with Joseph is disclosed and then repeatedly stated, precisely while Joseph is a slave. Joseph, Potiphar's wife repeatedly tells us (and everyone else), is 'a Hebrew'. This word occurs five times in the Joseph story (39:14, 17; 40:15; 41:12; 43:32). In each case it refers to foreigners, and in each case it has a derogatory connotation. Scholarly research is fairly confident that the term 'Hebrew' was not initially the name of an ethnic or national group. Rather, it referred to a social class or status.

Another occasion when the term 'Hebrew' is used extensively is in the exodus story, and here it is clearly used to refer to those of a low social and legal status. The references in the Joseph story, then, do not say anything about Joseph's ethnicity or nationality, but a great deal about his low social and legal status. This is why Yahweh is with him in a special way. He is no longer the favourite son of a reasonably prosperous farmer; he is a slave. And this God, Yahweh, is particularly concerned with slaves and those on the margins of society.

REFLECTION

What difference does this discussion of the term 'Hebrew' make to your understanding of the Joseph story?

DREAMS *in* PRISON

Chapter 40 begins with a signal of time having passed. The final words
of chapter 39 inform the reader that 'the Lord' (Yahweh) is with Joseph
and causes him to prosper. Now, after some time, we find Joseph
drawn into different work from his normal work in the prison. The
dreamer now becomes the dream interpreter.

This shift from dreamer to interpreter is worth noting. Having
dreamt two dreams at the beginning of the story, Joseph does not
dream again in the story. But he does interpret the dreams of others.

The dreams of Pharaoh's servants

God's presence with Joseph has brought Joseph among the élite of the
prison, including two servants who serve Pharaoh. We are not told of
their crimes, but, like Joseph, they have offended their high-ranking
master. Because their master is above Joseph's master, and perhaps
because Joseph is a Hebrew, Joseph serves them in prison.

Again, the narrator tells us that time has passed (v. 4). We are not
to imagine that all this took place quickly, even with God's favour.
Joseph is 'doing his time'! Time is interrupted, however, by dreams.
Remarkably, both the cupbearer and the baker dream a dream on the
same night, although we are informed that each dream will hold its
own meaning (v. 5). Joseph encounters them on his normal morning
rounds, the day after the night of their dreams. Capable servant that he
is, he notices that they are downcast (v. 6). Ironically—and perhaps the
reader is meant to smile at this—here they are in prison and they are
dejected because they do not have anyone to interpret their dreams
(v. 8).

These dreams are an implicit invitation to Joseph. Will he act? When
he dreamed his two dreams, his family interpreted them. What will he
do with these two dreams? Joseph now moves into the role that will
define his identity for the remainder of the narrative. First, he uses a
rhetorical question to remind his fellow prisoners that interpretations
come from God, and not only from the professional interpreters in the
court of Pharaoh (v. 8b). Having done this, he immediately offers
himself as someone who is able to interpret what God is saying. This is
a bold move on the part of Joseph, allowing himself to be used by God.

Planning for the future

Joseph is able to interpret the cupbearer's dream with ease. The dream is not self-evident in its interpretation, but Joseph has no difficulty in offering an interpretation. So confident is he of his interpretation that, without a pause, he firmly but politely asks the cupbearer to act on his behalf when he is restored to favour before Pharaoh (v. 14). What is most important in this scene is that Joseph takes control of his life. He appears to have matured. There are no signs here of the spoiled young man of chapter 37. Here we find someone who is sensitive to the pain of others and who reaches out to them.

The baker is portrayed as being more apprehensive than the cupbearer, for he only relates his dream once he has heard the favourable interpretation given to his colleague (v. 16). Joseph again interprets the dream without difficulty, although this time the news is not good. The fact that Joseph says nothing to the baker about securing his release is further evidence of Joseph's confidence in his interpretation.

Lifting heads

The three days pass, and the dreams are fulfilled as Joseph proclaimed. Joseph's play on words, when he relates the interpretation of the dream to the baker, is insensitive in the circumstances. Having told the cupbearer that Pharaoh will 'lift up your head and restore you to your office', he tells the baker that 'Pharaoh will lift up your head—from you!—and hang you on a pole' (v. 19). The phrase 'lift up the head' refers to the formal recognition that a plaintiff receives before the king, and so is appropriate in verses 13 and 20, but is extremely inappropriate in verse 19. Joseph's insensitive 'bedside manner' with the baker reminds the reader, perhaps, that he has not matured as much as we might have imagined.

Seeing that Joseph's interpretations are fulfilled raises the reader's hope that Joseph's own dreams too will come true (as interpreted by his family). But the final sentence of the chapter cuts this hope short. The cupbearer does not remember Joseph; he forgets him (v. 23). We will have to read on to see in what way Joseph's head is lifted up.

PRAYER

Help us, gracious God, to be attentive to the needs of those
around us, even when we ourselves are in situations
of darkness and despair.

DREAMS *in the* PALACE

Time passes. In one short narrative sentence, two full years pass. The Hebrew phrase 'and at the end of two years of days' (v. 1) hints at the relentless and tedious passing of time. But once again the passage of time is interrupted by dreams. Again there are two dreams. The reader again wonders whether, this time, things will work out for Joseph.

The reader (like Joseph) is required to wait, however. Pharaoh's dreams, like Joseph's and those of the cupbearer and baker, draw on the ordinary images of an agricultural society. In the case of Pharaoh's dreams, though, these images become grotesquely distorted, with the gaunt cattle devouring the sleek, and the thin ears of corn consuming the healthy. Indeed, so horrible is the image that Pharaoh is relieved to wake and find it a dream (v. 7). In the Hebrew text, the reader is invited to experience the dreams directly as Pharaoh does, through the repeated use of the phrase 'and see/behold'. Verse 2 begins, 'And see/behold, from the Nile...', as do verses 3, 5 and 6. We then experience, with Pharaoh, the relief on waking (v. 7): 'And see/behold, it was a dream!'

Pharaoh's usual resources, his magicians and wise men, are unable to interpret these disturbing dreams, and their failure sets the stage for Joseph.

Joseph before Pharaoh

Joseph has no direct access to Pharaoh, of course, and so must rely on the kindness of others (40:14). The cupbearer finally delivers: at last he 'remembers' (compare 40:14 with 41:9). He recounts his experience in prison with Joseph, but leaves out an important detail, namely the identity of the one to whom interpretations belong (40:8).

Now the pace picks up. Time accelerates as Joseph is summoned, has to shave (according to Egyptian custom) and changes his clothes. In the rush, the attentive reader should not neglect to notice that Joseph is once again clothed in the clothing of favour. His father clothed him, Potiphar clothed him, and now Pharaoh (or perhaps the captain of the guard) clothes him (v. 14). How long will he wear these clothes, given that he did not wear the others for any length of time?

Joseph immediately makes it clear to Pharaoh that he is not simply another expert. Once again he bears testimony to God—in the palace of the Egyptian Pharaoh. Joseph's phrasing is careful, as it should be, showing his awareness of where he is. 'Elohim/God,' he says, 'will answer Pharaoh with peace' (v. 16). This is ambiguous, implying perhaps that the interpretation will be favourable to Pharaoh, or, more likely (from Joseph's perspective), that God will provide an accurate interpretation and so bring Pharaoh's troubled mind to peace. One has to be careful how one talks to the powerful, and Joseph shows that his years as a servant have taught him how to talk to power.

Pharaoh now retells the dreams, emphasizing their horror and once again using the phrase 'and see/behold' regularly. The dreams have had a profound effect on Pharaoh. The retelling slows the action, building some narrative tension.

When Joseph speaks again, he does not hesitate. Like his own dreams (but unlike those of the cupbearer and the baker), both dreams have the same message. And, Joseph makes clear (vv. 25, 28, 32), the message is from God to Pharaoh: 'God has revealed to Pharaoh what he is about to do.' Once again, God reveals the future to one outside the covenant family (see also 20:3), in this case to an Egyptian. God, it would seem from this narrative, desires to address all nations, using Abraham's family as the vehicle of blessing to all families (12:3). Indeed, two dreams, Joseph informs Pharaoh, indicate God's urgency (v. 32).

Theological reflections

What these comments also indicate, however, is a theological perspective in which God is the agent of abundance and of famine. God does these things. God's compassion, in this account, lies in the warning to someone who has the power to respond responsibly. So Pharaoh is warned. Why, some of us would ask, does God do such things? Why does God actively initiate famine? Is it, as we might infer from this story, in order to expose how humankind does or does not take responsibility for the resources it has? Or is the question itself, and the theological perspective from which it comes, the problem? The Joseph story (unlike the book of Job) does not deal directly with these questions; its focus is elsewhere.

PRAYER

Grant us patience, merciful God, to wait for you to act.

89 GENESIS 41:33–57

JOSEPH ADVISES PHARAOH

Without a pause, Joseph changes from interpreter to adviser (vv. 33–36). This is a daring move indeed, but Joseph grasps the momentum of the situation to suggest to Pharaoh what he might do in response to the dreams and their interpretation. Again, Joseph has no doubt that his interpretations are accurate. A plan of action is, therefore, required. God has spoken and now humans must act.

Joseph's advice has a number of elements. First, the right person should be appointed to take charge of the task as a whole, someone who is discerning and wise. Second, supporting this person, presumably, a number of more local commissioners should be appointed. Third, their primary task should be to tax one-fifth of the produce during the years of plenty and to hold it in reserve for the period of famine. This third element of advice is not as clear in the Hebrew as the NRSV makes out (v. 34). The meaning of the verb here is not clear, and some scholars have suggested that it may refer to dividing the land into five parts or placing the land under a quasi-military authority. The verb appears to have something to do with the number five, however, so the NRSV translation is a plausible one.

Pharaoh's response

Joseph's boldness may have caused some readers to hold their breath, waiting for Pharaoh's response. When it comes, surprisingly perhaps, there is no censure. Joseph's advice is received as good advice. Wise leader that he appears to be, Pharaoh does not simply appoint Joseph. This would almost certainly have been counter-productive, given that Joseph is a foreigner, of low status, and just out of prison. Instead, Pharaoh poses a question to his officials (v. 38). While it may be a rhetorical question, it serves nevertheless to provide some sense of consensus. There are no objections, so Pharaoh goes ahead and appoints Joseph. Remarkably, Pharaoh openly acknowledges God's presence with Joseph (v. 39).

The focus now shifts quite markedly on to Joseph. He becomes the object of Pharaoh's speech and actions. Just as Potiphar trusted him with everything in his house, and the captain of the guard trusted him with the care of the prison, so now Pharaoh places Joseph over his palace, his people, and the whole land of Egypt. But like Potiphar, Pharaoh makes it clear who is ultimately in charge (v. 40b).

Having appointed him, Pharaoh equips him, granting both the symbolic and pragmatic requirements of his new status and office (vv. 42–45). Once again Joseph is clothed in new garments. He is also given a new name, an Egyptian name, and he is married to an Egyptian, the daughter of a priest. The Hebrew has become an Egyptian! None of this induces a theological disclaimer from the narrator (or even a later editor). Clearly, whenever this story came to its present final form, there was no problem with a son of Israel marrying a foreign wife.

Joseph's rise

The young herd-boy has come a long way, although the path has not been easy. According to verse 46, 13 years have passed since he was shepherding with his brothers. Most of these years have been years of slavery. How will Joseph cope with fame, fortune and power? He did not do very well when he was younger, but perhaps he has grown up.

Joseph begins well, immediately implementing the plan he had outlined to Pharaoh. During the years of plenty, he too is fruitful, fathering two sons, both of whom are named in such a way as to remind Joseph of where he has come from and what he has become, and of God's role in his life (vv. 51–52).

Pharaoh's dreams and Joseph's interpretation are fulfilled. Seven years of abundance are followed by seven years of famine. But Egypt is prepared, thanks to God and Joseph. One ominous note is sounded, however, for we are told that Joseph sold grain he had stored to the Egyptians (v. 56). Having taken their surplus in the years of plenty by means of a tax, they are now made to pay for it in the years of need. This point is taken up again by the narrative in 47:13–26.

Joseph may have forgotten 'his father's house' (v. 51), but his plan will soon reunite the family. Very soon 'all the world came to Joseph in Egypt to buy grain' (v. 57). Among those who would come would be Jacob's family.

PRAYER

Grant that all our leaders, gracious God,
may be discerning and wise.

The FAMILY'S FIRST JOURNEY

The scene shifts again, this time from Egypt to Canaan. What unites these very different contexts is the famine. When Jacob (as he is called in verse 4, but note the name Israel in verse 5) hears that there is grain in Egypt, he does not hesitate—although his sons do (v. 1b). He orders them to go there and buy grain. The brothers have either become lethargic from the lack of food (a common symptom of malnutrition) or they have some premonition of what awaits them.

Jacob has not changed in at least one respect: he still favours the sons of Rachel. So he sends the remaining ten brothers to Egypt, keeping Benjamin with him. Israel's fear for Benjamin's safety is not unfounded, for he has already lost one favourite son. There is a sense of justice in this, too, for Benjamin was almost certainly too young to have participated in his brothers' dastardly deed. This trip to Egypt will reunite those brothers who last met in the fields near Dothan.

Back to Egypt

The scene shifts back to Egypt. The narrative pace quickens, and without much preamble the brothers are bowing before Joseph, as Jacob's interpretation of his dream predicted they would (37:10). Wherever Joseph goes in Egypt, his assistants shout for those before his chariot to bow the knee (41:43). Now his brothers bow their knees (v. 6), even though no one tells them to.

Immediately Joseph recognizes them, while they remain unaware of who he is. He has changed, but they have not (although how much each party has changed remains to be tested more deeply). This asymmetrical knowledge sustains the narrative for the next few scenes, and the reader anxiously waits for the anticipated moment of recognition or revelation. Joseph's first response is a strange, though perhaps not unexpected one. He pretends to be a stranger, and he speaks harshly to them (v. 7). The absence of peace (*shalom*) continues!

It is only when they bow before him, we are told, that Joseph remembers his dreams (v. 9). His second, more reflected, response is also odd, and this time the reasons are harder to find. Why does he accuse them of being spies, and what is the relationship of this charge to his dreams? If Joseph's response is not easy to fathom, neither is the response of the brothers in turn (v. 13). Perhaps the incoherence of both Joseph's and the brothers' behaviour is the narrative's signal that communication is completely broken between them.

Power

The Joseph story is in many respects a story of power. As his father's favourite, Joseph had power, and used it. As a group, his brothers had power, and used it to sell him into slavery. Now Joseph has power, and again he uses it to reassert his charge against them (v. 12). But he offers them a way out, a test. The test is based on the knowledge they have volunteered, and as such makes some sense. If they are indeed ten of twelve brothers, with one 'no more', then there should be one more brother. One of them must go and fetch Benjamin.

Swearing an oath on the name of Pharaoh (twice), Joseph allows no further discussion, but places them in prison. Having allowed them to sweat for three days (the same amount of time that Abraham had in Genesis 22 to prepare for his test), he summons them and puts his test before them. Having had time to think, he has modified the test. Instead of one going back to Canaan to fetch Benjamin, one is to remain in prison, and the rest are to return. Why Joseph changes the test is not clear, but the most likely reason is that he has come to realize that one brother would not be able to carry sufficient grain back to Canaan to sustain the family there (see v. 19b). So perhaps Joseph's change of plan is motivated by compassion for the rest of the family back home.

This time Joseph does not swear an oath on Pharaoh; instead he invokes God (v. 18). This shift may be significant, for it has been unclear from the narrative quite where Joseph stands with God since his rise to power. Publically the brothers agree—for what else can they do?—but privately there are only recriminations and guilt (v. 21). At last the reader is given some clue to Joseph's behaviour. Is it perhaps to induce in his brothers the despair that he felt when they abandoned him to the pit and slavery? The earlier narrative did not tell us that Joseph pleaded for his life, but his brothers now remember his cries vividly. From Reuben's reaction it appears that the brothers imagine Joseph to have died (v. 22), but he is not dead: he is very much alive and in control of their lives.

PRAYER

Forgive us, Father, for the hurt we inflict on others.

JOSEPH TESTS HIS BROTHERS

As the brothers apportion blame and expose their guilt among themselves, Joseph eavesdrops. Part of his disguise had been to use an interpreter when he spoke to them, so they are unaware that he can understand their language. This intimate scene fills Joseph with mixed emotions. He is unrelenting in his desire to torment his brothers, but he is also unable completely to conceal his longing to be a part of the family again. He has to turn away to prevent them from seeing him weep (v. 24). But once he has controlled himself, his resolve to test his brothers remains undiminished.

He selects Simeon, the second eldest, as the hostage. Significantly, he leaves the eldest son of the senior wife (Leah) to lead the brothers back to Canaan and bear the news to Jacob (just as Reuben had done after they had disposed of Joseph). But he holds as hostage the second eldest son of the senior wife. The test is now set. First, Reuben must once again come before his father with news of a missing son. Joseph has recreated the scene. A second element of the test is the question of whether the brothers will abandon Simeon, as they abandoned Joseph. Will they return with Benjamin to ransom Simeon? The third element of the test is how the brothers will react to their returned money.

Why Joseph returns his brothers' money is not clear. In the context of the ancient Near East, such a gesture could be understood as a sign of generosity, indicating that his brothers had been his guests. It could, however, be a way of tormenting his already terrified brothers still further. This indeed is the outcome (v. 28b). The returned money may be a sign of their betrayal, reminding the men that they once sold their brother. If they are honest, the brothers will return the money to Joseph when they go back, and in doing so will be symbolically returning the money they received when they sold him. When one of them sees the returned money, the response is despair and fear. Everything seems so out of their control, they can only imagine that somehow God is at work, although they do not understand what God is doing.

Before their father (again)

When the brothers come before Jacob, they recount, fairly accurately, what has transpired (vv. 29–34). The fairly lengthy recounting builds tension as the reader waits to find out how Jacob will react this time to the news that he has lost another son.

But before we hear of Jacob's response, there is a rather odd scene in which the brothers empty their sacks and 'discover' their money amid the grain. How does this relate to verse 28? Either the brothers have staged the scene, having withheld this information from their father deliberately, or it indicates the combination of two different sources of the Joseph story. There is also a third option: if only one brother had opened his sack in order to feed the animals on their journey (vv. 27–28), then only one brother would have discovered the returned money. Back at home, however, they empty all the sacks and discover that all their money has been returned. The effect of this on them is that they are again frightened (or 'dismayed', as the NRSV translates it). Significantly, this reaction is immediately followed by Jacob's first words since their return.

Blood money

Having heard their story and seen the money, Jacob might wonder whether he is being told the truth. Perhaps his sons have sold Simeon, which is why they have money. Perhaps, Jacob might be thinking, his sons also sold his beloved Joseph! Such thoughts may well lie behind the words that Jacob then speaks out aloud (v. 36).

Jacob's words are full of loss and are intensely personal. The Hebrew syntax is revealing: 'Me you have bereaved. Joseph is no more. And Simeon is no more. And you would now take Benjamin. To me has this all happened.' Although rather self-centred, Jacob does not hide his feelings. Both these aspects confirm what we have come to know of Jacob's character. He is self-centred and he feels deeply.

Reuben tries to intervene, trying once again to rescue the situation (v. 37). But as before with both Joseph and Simeon, he is powerless now. Jacob simply ignores his offer, refusing even to contemplate sending Benjamin to Egypt. Even here, Jacob is true to form, still having his favourites, still being insensitive to how his other sons may feel about his blatant expression of favouritism, and still thinking of himself.

PRAYER

We pray this day, Lord God, for all those who are dominated and controlled by others more powerful than them.

The FAMILY'S SECOND JOURNEY

The famine is unrelenting, as it can be in this region, and soon the grain they have brought from Egypt is finished (v. 2). So Israel (as he is now called) once again instructs his sons to return to Egypt to buy grain. He seems to have completely forgotten his son Simeon, a hostage in Egypt. He seems also to have blotted out the demand that Benjamin must accompany his brothers.

It is Judah who bluntly reminds his father that there is a cost involved in going back to Egypt. He states in unambiguous terms that unless they take Benjamin with them, there is no point in going to Egypt. Israel (again the name change) responds with a fresh attack on his sons' actions, once again seeing himself as the prime victim. The brothers try to explain the context of their disclosure, making it clear that 'the man' in Egypt was particularly interested in their family (v. 7). Before Israel can respond, Judah continues, putting before his father a carefully formulated proposal.

Judah's proposal has a number of elements to it, including taking personal responsibility for Benjamin, the urgent needs of the family as a whole for food, and an indication that further procrastination is pointless. Reuben and Judah had both failed to protect Joseph; now they have a second chance. Reuben's earlier attempt had been dismissed by his father; now it is Judah's turn to try to redeem himself.

It is the reality of the famine that breaks Israel's resolve. The needs of his extended household eventually outweigh his own personal desire to keep Benjamin by his side. Instead of being passive, Israel now becomes proactive, instructing his sons to take luxury goods as gifts to Egypt, as well as money to buy grain plus what was returned the previous time (vv. 11–12). Significantly, the luxury goods they take as gifts overlap in part with the trade goods of the caravan that took Joseph to Egypt (see 37:25). Here Israel behaves as any household head in his world would, preparing gifts to be given to another household head.

Finally, Israel acknowledges Simeon (v. 14), praying that God will deliver his sons and return them to him, although he clearly does not hold out much hope. His final words are words of bereavement.

Back to Egypt

The return trip to Egypt is narrated briefly, in a single sentence. Before we know it, we are back with the brothers in Egypt. Joseph has eyes only for Benjamin. Benjamin's presence also changes Joseph's demeanour towards his brothers, for he orders them to be taken to his home for a meal (v. 16). That an animal is to be slaughtered is a sign of a generous welcome and of being honoured guests.

This radical change in behaviour on Joseph's part confuses the brothers and generates more fear. Once again, the narrator allows us access to their 'thoughts' (in the Hebrew, v. 18). One of the features of this narrative is that we as readers are able to 'hear' what characters are thinking.

Ironically, the brothers fear that they will be enslaved (as they enslaved Joseph). Ironically too, when they sold Joseph for profit they did not declare it, but now they declare the returned money (v. 21), even though they had nothing to do with it. Perhaps the brothers are growing in responsibility and openness. Perhaps Joseph's test is having its intended effect.

Joseph's attendant allays their fears, and then makes an enigmatic theological comment about God's role (v. 23). The brothers are probably mystified by this comment, but we as readers recognize it as a central theme of the narrative, namely, God's concealed guidance. Before the brothers can probe or discuss this theological comment, Simeon is restored to them—another sign, perhaps, of God's hand in these affairs.

The brothers, now united, except for Joseph, are hospitably received in Joseph's house. They in turn prepare the gifts they have brought. The scene is now set for Joseph's arrival.

REFLECTION

Do you see any growth in the brothers? Have they become 'better' people? Is this part of Joseph's plan, to reform them? Or is Joseph simply wanting to punish them?

JOSEPH OBSERVES HIS BROTHERS

This scene is a remarkable combination of intimate sharing, detached observation and manipulation. It begins with a formal presentation of gifts and obeisance (as Joseph's dreams prefigured). This is followed by an extensive intimate conversation in which Joseph asks a number of personal questions about their (and his) family (vv. 27–28). When it comes to his question about Benjamin, he does not even wait for an answer. Before the brothers can reply, he bestows a blessing on Benjamin (v. 29).

The brothers must have been a bit puzzled by this behaviour, particularly as, immediately afterwards, Joseph rushes from the room. But the focus now is not on the brothers, but firmly on Joseph.

Joseph wept

Once again (see 42:24), Joseph is overcome with emotion (43:30). The narrator sets up this scene with great care. Having consistently referred to Joseph's brothers as 'the men' (43:16, 18, 24), he singles out Benjamin as 'his brother' (v. 30). Note too that Benjamin is identified initially as 'his mother's son' (v. 29): mothers continue to play a sublimated but significant role in this narrative.

Separation and favouritism

When Joseph returns, having regained control of himself, the meal begins. We are alerted to three aspects of this meal. First, the Egyptians eat separately, because, we are told overtly by the narrator, Egyptians did not eat together with 'Hebrews' (v. 32). Again, as we have already seen in the episode with Potiphar's wife, there is unmistakable discrimination here. The brothers are seen as belonging to the 'Hebrews', a socially displaced people. Notice once again that the designation is used by others, not by the brothers themselves.

The second aspect of the meal is more perplexing to the brothers. While they probably expected to be seated separately from Joseph and the other Egyptians, they could not have expected to be seated in order of their ages (v. 33). Joseph's motives for doing this are not given to us, so we can only speculate. Was he simply (and unconsciously) following local custom (whether his family's or an Egyptian custom) or was he trying to communicate something to his brothers? If the latter, what was he wanting to communicate? Was he wanting to provoke further fear, or was he yearning for them to make the connection and so to recognize him?

The third aspect that we are meant to notice is the favouritism shown to Benjamin. Like his father, Joseph cannot resist demonstrating his favouritism. In front of his brothers he ostentatiously favours Benjamin. But this is not the final word on the meal, for it continues uninterrupted by any conflict or fear. 'So they drank and were merry with him' (v. 34).

Manipulation

While we might have imagined that this was the moment for disclosure, reconciliation and reunion, Joseph has other plans. In chapter 44 he sets another test for his brothers. The test is similar to the first, but with a added twist. Joseph commands that his silver cup be placed in Benjamin's sack.

His primary motive is probably to keep Benjamin in Egypt. If this is the case, then Joseph seems quite willing to give up on his relationship with his other brothers and the rest of his family. Or perhaps, as before, Joseph is not capable of thinking clearly when it comes to his family. Perhaps he does not know what he wants, whether to punish or reward, whether to reject or accept. The idea that Joseph may be making it up as he goes along seems to be supported by the ad hoc arrangements. The steward who is instructed to put Joseph's cup in Benjamin's bag is only told the next day to pursue the brothers (44:4). Perhaps the cup was initially intended as a gift to Benjamin, but later Joseph changed his mind and turned it into a trap.

Joseph is clearly the one with power, the one who is in control, but is he in control of himself? More ominously, has Joseph developed delusions of divinity? The steward had earlier informed the brothers that it was God who had put treasure in their sacks (43:23), yet we as readers know that it was Joseph's doing. Is the steward simply making fun of them, or is the narrator trying to tell us something?

REFLECTION

Do you see any growth in Joseph? Has Joseph grown as a character? What are his strengths and what are his weaknesses?

94 GENESIS 44:3-17

DECEPTION & DIVINATION

The day dawns, and the readers of this story wonder what lies in store. The brothers set out on the journey to Canaan, but this time it is forcibly interrupted by Joseph's steward, who has been given his lines.

An immediate question that comes to mind when we read Joseph's instructions to his steward is whether the silver cup secreted in Benjamin's sack is indeed a cup of divination (v. 5) or whether this is just another ruse. The use of a cup for divination was a widespread practice in antiquity, with small objects being placed in the liquid in the cup and the diviner then interpreting the emerging effects. If it is genuinely used by Joseph for divination, then Joseph has embraced the religion of Egypt quite substantially. But what is the narrator saying then? Is this practice unproblematic for someone who worships Yahweh? In other words, do such practices have a place within Yahweh worship? Or is the narrator making some subtle critique of Joseph, alerting the reader to Joseph's need to resort to such devices? What about the dreamer and interpreter of dreams: what has become of him? Does God no longer communicate with and through Joseph as before? Has Joseph's power corrupted his relationship with God? Does Joseph falsely imagine that his power over Egypt and over his brothers has made him like God? Questions abound, and we are meant to ask them. The ambiguity of this reference to a cup of divination demands that we pay careful attention to the religious dimension.

The other option is that it is just a ruse, used to frighten the brothers further. In other words, Joseph is pretending that this cup and he himself have special powers to discern the future. This option fits in well with Joseph's previous behaviour, as he continues to manipulate and torment his brothers.

When confronted with the charge of theft, the brothers are dumbfounded. They protest their innocence, citing their honesty in returning the money they found in their sacks before. They are so sure of their innocence that they make a rather rash commitment (v. 9). Clearly they have not made a connection between this situation and the previous one. Knowing what he knows, however, the steward

206

rather cleverly amends the consequences for those found guilty of the crime (v. 10). The steward is either ad-libbing or he has been instructed by Joseph on the required outcome of the confrontation. Given verses 4–6, the latter is more likely.

Theatrically, the steward begins with the eldest and works his way finally to the youngest, where he and the reader know that the cup is located. We experience no real tension, knowing in advance what is going on. However, the brothers' growing relief as sack after sack does not contain the cup (strangely, there is no mention here of the returned money) is suddenly shattered as the cup is discovered in Benjamin's sack. The brothers, not the reader, are being tormented!

The brothers' grief is immediate (v. 13). No words are necessary, for they know full well that the inexplicable has happened. Dejected, they return to the city.

In Joseph's house again

The brothers (now named as such), led by Judah, immediately cast themselves (again) at Joseph's feet. They say nothing. Joseph goes on the offensive, pretending that he was able to foresee their crime. Note that he speaks to them in the plural (which is clear in the Hebrew of verse 15). Judah, their spokesperson, is at a loss to explain what has happened, perhaps assuming that Benjamin (or others of the brothers) actually did steal the cup. He seems to admit as much (v. 16b). Crushed, he accepts the consequences. There appears to be no fight left in him.

Joseph turns the screw as he brings his plan to its intended conclusion. Now it is clear what he has been up to: he wanted to isolate Benjamin from his brothers, perhaps wondering whether they would abandon Benjamin as they had abandoned him so many years ago. This is the test. Joseph dangles their freedom before them, saying with grim humour that all the brothers except Benjamin are free to return to their father in peace (v. 17). Judah and the reader know, however, that to return without Benjamin is to perpetuate the absence of peace in the family.

REFLECTION

Do you think Joseph's relationship with God has undergone any changes since his elevation to leadership?

95

JUDAH'S SPEECH

What follows (vv. 18–34) is a remarkable speech. Into the tension of this moment, Judah presents a compelling retelling of their story, coming close to revealing the dreadful secret that lies at the heart of this family (vv. 20, 29).

Brothers as servants

Assuming the leadership role, Judah makes it clear, repeatedly, that they are Joseph's servants. Whether this is simply a strategy for survival or whether it indicates a genuine attitude is not clear. The brothers have been severely shaken by what has happened and know that they are not in control of their destiny. Joseph is, and so Judah appeals to him, using terms of deference.

What Judah's speech tries to do is to allow Joseph to see what has transpired from the perspective of the brothers. Having been on the receiving end of Joseph's apparent anger and arbitrary behaviour, Judah begins (v. 18) by asking for a fair hearing. Joseph has not been a good listener, nor has he had to be; he is in charge! But Judah asks to be heard. Having received some sign that Joseph is listening, for he does not interrupt, Judah continues, slowly recounting the story from his perspective, but in a way that does not place Joseph's actions in a bad light. Indeed, Judah uses the honorific 'lord' repeatedly to indicate clearly that he is not challenging Joseph's authority. He simply wants to tell his story.

Jacob and Benjamin

In retelling the story so far from his perspective, Judah omits any reference to Joseph's strange and intimidating actions. Instead, he concentrates on the effect of the events on his family, particularly his father. Unwittingly, Judah focuses on the two most significant people in Joseph's life, his father (Jacob) and his brother (Benjamin). The fact that Judah understands the effect of the events on his father shows his own growth. The selfish person who thought only of material gain when he sold his brother into slavery (37:26–27) has changed. He is now able to appreciate the perspective of another.

What probably moves Joseph to declare his identity is Judah's repeated reference to Jacob as Joseph's 'servant' (vv. 24, 27, 30). While Joseph may find some satisfaction in hearing his brothers refer to themselves as his servants, he must have baulked at hearing his father described as such. What is more, Judah's speech contrasts the reference to Jacob as Joseph's servant with the phrase 'my father' (vv. 30, 32, 34 twice), describing his own relationship with Jacob. How Joseph must yearn to speak of Jacob as 'my father'!

A profound change

Furthermore, Joseph now knows how his father reacted to the news of his death. And yet he is not dead; he is alive! Remarkably, Judah has managed to touch Joseph deeply. The power of Judah's speech resides in the way it tries to represent the perspective of another—his father. Judah, it seems, has passed the test. He is now a different person. He can now place the needs of others before his own needs. He has taken responsibility for his actions and he has made a choice for others. He has found his self-respect. Self-respect leads to self-sacrifice: he offers himself instead of Benjamin (v. 33). There is no new information in Judah's speech, and yet the perspective is entirely new. This is one of the longest speeches in the book of Genesis and one of the most profound.

REFLECTION

Re-read the Bible passage and then formulate a prayer that captures the challenge of Judah's transformation for yourself.

96

JOSEPH REVEALS HIS IDENTITY

Now it is Joseph's turn to react. How will he respond to Judah's impassioned and selfless plea? Having controlled his emotions on two previous occasions (42:24; 43:31), Joseph now is unable to control himself. His inner struggle to conceal his identity collapses. Sending out those who know him, he then reveals himself to those who do not.

Amid tears, he declares his identity: 'I am Joseph' (v. 3). He then appropriates Judah's final words, in which Judah made reference to 'my father' (44:34). He makes these words his own, wondering aloud whether it can really be true that his father ('my father') is still alive. There is no response! The effect of Joseph's declaration is devastating. Joseph the Egyptian official was frightening; Joseph their revealed brother is terrifying. They are deeply traumatized.

Seeing this, Joseph summons them closer, yearning for recognition. But more explanation is necessary, so Joseph begins by allaying their fears. It seems that his appetite for retribution has been sated. He is able at last, like Judah, to see things from another perspective. His life since being sold as a slave takes on fresh significance. Thoughts that have so far been repressed are now articulated. God was at work, using him to save the lives of others. Suddenly, for this is how it comes across in the text, his role in the famine takes on added significance, not only in preserving lives in general (v. 5), but the lives of his family in particular (v. 7). It is almost as though, having revealed himself, he now receives revelation.

Here, we and his brothers encounter a quite different Joseph. His recognition of God's role seems to have changed him. Before they can respond, Joseph rushes on, filled as he now is with the prospect of being united with his father and the rest of the family. His purpose is clear, which is to provide for his family in Egypt for the duration of the famine (v. 11). Clearly the brothers are still bewildered, for Joseph reassures them once again that it is indeed he who stands before them (v. 12). The old Joseph is not entirely gone, however, for he wants his father to know of his power and what he has accomplished (v. 13). Perhaps here we have an insight into the cost of favouritism on the favourite. Perhaps Joseph grew up never quite knowing whether he could live up to his father's high view of him.

At last there is physical contact and tears (v. 14), beginning with Benjamin and then extending to the other brothers. This is followed by conversation. They have come a long way. Long chapters and many years ago, they were unable to speak to each other in peace (37:4); now it seems they can.

All the commotion and weeping in Joseph's house has been heard (v. 2). Now the details reach Pharaoh's palace. From the perspective of the palace, this is the first they know of Joseph's family. Apart from Joseph's household, few others knew of the earlier visits. Pharaoh's response is a generous one, reaffirming Joseph's offer and giving them legal sanction. Indeed, Pharaoh exceeds Joseph's offer (vv. 19–20).

Back to Canaan

'The sons of Israel' as they are referred to here (v. 21) get ready to leave. Joseph provides them with all they need for the return journey. The detail demonstrates both his care and his resources. Two notable things happen, however, during the preparations. As we might expect, Joseph favours Benjamin, heaping lavish gifts on him. Surprisingly, he does let Benjamin go, understanding, no doubt, how important it will be for his father to have Benjamin back with him. The second thing that deserves some comment is Joseph's final sentence to them: 'Do not quarrel along the way' (v. 24b). Is this an attempt at humour, or is Joseph being a bit condescending and bossy towards his brothers? Unfortunately, the verb here is not easy to translate, although a more accurate translation may be something like, 'Do not be perturbed on the journey'. If this is correct, then Joseph is only saying that they should not worry about anything on their journey.

The return journey is described briefly, as is the brothers' report to Jacob. The attention of this short account is on Jacob, as it should be. He is stunned (v. 26), and cannot believe them. The Hebrew verb conveys the idea of being feeble, numb or cold. He cannot allow himself to believe the impossible. It is only as he takes in the wagons waiting to transport him to Egypt that the truth slowly sets in. Gradually he allows himself to believe. His deepest, unimaginable desire has been fulfilled: he will see his favourite son before he dies (v. 28).

PRAYER

Enable us, God of life, to reach out to those from whom we are estranged. May our talk and our touch rekindle relationship and life.

JACOB & HIS FAMILY GO *to* EGYPT

The narrative focus shifts for the moment to Israel (for the name changes again), reminding us that this is his story as well. Indeed, as 37:1–2 makes clear, the story of Joseph is the story of Jacob/Israel. Knowing that Joseph lives, Israel sets out immediately, but pauses in Beer-sheba, his father Isaac's dwelling place, to offer sacrifices to 'the God of his father' (v. 1). This formulation (literally, 'the gods/Elohim of his father' in the Hebrew) probably goes back to a time when each clan had its own gods. In this narrative, however, the old formulation has taken on new meaning and refers quite clearly to a single God.

This is a momentous point. Israel is about to leave the land to which his ancestors were led by God. It is doubly appropriate, therefore, that Israel pauses before he leaves. Even the thought of his beloved Joseph does not overrule the necessity to acknowledge God. And God is faithful, for during the night God speaks to Israel (vv. 2–4), reassuring him that it is permissible to leave the land. This is the first time that God speaks overtly in the Joseph narrative. God's promise is fourfold. First, God promises to make Israel's descendants into a great nation. This very family that has been under threat from famine will increase and become many. Second, God will go with Israel. God is not restricted to a particular place. Third, God will bring Israel (or his descendants) back to this land that they are now leaving. Fourth, God promises Israel, the father, that his favourite son, Joseph, will be the one to close his eyes when he breathes his last.

With God's reassurance, Jacob (for the name shifts again) continues his journey to Egypt. Once again Jacob is on the move, leaving Beer-sheba for the second time in his life (see 28:10). Now, as then, God promises to be with him (28:13–15). He himself will not see his own land again. For now, however, his thoughts remain fixed on seeing his son Joseph. Although instructed by Pharaoh (45:19–20) to leave his possessions behind, Jacob the proud and self-reliant wanderer knows better, and so takes all that is his with him (vv. 6–7).

Jacob's descendants

The genealogical list in verses 8–25 (or 8–27) interrupts the narrative flow, and may be a later insertion. Both the theophany in verses 2–4 and the genealogy are somewhat out of place, in that they introduce two different genres into the Joseph narrative. While there is no reason why a narrative should not contain other genres as an integral part of it, the Joseph story so far has shown no propensity to do this. As we read on, we will see that the narrative becomes more and more difficult to follow, an indication perhaps that various redactors revised this part of the narrative over time.

The genealogy itself appears to be constructed so as to produce the number 70 (see Deuteronomy 10:22), for it includes Joseph and his sons (who were already in Egypt) and allocates ten sons to Benjamin, which does not fit with the narrative. Furthermore, according to Genesis 38, Er and Onan are already dead, and so could not have left Canaan with the family (v. 12). It would appear, therefore, that a later genealogy has been inserted here as a memorial to those who left Canaan, even though it may not be historically accurate (see also the genealogical list in Numbers 26). Symbolically, it is important.

Meeting

The narrative continues in verse 28, with Jacob sending Judah ahead to obtain directions to Goshen, the region that Joseph promised them (45:10). Judah has not only gained self-respect; he has also gained his father's respect and confidence. It is appropriate therefore that it is the two most reformed brothers, Judah and Joseph, who usher in the new era. As Judah travels from Jacob, so Joseph travels to Jacob. Jacob is now the meeting point of this reconstituted family.

Joseph comes in his chariots, but his father does not bow before him, as Joseph's second dream might suggest. Instead, Joseph embraces his father and weeps on his neck for a long time. The Hebrew verb used in verse 29b is significant: Joseph 'appeared' to his father. This expression has been used by the narrator prior to this only for God's appearing (see, for example, 12:7; 18:1). From Israel's perspective, Joseph's presence is indeed miraculous, so much so that Israel declares that he is ready to die, now that he has seen his favourite son (v. 30).

PRAYER

Thank you, loving God, for our families and for those times when we are able to meet together. May you always be a part of our families.

SETTLING *in* EGYPT

The journey from Canaan to Egypt is complete, and there will be no return for a long time. Israel/Jacob's family is now in Egypt, but they have yet to settle. Joseph sets about arranging this, starting by securing Pharaoh's consent. Although the beginning of this section reads as if Pharaoh is finding about Joseph's family for the first time, this may simply be a narrative technique to represent how it appears from Israel's perspective. Joseph prepares both his family and Pharaoh. Here we see Joseph the statesman at work.

The audience with Pharaoh

Joseph has briefed his family well, anticipating the concerns that Pharaoh might have in trying to accommodate this influx of refugees. Choosing five of his brothers as representatives of the family (47:2), Joseph presents them to Pharaoh. Their responses are clear and diplomatic, assuring Pharaoh that they already have a livelihood, that they are resident aliens (so acknowledging that their real home is elsewhere), that they consider themselves his servants, and that they are content to occupy land on the edge of Egypt's territory, in Goshen.

Pharaoh consents to their request, dealing directly with Joseph, thus making it clear that he holds Joseph responsible (vv. 5–6). He also suggests that selected members of the family may be given responsibility for Pharaoh's own herds. Although framed as a suggestion, what Pharaoh is implying here is that he expects actual service from some of Joseph's family. In some sense, they are servants of the Egyptian state. Monarchs do nothing for free!

There is nothing in Pharaoh's response, however, to confirm Joseph's claim in 46:34 that 'all shepherds are abhorrent to the Egyptians'. There is also no independent verification of this from Egyptian sources. It may be, therefore, that Joseph says it either to prepare his family for a possible frosty reception or to protect them from the kind of discrimination he has encountered as 'a Hebrew'. In other words, he might be wanting to indicate that any reserve they encounter will be due to their profession, not their person. Whether this is true or not, Joseph seems to be trying his best to help his family fit into the society that has become his own. As it turns out, the audience goes well, even though Pharaoh concludes the negotiation with Joseph rather than his brothers. Joseph has become Egyptian and has therefore ceased to be 'a Hebrew'; this is not the case with his family.

Having concluded the negotiations, Joseph then brings his father before Pharaoh (v. 7). Jacob (again the name shift) blesses Pharaoh, a common form of greeting in the ancient Near East, although it may also convey here a sense of Jacob's superior stature (from the viewpoint of the narrator). The greater blesses the lesser. Jacob is a refugee, but he does not allow this reality to limit his identity.

The exchange is formal and dignified, although Pharaoh is obviously impressed by Jacob's age, a clear sign of blessing (v. 8). Jacob does not answer Pharaoh directly, emphasizing the content of his years rather than their number, and locating his life within those of his ancestors (v. 9). He stands before Pharaoh not as an individual but as the representative of a long lineage. Perhaps he is, in a subtle way, rejecting the notion that his people are 'Hebrew'.

In Goshen

Joseph's thorough preparations accomplish what he had hoped for. The family settles in 'the best part of the land' (47:11). The exact location is not clear: even the biblical text offers us different names. 'Goshen' as the site of the settlement is consistently used (46:29, 34; 47:1, 4, 6), but in 47:11 the text reads 'in the land of Rameses'. Apparently, there is more than one tradition behind this part of the text.

Joseph's final act of settlement is to secure food for his family. Having just arrived, they would not yet be able to make their own way on the land, and so have to be assisted. This Joseph does, supplying food for the entire family (v. 12).

PRAYER

We pray today for all those who are refugees, that they may find a place to call home.

The FAMINE CONTINUES

This episode may well be one of the most important in the entire Joseph story. How we interpret Joseph's actions in this scene will determine to a large extent our final opinion of Joseph.

Paying for food

The main narrative picks up from 41.56. The famine is no longer the backdrop to the story of Jacob's family; it now becomes the focus in itself. We left this subplot of the narrative with Joseph opening up the storehouses and selling grain to the Egyptians (and those who came from other countries). When the people cried to Pharaoh, he told them, 'Go to Joseph; what he says to you, do' (41:55).

Because it has been a while since the reader followed this aspect of the story, the narrator summarizes and sets the scene in verse 13. We pick up the story with Joseph collecting money as payment for the stored grain. As the commentator John Skinner has said, 'Joseph is here represented as taking advantage of the great famine to revolution-ize the system of land-tenure in Egypt for the benefit of the crown.'

Joseph does precisely this, in three carefully managed stages. Stage one is selling grain back to those from whom it was taken in the form of tax. The people pay for it with money, and their money is brought by Joseph into Pharaoh's palace. When the people's money is exhausted (v. 15), they plead with Joseph for food, knowing that there is food (see 41:49). Joseph is unrelenting in his financial policy, which now moves into stage two. Stage two requires that the people now pay for food with their livestock. The fact that this would have affected the livelihoods of many is not taken into account by Joseph. The people are desperate, so they bring their livestock and exchange it for food.

But this only sees them through one more year of famine (vv. 17–18). When this food is used up, they again come before Joseph, but this time they grovel, referring to him as 'my lord' (v. 18). They now know that he literally has the power of life or death. This leads to the final stage, stage three. The desperate people offer both their land and themselves to be bought in exchange for food and seed (without which they can grow no food in those areas where it is still possible to produce food, v. 19). Joseph buys their land for Pharaoh and, 'As for the people, he made slaves of them from one end of Egypt to the other' (v. 21). The Masoretic Hebrew text is not clear at this point, reading 'he moved the people into the cities'. Joseph's strategy may well have been to bring people from the vulnerable rural areas into the cities, close to the supply of grain and other state resources. This reading does not mesh with verse 25, however, where it is clear that the people are indeed slaves. The Samaritan Pentateuch and the Septuagint both have 'he made slaves of them'. The Hebrew text is understandably embarrassed by what has become of Joseph, and so the text is amended to cover his crime.

Verse 22 indicates an exception to Joseph's policy. The priests did not need to sell their land in order to survive, the reason being that they received provisions from Pharaoh. Here we have a very clear picture of what is known as the city-state. The city-state is ruled by a monarch, who is supported by court officials like Joseph, religious functionaries like these priests, and a standing army. The city is sustained by the surplus produce of the people on the land through forms of taxation, and the people in turn benefit by receiving protection. As in this case, times of famine and drought enabled court officials to buy the livestock and land of the farmers who owned the land in the area controlled by the city-state. In such circumstances, local farmers tended to remain on the land, no longer as owners but as tenant farmers.

This is what we find in verses 23–24. As tenants on the land they once owned, they must pay Pharaoh one-fifth of their produce. A new system is in place, and it is a system instituted by Joseph.

The people's response

The people's response may be interpreted in two ways. First, they genuinely embrace their servitude as the price they are willing to pay for survival. Second, they tell Joseph and Pharaoh what they want to hear. The powerful love to hear that those they control are grateful, and so they say what needs to be said publically. Back home, in the privacy of their own communities, they may say other, less obsequious things.

What makes this section so hard to interpret is the difficulty of determining the narrator's point of view. Is he/she approving of Joseph's actions, or is there a veiled critique here?

PRAYER

Deliver us, God of righteousness, from unjust structures.

JOSEPH'S PROMISE

This section begins with confirmation that 'Israel' settled in the land of Goshen. The following verbs then shift into the plural, nicely captured by the NRSV, indicating both the family and the nation. For now, the fact that Israel's family gained possessions and multiplied is not seen as a problem; later it will be (Exodus 1:9).

Jacob's family and the Egyptians

It is worthy of note that there appears to be little connection between the previous section and this one. How is Jacob's family coping with the famine in Egypt? Are they having to sell their livestock and indeed themselves in order to survive, or is Joseph taking care of them?

In 47:12 we were told that Joseph did provide food for his father's household. But was this provision ongoing or only for the beginning of their stay? It is difficult to imagine Joseph not supporting his family, given his position of power. The verb form in 47:12, however, would suggest that it was a one-off provision. We have already seen that Pharaoh expects Jacob's family to serve him (47:6), and we read in 47:15 that 'the money from the land of Egypt and from the land of Canaan was spent'—although this may refer to the money of other refugees from Canaan, not Joseph's family. The very next sentence perhaps confirms this, for we read that 'all the Egyptians came to Joseph'. From then on, the only references are to Egyptians. The weight of textual evidence, therefore, would suggest that it was the Egyptians who were made slaves and not the other peoples, including Jacob's family. But how could such a distinction be maintained in a large country with a city-state economic policy in place, which presumed state ownership of the land and a 20 per cent taxation?

Either the text is composite here, preserving different traditions, or these questions are not the concern of the narrative. The implications, however, are substantial. If Joseph did protect his family from the state's systems of land ownership and taxation, then it is not surprising that the new pharaoh who arose over Egypt in Exodus 1 sought to redress the situation. If, on the other hand, Joseph did not give his own people preferential treatment, then it was he who effectively enslaved his own people, and they remain in this condition until we next encounter them in the book of Exodus.

All of this speculation, however, presumes that the narrative of Genesis continues into Exodus. The possible connection between Genesis and Exodus will be touched on briefly later.

Jacob's final request

The Genesis narrative continues in this section without raising or offering any clear resolution to the implied questions. Instead, the narrative shifts from settlement to Jacob's final request. With name changes between Jacob and Israel occurring from one verse to the next (vv. 28–29, suggesting that the names are interchangeable), Jacob summons Joseph, his favourite son, and makes him promise to bury him among his ancestors. Like Abraham before him (24:2), Jacob invokes what is clearly an ancient primal custom of swearing by the genital organs. This is another sign of the antiquity of the oral traditions on which this story is probably based. The story as we now have it was almost certainly written long after the period it describes, but its sources include oral and written stories that are far more ancient. For Jacob, Egypt is simply another place of sojourn; it is not home. If land is 'storied space', as an African colleague has suggested, then only Canaan is the land in which he wants to be buried, for it is there that the stories of his ancestors are located.

Having obtained a solemn oath from Joseph, Jacob bows and worships (whether on his bed or staff is not clear from the Hebrew). The old man uses his failing energy to secure a promise that he will be taken home when he lies down with his ancestors. Burial is a serious matter to most peoples, and where one is buried is crucial. Burial in an inappropriate place may lead to dislocation from the ancestors and so misfortune for the living.

PRAYER

May we all, God of our eternal rest, be buried by our families in our 'storied space'.

JACOB BLESSES JOSEPH'S SONS

Time, it appears, has passed and Jacob is dying. Now is the time to set things in order. Recognizing the moment, Joseph takes his two sons to Jacob. Jacob senses why Joseph has come and so recounts God Almighty's (El Shaddai; see also 17:1) promise at Luz of descendants and land (35:11). Graciously, Jacob now formally adopts Joseph's sons into his clan. Joseph does not even have to ask, although he must have worried about how his sons would be perceived by the family, born as they were in a foreign country to a foreign mother. None of this worries Jacob, who makes it clear that Ephraim and Manasseh will be his, just as Reuben and Simeon are. Indeed, Jacob seems to be saying here that Joseph's sons will have the same high place in Jacob's household as the two eldest sons of Jacob's senior wife, Leah (v. 5).

Jacob does make a distinction, however, between the two grandsons before him, Ephraim and Manasseh, and any other sons that may be born to Joseph. Such sons will not stand alongside Ephraim and Manasseh in the lineage, but under them (v. 6). Quite why Jacob does this is not clear.

Fragments

Verse 7 bears little relation to what precedes or follows it, and may be a clumsy insertion by some redactor who wanted to preserve this fragment. Or, the narrative may be trying to capture the rambling thoughts of a senile Jacob. In the midst of blessing Joseph's sons, his thoughts drift back to the love of his life, Rachel.

Similarly, verse 8 is either a clumsy inclusion or the narratively simulated forgetfulness of an old man. The name change from Jacob to Israel is not conclusive, as we have seen elsewhere. What follows is deeply moving, capturing as it does the joy of an old man who could not imagine he would ever see his favourite son again, let alone that son's children. Now he has Joseph's sons perched on his knees.

Joseph now formally brings them before his father, he himself having bowed before his father (and not the reverse as his dream seemed to imply). Joseph leads Manasseh, the firstborn, towards Israel's right hand (the hand of the richer blessing) and Ephraim, the younger, towards Israel's left hand. The almost-blind Israel, however, deliberately crosses his hands, bestowing the higher blessing on Ephraim. The subsequent history of Israel gives this scene added weight, for Ephraim did become the greater political entity. Hosea, for example, often refers to the northern kingdom simply as 'Ephraim'. Whether Israel's blessing accomplishes this destiny or whether Ephraim's history is being read back into the narrative is impossible to determine. Like so much of the book of Genesis, the history of its composition here is complex.

It is interesting to note that this chapter begins with Joseph taking Manasseh and Ephraim (using that order) to his father. As soon as Jacob begins speaking of them, however, the order shifts to Ephraim and Manasseh (v. 5). According to the narrative, Joseph does not interrupt the blessing, but immediately afterwards (v. 17) intervenes and tries to correct Israel's error. Israel dismisses Joseph's concern, stating clearly that he knows what he is doing. He has a premonition, and has blessed accordingly. His own father, of course, did likewise, blessing him with the firstborn's blessing instead of Esau (27:27–29). What Isaac did unwittingly, Israel now does in full cognizance of what he is doing.

The blessings

The first part of the blessing (vv. 15–16) is in the form of poetry. Israel uses a threefold invocation of the deity, invoking the God of his ancestors, the God who has been his shepherd, and the angel who has protected him. In this beautiful invocation he sums up the three major ways in which God is manifest to him. God is the one whom he has 'inherited' from his ancestors, the one who has always been there before him. God is also his companion in a more personal way. Israel/Jacob the shepherd has come to know God as his shepherd. And finally, God is also the angel who intervenes in his life (28:12; 31:11; 32:1). It is God in all these forms that Israel passes on to 'the boys'.

PRAYER

Thank you, our God, for our grandparents and parents, and for those who have gone before us in the faith.

JACOB BLESSES HIS SONS

Having blessed Joseph's sons, Israel then blesses Joseph twice, once in private and once in public. The private blessing follows immediately after the blessing of Ephraim and Manasseh and their descendants.

Blessing Joseph (in private)

Israel makes promises on behalf of God to Joseph—his favourite to the end—in private (48:21–22). Using the plural form to designate both Joseph's descendants and Joseph as the representative of the clan, Israel promises God's presence and that God will bring Joseph back to the land of his ancestors. He also formally bequeaths to Joseph (using the singular now) a particular piece of land as an extra portion. Yet again, Joseph is singled out by his father.

The piece of land referred to here may be Shechem, for the Hebrew word used here for 'the portion' is a related word. If this is the case, however, then Israel is reconfiguring what actually took place in Genesis 34. Again, many hands have been at work, revising this text over time.

Blessing Joseph and his brothers

In chapter 49, after a short preamble, the narrative shifts into poetry as Jacob blesses all his sons. The narrative thread has been lost, and what we have here towards the end of the book of Genesis is a host of loosely connected fragments.

What follows in the poetry is a series of oracles describing the characters and fortunes of the twelve sons/tribes of Israel. It is unlikely that Jacob would actually have said all these things on his deathbed, for many of them only have significance for later periods of Israel's history. Once again, later concerns have been read back into the stories of the ancestors.

In each oracle, Jacob takes some incident from that son's past or some aspect of his character and uses it to frame the future of that son's clan. In many instances we learn more about Joseph's brothers from this blessing than we have heard so far in the narrative.

Reuben is characterized both by his strength and by his unpredictable nature (vv. 3–4). Because of the latter, and because he committed an incestuous act with Bilhah, his father's wife (35:22), he shall no longer excel. Simeon and Levi have violent natures in general (vv. 5–7), and because of this and the particularly brutal attack on Hamor's city (34:25), they are condemned. Judah is remembered for restoring Benjamin and Joseph, and he is the first of the sons so far to be blessed (vv. 8–12). His brothers shall praise him and he shall subdue his enemies; he has a formidable presence and royal rule is promised to him, along with a lavish lifestyle. Zebulun will occupy territory close to the sea (v. 13). Issachar is a hard worker, but will give in to an easy life and so be enslaved (vv. 14–15). Dan, although appearing insignificant, will be formidable in battle, bringing justice to his people (vv. 16–17). Gad, similarly (and there is a pun on Gad's name here), will use guerilla-type tactics to respond to those who attack him (vv. 18–19). Asher will be a producer of good food (v. 20). Naphtali is gentle and produces beautiful offspring or words (v. 21, depending on the obscure Hebrew). Joseph is fruitful and strong; because of this, he will generate jealousy from others, but he will prevail because of God's strong presence with him (vv. 22–26). Benjamin is predatory in battle (v. 27).

In verse 28, the narrator addresses the reader directly, assuring us that each 'tribe' has received 'a suitable blessing'. This summary verse, which jumps forward to a time when the sons have become tribes, may be the work of another hand.

Jacob's charge

Verse 29 returns to Jacob, who prepares his sons (not tribes) for his death and charges them to take him home and bury him there among his ancestors. He gives detailed instructions about where he wants to be buried. Although not previously mentioned, it appears from this that Isaac, Rebekah and Leah have been buried with Abraham and Sarah—or so Jacob tells his sons.

Having dealt in detail with this important matter, Jacob lets go of this life and is 'gathered to his people'. What a lovely way to go! Jacob is at peace, but what about the brothers?

PRAYER

May we, God of Jacob, be surrounded by our family and friends as we approach death.

FINAL & UNFINISHED BUSINESS

Now that Jacob has gone to be with his ancestors, the story resumes its focus on Joseph and its narrative flow. Filled with grief, Joseph falls upon his father, weeping. The enigmatic Joseph who can be so calculating and cruel is also the Joseph who weeps with ease. The brothers say nothing. Perhaps their silence 'speaks' of their sense of alienation from their father, who always favoured only a few of them. For most of them, too, their father's blessing has been somewhat ambiguous, so perhaps there is not much for them to say.

Preparing Jacob for burial

Fulfilling his father's final request is Joseph's priority, so he embalms his father, according to the Egyptian custom, and seeks permission from Pharaoh to return home to bury his father. Pharaoh, like the Egyptians generally (v. 3), is supportive of Joseph. Jacob's body is carried back to Canaan for a state funeral, accompanied by the leadership of both communities. The proper procedures of mourning are performed, and everything is done as Jacob had desired. This is not the exodus, but it is a foreshadowing of it. Here, no thought is given to returning to Canaan to resettle there. They are returning only to bury Jacob. Indeed, when the local Canaanites observe the mourning, they perceive the participants as Egyptians mourning, not their own people (v. 11b).

Reconciliation

The death and burial of Jacob, and perhaps also the trip 'home' to Canaan, bring up the unfinished business among the brothers. Fearing (again) that Joseph may now seek retribution for their betrayal long years ago, the brothers panic (v. 15). What if it was the presence of their father that prevented Joseph from striking out against them?

They construct a story in which Jacob apparently tells them to beg Joseph to forgive them their crime against him (v. 17). Whether Jacob actually said this, we do not know, although it would be nice to think that he had. But such was Jacob's preoccupation with Joseph (and himself) that it is unlikely. So the brothers have to construct the kind of father they wish they had had.

Importantly, this ruse does give the brothers an opportunity to say that they are sorry and to ask for forgiveness. This has not yet happened! The way the brothers phrase their contrition is significant, invoking God and their father: 'please forgive the crime of the servants of the God of your father' (v. 17). Although the NRSV does not capture the point, it appears that the brothers did not actually come before Joseph personally. Instead, they 'sent a message to Joseph saying…' (v. 16). It is only when Joseph weeps (for the third time in the narrative) that they have the courage to face him in person.

Joseph's response is wonderfully gracious, assuring them that they have no need to be afraid. As he did when he first confronted them in his house, he again offers a theological perspective on all that has happened. Having reiterated his sense of God's purpose in the events (v. 20), he also assures them of his ongoing support for them and their children. What seals the genuineness of Joseph's response is the next sentence: 'And he reassured them and he spoke to their heart' (v. 21 in Hebrew). Finally there is restored communication.

Joseph is not, he assures them and us, God (v. 19). Although he has tremendous power, and although he has used this power in ways that are not always godly, he knows that he is not God.

Conclusion

The story of Joseph, Jacob, and indeed Genesis, comes to its conclusion. Joseph remains in Egypt, showing none of the need that his father showed to return home. Long after the famine has ended, Joseph stays in Egypt. He lives a long life and is privileged to see his children's children and their children. It is only many, many years later—years that the narrative does not recount—as he nears death, that Joseph speaks of the land of his ancestors. Why neither he nor any of the family that he now heads has returned remains untold. God, it seems (v. 24), is required to initiate their return to Canaan. When this does happen, Joseph tells his brothers, they must take his bones to be buried with the ancestors that have gone before him.

This is where the book of Genesis concludes, waiting for God to act. And act God does—but that is another story.

PRAYER

Thank you, God who speaks, for these stories. May you bring them to our memory again and again, revealing always more of your word to us.

NOTES

NOTES

NOTES

NOTES

NOTES

NOTES

NOTES

NOTES

NOTES

NOTES

NOTES

NOTES

THE PEOPLE'S BIBLE COMMENTARY

VOUCHER SCHEME

The People's Bible Commentary (PBC) provides a range of readable, accessible commentaries that will grow into a library covering the whole Bible.

To help you build your PBC library, we have a voucher scheme that works as follows: a voucher is printed on this page of each People's Bible Commentary volume (as above). These vouchers count towards free copies of other books in the series.

For every four purchases of PBC volumes you are entitled to a further volume FREE.

Please find the coupon for the PBC voucher scheme opposite.

All you need do:

- Cut out the vouchers from the PBCs you have purchased and attach them to the coupon.

- Complete your name and address details, and indicate your choice of free book from the list on page 240.

- Take the coupon to your local Christian bookshop who will exchange it for your free PBC book; or send the coupon straight to BRF who will send you your free book direct. Please allow 28 days for delivery.

Please note that PBC volumes provided under the voucher scheme are subject to availability. If your first choice is not available, you may be sent your second choice of book.

THE PEOPLE'S
BIBLE COMMENTARY

VOUCHER SCHEME COUPON

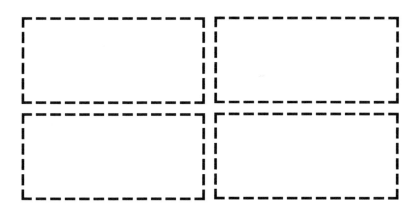

Customer and bookseller should both complete the form
overleaf.

Name: . . . .

Address: . . . .

. . . .

Postcode: . . . .

My choice of free PBC volume is:
(Please indicate a first and second choice;
all volumes are supplied subject to
availability.)

❑ Genesis

❑ Exodus

❑ Leviticus and Numbers

❑ Deuteronomy

❑ Joshua and Judges

❑ Ruth, Esther, Ecclesiastes,
   Song of Songs, Lamentations

❑ 1 & 2 Samuel

❑ 1 & 2 Kings

❑ Chronicles to Nehemiah

❑ Job

❑ Psalms 1—72

❑ Psalms 73—150

❑ Proverbs

❑ Isaiah

❑ Jeremiah

❑ Ezekiel

❑ Daniel

❑ Hosea to Micah

❑ Nahum to Malachi

❑ Matthew

❑ Mark

❑ Luke

❑ John

❑ Acts

❑ Romans

❑ 1 Corinthians

❑ 2 Corinthians

❑ Galatians and Thessalonians

❑ Ephesians to Colossians
   and Philemon

❑ Timothy, Titus and Hebrews

❑ James to Jude

❑ Revelation